Enoch Mellor

Priesthood in the Light of the New Testament

The Congregational Union Lecture for 1876

Enoch Mellor

Priesthood in the Light of the New Testament
The Congregational Union Lecture for 1876

ISBN/EAN: 9783337253400

Printed in Europe, USA, Canada, Australia, Japan

Cover: Foto ©Lupo / pixelio.de

More available books at **www.hansebooks.com**

PRIESTHOOD.

PRIESTHOOD

IN THE LIGHT OF

The New Testament.

THE CONGREGATIONAL UNION LECTURE
FOR 1876.

BY

E. MELLOR, D.D.

A. S. BARNES AND COMPANY,
NEW YORK, CHICAGO, AND NEW ORLEANS.
1876.

(All rights reserved.)

ADVERTISEMENT

BY THE COMMITTEE OF THE CONGREGATIONAL UNION OF ENGLAND AND WALES.

THE CONGREGATIONAL UNION LECTURE has been established with a view to the promotion of Biblical Science, and Theological and Ecclesiastical Literature.

It is intended that each Lecture shall consist of a course of Prelections, delivered at the Memorial Hall, but when the convenience of the Lecturer shall so require, the oral delivery will be dispensed with.

The Committee hope that the Lecture will be maintained in an unbroken Annual Series; but they promise to continue it only so long as it seems to be efficiently serving the end for which it has been established, or as they may have the necessary funds at their disposal.

For the opinions advanced in any of the Lectures, the Lecturer alone will be responsible.

18, SOUTH STREET, FINSBURY,
January, 1874.

CONTENTS.

LECTURE I.

	PAGE
THE PRIESTHOOD NOT AN ORDER IN THE NEW TESTAMENT	1

LECTURE II.

THE PRIESTHOOD NOT AN ORDER IN THE NEW TESTAMENT (CONTINUED) 37

LECTURE III.

THE CHRISTIAN PRIESTHOOD—ITS ALLEGED ORDERS AND LINEAGE 79

LECTURE IV.

THE PRIESTHOOD: ITS FUNCTIONS—AT THE ALTAR. 137

LECTURE V.

THE PRIEST AT THE ALTAR (CONTINUED): THE LORD'S SUPPER—CONSECRATION AND THE REAL PRESENCE 189

LECTURE VI.

THE PRIEST AT THE ALTAR (CONTINUED): THE
LORD'S SUPPER 255

LECTURE VII.

THE PRIEST AND THE CONFESSIONAL . . . 301

LECTURE VIII.

THE PRIEST AND THE CONFESSIONAL (CONTINUED). 345

APPENDIX 397

PREFACE.

THE following Lectures have been prepared and delivered at the request of the Committee of the Congregational Union of England and Wales. They are not considered by the author as by any means exhaustive, but he trusts that they may furnish some contribution towards the discussion and settlement of a question which is the most prominent in our times, viz., the Priesthood and its claims. He had hoped to embody in this volume another Lecture, treating of the intimate relations subsisting between Sacerdotalism and Scepticism, but the pressure of other work has interfered with its preparation.

LECTURE I.

THE PRIESTHOOD NOT AN ORDER IN THE NEW TESTAMENT.

LECTURE I.

THE PRIESTHOOD NOT AN ORDER IN THE NEW
TESTAMENT.

I HAVE designated the subject upon which I purpose to treat in the following lectures *the Priesthood*. The expression is not wholly free from ambiguity, and it may be well, at the outset, to define the sense in which it will be employed in these pages. My purpose is to show that in the gospel dispensation there is no official human priesthood analogous to that which prevailed in Judaism, and to vindicate the universal and inalienable spiritual priesthood of every man who is a child of God through faith in the Lord Jesus Christ. In the term priesthood, in its usurped and non-Christian signification, I include not merely the function of offering gifts and sacrifices unto God, but any form of official mediation between man and God by which it is assumed that in virtue of ordination, or any exterior rite whatever, certain persons acquire prerogatives which enable them, exclusively, to dispense salvation to others.

Whosoever claims, not in virtue of his faith, or his sanctity, or his habitual communion with Heaven, but in consequence of an exterior and ceremonial designation to an office, to be a representative to God, or a mediator with Him, or a messenger from Him, and to be on this ground alone the almoner and channel of His grace, this man is a priest after a fashion which commits a serious violence against both the letter and the spirit of the New Testament.

While it is admitted that priesthood and sacrifice have in many ages and nations been so strictly correlative that they suggested each other as by an inseparable association, yet the prerogatives of a priest may include an authority and a mediation in which sacrifice forms no part. Hence a teaching priesthood may be as little in harmony with the gospel as a sacrificing priesthood, and may be as fatal to the freedom and development of the higher life of man. Where the title of the instructor reposes, and that avowedly, not on inner qualifications, but on lineage constituted by imposition of hands or other ceremony, and where faith and submission are demanded, not on the ground of an intelligent apprehension of the doctrines inculcated or the duties enforced, but on the naked authority of the title in question, we have all that is *essential* in the priest, though no victim is immolated, and no incense rises towards heaven. In short, whatever may be conceived as being the relations which subsist between man and God, the assumption that these can and must be devolved by the great proportion of the race upon a separate order, without whose *official* mediation the flow of heavenly blessings is absolutely arrested, is an assumption which embodies that idea of the priesthood which the genius of the gospel both disallows and condemns. Hence the expression "Christian priesthood" denotes elements that are absolutely incompatible when applied to any clerical caste. It may be pardonable rhetoric, but it is indefensible theology. So far forth as this caste is a priesthood, it is not fulfilling a Christian commission; and so far forth as it is fulfilling a Christian commission, it is not a priesthood. This is the position which, in the course of these lectures, it will be my endeavour to elucidate and establish.

The region within which the evidence admissible in this discussion is to be found is the New Testament, and this as exclusive alike (though for different reasons) of the Old Testament and the post-apostolic Fathers. The question is not concerning the Jewish priesthood, nor is it concerning that system of sacerdotalism which, after certain processes of nebulous development, began to acquire definite consistency and form towards the close of the second century. Of the Divine authority of the former there is no dispute between myself and the modern defenders of the priesthood. The conflict, however, is becoming every day more strenuous and even fierce in respect to the Divine authority of the latter, which, with an amazing confidence, is alleged to have preserved its succession uninterrupted down to these times; and which, if it be a priesthood that in its official capacity is sealed of heaven, has in various ages exhibited a marked indifference both to doctrine and morals, matters which we should have deemed of the first importance in settling the claims of any order of men to be accounted the representatives of God in a spiritual kingdom.

In restricting the field of evidence to the New Testament, and especially to the Acts of the Apostles and the epistles, I am aware that some discourtesy seems to be cast upon Tradition and the authority of the Fathers. But no discourtesy is intended. It is simply assumed that the writings of the apostles contain all that is essential and authoritative in doctrine; that with these no tradition and no *consensus patrum* can be co-ordinate; and that by these all subsequent teachings must be tested. To those who regard the body of the apostolic writings as having all the obscurity of a sacred riddle, which was designed to be solved by the Church of the ante-Nicene age, or by the Church of all future time, as one by one doctrines became developed, ripened, formulated, and dogmatically declared, these lectures will have no value. The theory that the apostles are to judge the Fathers, and the theory that the Fathers are to be the final interpreters of the apostles, are fundamentally at variance with each other, and originate divergent and irreconcilable systems of both ecclesiastical doctrine and practice.

And it must, in fact, be noted that we have patristic authority against deferring to patristic authority, which not only seriously disparages the so-called consent of the Fathers, but vindicates in the most vigorous and resolute manner the supremacy of the Scriptures as the judge in matters of faith. It was a significant piece of strategy on the part of the writers of the Tracts for the Times, in view of their purpose to revive Catholic doctrines and practices, to rehabilitate the credit of the Fathers, which had been so mercilessly assailed in the writings of Daillé and Middleton and others. The depreciation, in fact, had become undiscriminating and excessive, depriving those ancient writers even of that common respect which is due to men of whom many had relinquished heathenism in homage to a faith which braved without blenching the persecutions of the imperial power. And the reaction was sure to come sooner or later. But the pendulum swung once more to the opposite extreme, and the Tractarians, not content with assigning to the Fathers such merit as from their learning, piety, and self-sacrifice they were entitled to claim, raised them to a position of authority which nothing but their inspiration could justify. As seen through the mist of antiquity they became demigods, whose utterances, never too accordant, were to rule the Church in all future time. But did the Fathers themselves assert such a despotic sway? It is notorious they did not. In the famous contest which Augustine had with Jerome, that monk so rich in learning, and so full of bitterness and objurgation, when the latter sought to overwhelm his antagonist with some half-dozen Greek theologians, the bishop of Hippo replied: "I confess that I only owe to those books of Scripture which are now called canonical that reverence and honour to believe steadfastly that none of their authors

ever committed any error in writing the same. . . .
But as for all other writers, however eminent they are
either for sanctity or learning, I do not so read them
as to think that anything is true because they have
so thought, but because they have persuaded me that it
is taught by these canonical writers, or by probable
reason. Nor do I think that you, my brother, are
of a different opinion. I do not think that you expect
your books to be read as if they were the productions
of prophets or apostles, concerning the infallibility of
whose writings it is not lawful to doubt. As for the
writings of those later authors, which are contained
in innumerable books, but are by no means to be es-
teemed as of equal value to the canonical Scriptures,
even though the same truth may be found in them,
it is of greatly inferior authority. Therefore, if the
reader encounter any passages in their writings which
we think to be disconsonant with the truth, because
possibly they are not understood, he is at liberty to
accept or reject them according to his judgment."[1]

This testimony of the great African bishop would be
sufficient if it stood alone. But Jerome himself, in his
preface to his second commentary on Hosea, says that
authors are to be judged "not by the dignity of their
names, but by their real worth, and that we must consider not whom we are reading, but what. So that
whether he were a bishop or a layman, a general and
lord, a soldier and slave; whether he lie in purple and
silk or in the coarsest rags, he must be judged not by

[1] "Epis. ad Hieron." fol. 14. Paris, 1579.

his degree of honour, but according to the merit of his works."[1]

Speaking of the Fathers in general, and even of such as lived before his time, and therefore nearer to the fading twilight of apostolic days, he says: "It may be that they have erred unintentionally, or have written in another sense, or their writings have been little by little corrupted by unskilful copyists; or else, before the birth in Alexandria of that (as it were) southern devil Arius, they spoke some things innocently and too unwarily, which could not escape the cavils of perverse men."[2]

The abject and implicit homage which has been claimed for the Fathers is thus seen to be repudiated in advance by the Fathers themselves, who, at least by precept, if not always by example, enjoined an unquestioning submission to the authority of the Scriptures. And they were wise in thus protesting, as if prophetically, against the superstitious regard which has been accorded to them for centuries; wise, if we consider the extraordinary opinions which they individually held; wise, if we consider the irreconcilable nature of their opinions on the same matters; wise, if we consider the conflicting nature of their opinions at different periods of their lives, and according to the polemical purpose they had to serve; wise, if we consider the extensive range they allowed to a prudential deceit and falsehood, euphemistically termed "economy;"

[1] Hier. "Com. 2 in Oseam." Præfat.
[2] Hier. L. 2 "Apol. *contra* Ruff."

and wise, if we consider the distinct sanction which they gave to demonolatry, and reverence for relics and rags. To deny a guilty complicity in false miracles on the part of some even of the most illustrious of the Fathers, is to abdicate the functions of common sense, or to suppose that they had been abdicated by the Fathers themselves.

By no writer have their real position and claims been more admirably put than by Jeremy Taylor, who in his "Liberty of Prophesying" says: "Why the bishop of Hippo shall have greater authority than the bishop of the Canaries (*cæteris paribus*), I understand not. For did they that lived (to instance) in St. Austin's time believe all that he wrote? If they did they were much to blame, or else himself was to blame for retracting much of it a little before his death. And if, while he lived, his affirmative was no more authority than derives from the credit of one very wise man against whom also very wise men were opposed, I know not why his authority should prevail farther now. For there is nothing added to the strength of his reason since that time, but only that he hath been in great esteem with posterity. And if that be all, why the opinion of following ages shall be of more force than the opinion of the first ages, against whom St. Austin in many things did clearly oppose himself, I see no reason. Or whether the first ages were against him or no, yet that he is approved by the following ages is no better argument; for it makes his authority not be innate, but derived from the opinion of others, and, to be *precaria*, and to depend upon others, who, if they should change their opinions (and such examples there have been many), then there were nothing left to urge our consent to him, which, when it was at the best, was only this, because he had the good fortune to be believed by them that came after, he must be so still; and because it was no argument for the old doctors before him, this will not be very good on his behalf. The same I say of any company of them (I say not so of all of them, it is to no purpose to say it), for there is no question this day in contestation in the explication of which all the old writers did consent. In the assignation of the canon of Scripture they never did consent for six hundred years together; and then by that time the bishops had agreed indifferently well, and but indifferently upon that, they fell out in twenty more; and except it be in the Apostles' Creed and articles of such nature, there is nothing which may with any colour be called a consent, much less tradition universal." [1]

The principle, therefore, which will guide us in the investigation of the subject we have undertaken is, that nothing can be accounted Christian doctrine which is not found in the writings of the New Testament, and that no system of Church polity and organisation can be regarded as *exclusively* apostolic and authoritative which has not the same inspired support. The question which we have now to consider is, What says the New Testament touching the existence of an official human priesthood in the Christian Church? and

[1] "Liberty of Prophesying." Sect. viii.

the answer to this question will involve the establishment of the following positions.

1. That there is no such priesthood acknowledged in name.

2. That there is no such priesthood acknowledged in office.

3. That there is no such priesthood acknowledged in specified qualifications.

4. That such priesthood is precluded by the whole genius of the Christian dispensation.

I.

There is no official human priesthood acknowledged in name.

The fact that the word priest ($ἱερεύς$) is not applied in the New Testament to any office-bearer in the Church of Christ, is of itself a circumstance of no mean signification. It cannot be an accident. Such a supposition is forbidden, both by the uniformity of the fact and by the inveteracy with which the name had clung to the sacerdotal office among both the Jews and the nations of heathendom. The suddenness with which a word saturated with official sacerdotalism was dropped as a designation of the ministers of the new faith, and this too by men who had used it daily in connection with the sacrificing priests of Judaism, could not be the result of caprice, but of a conviction that it could not aptly characterise the ministers of the gospel dispensation. Words are neither born, nor do they die, nor dissolve their ancient associations without cause; and if the preachers of the gospel were known to have been clothed with priestly functions as real in substance as those of the Mosaic economy, however differing in form, it is scarcely conceivable that the appellation by which the Jewish priests had been called would have been withheld from the administrators of the gospel. Throughout the Old Testament no nominal distinction is marked between those who sacrificed to Baalim and those who sacrificed to God. They are all termed *priests*, irrespective of the diverse faiths which they represented. Hence the word shows no partiality for one religion more than another, and was as ready to offer its services to the Christian dispensation as to the Jewish or Pagan religions, provided there had been any official functionary to whom the designation would have been appropriate. The absence of the word in such connection is a phenomenon which demands explanation, and the explanation devolves on those who represent the Christian ministry as a priesthood. That it should have been disused as a name of office by apostles, on the supposition that under the New Covenant all its significance had centred upon the High Priest of our profession, by whose redemptive work its typical import had been fulfilled, is natural. But such disuse is mysterious and inexplicable on the supposition that there still remained in the dispensation of the gospel a place for a priesthood, not in a figurative, but a real sense. The fact of this disuse is conceded by Bellarmine himself, who does not lightly acknowledge an argumentative pressure. While, however, he admits the statement of Chemnitz, whom he is assailing, that in the New Testament this name (priest) is not employed in the received signification, he proceeds to assign a reason why its employment is avoided, and this reason has been adopted by some of the Anglican school. "Because," he says, "in the time of the apostles the Jewish priesthood was still in force, and bloody sacrifices were offered in the temple at Jerusalem, the apostles, under the inspiration of their Lord, did not employ the names priesthood, sacrifice, temple, altar, and similar things, that they might the more easily distinguish the Christian from the Jewish sacrifices; and lest they should, by using the same words, be thought to renew, or confirm those rites. But a short time afterwards, on the overthrow of the temple at Jerusalem, and on the cessation of the Jewish sacrifices, the most ancient Fathers began freely to use all these names as they thought necessary."[1]

This explanation of Bellarmine is a pure hypothesis, for which there is not a shadow of evidence in the New Testament itself; nor have we anywhere an instance of the avoidance by apostles of terms which have a definite and characteristic meaning, simply on the ground that the same terms have been employed in other connections.

As to the importance of distinguishing Christian from Jewish sacrifices, what danger was there of confounding them when the whole stress of apostolic preaching was calculated to draw their hearers away

[1] Bellarmine, "Controver." ii. 332.

from the ceremonial of Judaism to the more spiritual realities of the Christian dispensation? Who was likely to confound the fishermen of Galilee, or Matthew the publican, or St. Paul, with the priests who were of the lineage of Aaron? or, when apostles wrote to Churches in various cities, who could imagine that in addressing the bishops of such Churches as *priests* (if they had ever done this), they would have created confusion between the priests of the Christian communities and those of the temples of Venus, Artemis, or Jupiter? The Jews had not relinquished their religious terminology in those heathen cities in which they had established colonies, lest, when they spoke of priest, sacrifice, and propitiation, they should be confounded with their heathen neighbours, or lest they should give encouragement to idolatry; and what more urgent need did there exist for the avoidance of these terms on the part of the early Christian teachers? But, in fact, the terms were not avoided. Temple, priest, and sacrifice, were employed and transfigured into glorious spiritual significations, in harmony with that dispensation of grace and truth of which Judaism had been the shadow and the preparation. And as to the name "priesthood" (ἱεράτευμα), it became a designation of the whole Church of God, and was never appropriated by apostles to themselves, or accorded by them to other teachers in the Church. Is it credible that if the priestly and sacrificial function of the ambassadors of Christ be that which by its mystery and glory casts every other into the shade, and if this were known by the apostles (as it must have been if there were any truth in the supposition), that they would have foregone the use of that very term which, more than any other, would express the nature of their commission? Was the Apostle Paul (to say nothing of his brethren in the apostolate) the man to make such a concession to the Jews, when we find him speaking of Christ as the Propitiation, and as our Passover, and thus fearlessly interpreting the types with which the Jews were so familiar by the great facts of the Christian Dispensation? Was he not rather the man to rescue the name from its simply Jewish and Pagan use, and to clothe it with the higher dignity of designating the ministers of a faith that was to fill the world?

In the light of these considerations, the common, unvarying, persistent repudiation by the apostles of the word "priest" as an appellation of the Christian minister possesses a striking significance. They do not denominate him a priest, because they do not consider him to be a priest. There is no need for the recondite, not to say whimsical reason of Bellarmine, which makes the apostles suspend the use of the term until the destruction of the temple at Jerusalem; while it must also be urged that it was not, as the Jesuit controversialist affirms, "soon," but at least a century after that event, that the ministry was denominated a priesthood as distinct from the laity.

Let us, then, endeavour to estimate the full significance of the fact that nowhere in the New Testament are those officers who are declared by sacerdotalists to be priests by pre-eminence, distinguished by this designation. We have letters to Jews and to Gentiles, and to both combined, but, throughout them all, the conception of a priest, as a Christian functionary —subordinate or supreme, stationary or itinerant, inspired or uninspired—is not even suggested in the faintest degree. This circumstance is of the gravest moment, even viewed apart from the inspiration which controlled and guided the thoughts of the apostles. Looking at their epistles as simply human productions, the absence of the sacerdotal element cannot fail to strike us, and to demand explanation. But when we regard the apostles as inspired expounders of truth, we cannot with reason or reverence assign any explanation of the uniform and consistent absence of the term "priest," except as we find it in the fact that all that was essential in the priesthood had been fulfilled in the great sacrifice of the Cross. Whether we consider the men who wrote the letters, or the Churches to which they were addressed, the more significant will the absence of the word " priest " appear. For if the apostles were, not in some indefinite metaphorical sense, but in a sense the most real, "priests," and if those whom they appointed to the work of the ministry were " priests," then — considering the awful prerogatives involved in the exercise of such a sacred and stupendous function—it is incomprehensible that the claim should not have been distinctly made, and made with a reiteration and emphasis that should have rendered it impossible for any reader of their epistles to resist the conclusion that their priesthood was their crowning distinction. And if they were priests, nothing could have contributed more directly and powerfully to root this conviction in the minds of the people than the constant assumption of the name. "Paul, a priest of Jesus Christ," would have been as easily written as "Paul, an apostle of Jesus Christ," and would have possessed the additional advantage of being a more precise designation. True, the Churches might have been amazed at the title when dissociated from its usual accompaniments; they might have wondered at the absence of altar, victim, incense, and sacred vestments. But this would have afforded an opportunity for the apostle to have expounded the infinite superiority of his priestly functions over those of the Jewish or heathen hierarchies, by asserting his power to imbue the water of baptism with a regenerative virtue; to transmute the common perishable elements of bread and wine into the body and blood of the Lord Jesus Christ, to be offered on the altar; and, by a judicial act, to open and shut the kingdom of heaven. The apostle magnified his office when his commission was rudely or ignorantly questioned, and proved that his credentials were as valid as those of his brethren who had been the companions of the Lord; and if the sacerdotal function had been the crowning and culminating duty of his apostleship, no respect for an expiring Judaism would have restrained him from asserting a power compared with which that of the Aaronic priests was but a shadow or a name. We have therefore a fact, admitted on every hand, that in the New Testament the word which was employed without scruple in both Judaism and paganism, as the specific designation of the chief functionaries of religion, is not employed as the designation of the apostles and ministers of Christ, and this fact finds its only sufficient solution in the circumstance that no sacerdotal position or action was assigned to the teachers of the new faith.

So much for the absence of the name of "priest." But the argument against the existence of a priesthood in the Christian Church, other than that of Christ Himself, acquires additional strength from the chief appellations which are given to the ministers of the word. These are *presbyters* (πρεσβύτεροι) and *bishops* (ἐπίσκοποι), which, as will be shown more at length in a subsequent lecture, were but designations for the same officers, the former having Jewish associations, and the latter Hellenic. The point of chief moment to be observed in this connection is that neither of these words, when it came into the New Testament, brought with it a priestly significance. The Jewish priest was not designated in his priestly capacity πρεσβύτερος, nor was the pagan priest designated ἐπίσκοπος, nor would either appellation have, of necessity, suggested to Jew or Greek any priestly function whatever; while the discarded term, ἱερεύς, could not have suggested any other, its whole import being not only religious, but *sacerdotal*. It is impossible to conceive of the argument based on the terminology of the New Testament against the priestly conception of the Christian ministry being stronger than it is made by these two considerations: that a definite, technical, acknowledged priestly term is declined by every writer, and that it finds its substitutes in terms which contain no priestly element whatever.[1]

II.

But if it be alleged that the question of a human official priesthood in the Christian Church is not to be determined solely on the basis of terminology, this is at once conceded, while at the same time it is maintained that no reason has been as yet assigned for the suppression of the name "priest" if its reality be admitted. When the fittest word for anything is systematically evaded, there must be a sufficient cause, and that cause has not been found in the adroit and ingenious theory of Bellarmine. Nor have we anywhere encountered a better theory to account for the absence of the *term* than that which is supplied by the absence of the *thing*. This explanation covers the whole ground, and fulfils all the conditions of a legitimate hypothesis. But it is not, we hold, a hypothesis pure and simple, but an inference justly drawn from the uniform teaching of the New Testament. The office of the human priest is not in the gospel dispensation, and hence the disuse of its common designation. To the consideration of this point—namely, the absence of the priestly *office* in the Christian Church, as seen in its organic working in the New Testament—we now proceed.

[1] See Appendix A.

A large portion of one whole epistle — that to the Hebrews — is devoted to the establishment of the exclusive priesthood of the Lord Jesus Christ. Into the authorship of this epistle it is unnecessary to enter, as, whether the writer were Paul, or Apollos, or Barnabas, or some other person, its value as evidence is admitted equally by the supporters and opponents of the doctrine of Christian sacerdotalism.

This letter assumes that a long-existing and divinely-established dispensation has virtually passed away. It addresses itself to the work of explaining the genius of that dispensation, shows its power, and still more its impotence; leads us into the temple, displays to us its arrangements, services, and ministrants; and then assures us in language which it ought to be impossible to misinterpret that the law thus embodied in elaborate symbolic ritualism was a "shadow of good things to come." The writer does not affirm that the Jews who witnessed or performed that pictorial and histrionic service realised the fact that it was exclusively typical and anticipative, but he declares that such was the nature of the Mosaic dispensation. The "sundry times" looked for their true antithesis and explanation to "these last days;" and "the divers manners" in which "God spake to the fathers by the prophets" pointed to the higher and fuller communication He has now made by and in His Son; a communication which is not only the fulfilment of past predictions, but a new and transcendent revelation of truths which never dawned on the vision of ancient seers. In language the most emphatic, this

¹ Heb. x. 1.

epistle declares that the typical and ritualistic dispensation is annulled.

"In that he saith, A new covenant, he hath made the first old. Now that which decayeth and waxeth old is ready to vanish away."[1] Of the Jewish priests, whose vocation was now expiring, the writer says: "For there is verily a disannulling of the commandment going before for the weakness and unprofitableness thereof. For the law made nothing perfect, but the bringing in of a better hope; by the which we draw nigh unto God. . . . And they truly were *many priests*, because they were not suffered to continue by reason of death: but this (priest), because he continueth ever, hath an intransmissible priesthood. Wherefore he is able also to save them to the uttermost that come unto God by him, seeing he ever liveth to make intercession for them. For such an high priest became us, who is holy, harmless, undefiled, separate from sinners, and made higher than the heavens; who needeth not daily, as those high priests, to offer up sacrifice, first for his own sins, and then for the people's: for this he did once, when he offered up himself. For the law maketh men high priests which have infirmity; but the word of the oath, which was since the law, maketh the Son, who is consecrated for evermore."[2]

The key to the whole of this reasoning of the writer to the Hebrews is to be found in the contrast so sharply defined and so continuously maintained be-

---

[1] Heb. viii. 13.   [2] Ibid. vii. 18-28.

tween many priests and one Priest, many sacrifices and one Sacrifice, oftentimes and once; and any interpretation which disturbs the unity which constitutes one member of the contrast destroys the conclusiveness of the argument which is pursued with such elaborateness of detail. Introduce "two" priests, "two" propitiatory sacrifices, and "twice" instead of "once," and the whole structure of reasoning falls to pieces. It is the perfection of the Saviour's person and the completeness of the Saviour's work which are here affirmed, and these must of necessity be prospective as well as retrospective. If they terminate one series of priests they must preclude another. Christ has put away sin—He has offered Himself once for sins for ever—He ever liveth to make intercession for us—He has sat down at the right hand of God. But if it were true that there still remain priestly functions in the Christian Church, what means the exalted and exclusive prominence which is here given to the priesthood of Christ? Now was the time, if there were other priests, that this truth should be distinctly set forth; for the writer is aiming, by a formal argument, to vindicate the Christian economy as the legitimate and preordained successor and fulfilment of Judaism, and also to conciliate the Jewish mind to the faith of the gospel. If then there were still, in spite of the one great oblation upon the cross, other sacrifices, other altars, other priests, and all these not metaphorical but real, what would have contributed more to abate and even remove the prejudices of the Jewish converts, who were still under the lingering spell of the temple ritual, than the assurance that nothing was changed in the New Testament but the forms of ritual and service? This was the time to justify and strengthen the tenacity with which the Hebrews clung to the visible ritual of a worldly sanctuary, by assuring them that though one line of priests was retreating from view with a vanishing economy, another line was inaugurated whose functions should infinitely surpass those of the men who had ministered in the temple at Jerusalem. But it was not another *line* that was inaugurated. There is neither multitude of priests nor succession. There is one Priest, and even He a priest who has finally accomplished the only sacrifice of expiation, and who is no longer visible to the Church on earth, but has passed into the heavens.

It avails nothing against these considerations to urge that Christ was the *High Priest*, and that His ministers fulfil the humbler functions, which correspond with those that fell to the lot of the ordinary priests under the Jewish dispensation. The sacrificial system of that dispensation was one great whole, and the writer to the Hebrews represents our Lord as embodying and fulfilling all priestly functions in His own person and work. He says: "Every priest (not merely every high priest) standeth daily ministering and offering oftentimes the same sacrifices, which can never take away sins: but this (or, He), after he had offered one sacrifice for sins for ever, sat down at the right hand of God."[1]

[1] Heb. x. 11, 12.

But the evidence against the sacerdotal nature of the Christian ministry becomes strengthened as we examine the last chapter of the epistle. The writer there speaks specifically of the supreme officers of the Church, and we may naturally expect that he will characterise them and their office in such terms as will not omit their most essential functions. If they be priests indeed, and priests by pre-eminence, he will not assuredly shrink from the name. What is the name by which he designates the officers? It is that of leaders or guides. "Remember them that are your leaders" (ἡγουμένων).[1] And he further unfolds the conception he has of this leadership in a manner which significantly precludes the idea of sacrifice, or of any truly priestly act. The leaders have "spoken the word of life," not performed some act of manual thaumaturgy, or offered some sacrifice, whether bloody or unbloody. And moreover they were officers who were to be imitated in that which undeniably was most essential to them as ministers of Christ, but which, as we shall see hereafter, is authoritatively ruled as *non-essential* to the modern priests—" whose *faith* follow, considering the end of their conversation. Jesus Christ the same yesterday, to-day, and for ever."[2]

But the absence alike of sacerdotal act and function becomes the more striking and unaccountable in view of another consideration, viz., that, according to the priestly conception of the ministry, the death and

[1] Heb. xiii. 7. [2] Ibid. xiii. 7, 8.

intercession of Christ are practically of no avail without the intermediate agency of a human priesthood. On this theory we have in Christ a fountain of grace, but it is a fountain inaccessible in itself, except to the comparatively few who have received official designation, and who thus become the conduits of its blessings to their fellow-men. And to this awful eminence they are raised, not, of necessity, by any spiritual sympathy with the Saviour; not by any holiness of character, or even any desire to attain such holiness; not by the possession of that faith which endures as seeing the invisible; but on the sole ground of a manipulative act which is supposed to establish their connection with a certain hierarchical lineage. But if this had been true, it was surely of the highest moment that the writer to the Hebrews should have given emphasis to the fact when contrasting two dispensations, and that with the object of exalting the later above the earlier. To say nothing of the earthly priesthood in the Christian Church when he was speaking of the earthly priesthood under Judaism, and especially when that new priesthood was as essential to the salvation of the world as the heavenly priesthood, was to leave the argument strangely incomplete. To speak of the one Priest, when in fact there were many, and when the work of the one Priest was abortive and inefficacious for the salvation of man without the mediation of other priests, was to mislead his readers. The author of this epistle, however, was neither a halting logician nor a deceiver. He meant to teach, among other things, that all official priesthoods were summed up in Christ, and he taught it with the clearness of a sunbeam. *One* priest in heaven, *no* priest on earth; these are the two correlative truths which no subtlety can separate from each other upon any principle of criticism which respects the unambiguous teaching of the Divine Word.

A final consideration drawn from this epistle in corroboration of the same great truths that all earthly priesthoods which had ever possessed Divine authority were absorbed in Christ, and that all earthly sacrifices which had ever possessed even a symbolically propitiatory value terminated in Him, is found in the last chapter. There we twice encounter the word sacrifice, but in neither case does it suggest the image of the official priest. There is a true sacrifice, but it is a "sacrifice of praise continually unto God."[1] And there are other true sacrifices which need no official priests to offer them, for the exhortation is addressed to the whole community. "To do good and to communicate forget not, for with such sacrifices God is well pleased."[2] And these are the only sacrifices mentioned throughout the whole of this epistle as being offered by any member of the Christian Church, whether he be in office or out of office, a fact which would have been inconceivable if there had been a special priesthood empowered, as its supreme and characteristic function, to offer "the tremendous sacrifice" of the body and blood of our Lord Jesus Christ.

[1] Heb. xiii. 15.   [2] Ibid. xiii. 16.

It has been seen that the teaching of the Epistle to the Hebrews, by whomsoever it was written, finds no place for a human priesthood in the Christian Church, and, in this respect, its teaching is in the strictest accordance with that of every other epistle. There is no idiosyncrasy of any apostle which inclines him in the direction of sacerdotalism. In this respect Paul, Peter, James, and John are at one. Between the most speculative of them and the most practical, the most logical and the most intuitional, there is no difference. Not one of them claims the name of priest except in a sense which is so palpably figurative as to forbid the intrusion of the sacerdotal conception. In one passage, striking for the boldness of the representation, the Apostle Paul introduces words of a strong priestly colouring. "I have written," says he, "unto you, brethren, putting you in mind, because of the grace that is given to me of God, that I should be the minister of God to the Gentiles, ministering the gospel of God, that the offering up of the Gentiles might be acceptable, being sanctified by the Holy Ghost." Here many of the terms employed are doubtless of a sacrificial character, but the sacrifice consists of the Gentile world. A similar allusion may be noted in his letter to the Philippians, where he says, "And if I be offered ($\sigma\pi\acute{\epsilon}\nu\delta o\mu\alpha\iota$) [that is, poured out as a libation or a drink offering] upon the sacrifice ($\theta\upsilon\sigma\acute{\iota}\alpha$) and service of your faith;"[1] an image which reappears in his second letter to Timothy—"I am ready to be offered up" ($\mathring{\eta}\delta\eta$ $\sigma\pi\acute{\epsilon}\nu$-

[1] Phil. ii. 17.

δομαι).² These metaphorical illustrations sustain no theory of sacerdotalism except one which it would have been well if it had maintained exclusive prevalence in the Church of God.

There is one passage which has been thought to yield considerable support to the assumptions of sacerdotalism, because in it the apostle claims for himself to be "a steward of the mysteries of God."[1] This word mysteries is supposed to denote certain sacramental acts which are the exclusive prerogatives of the priests; and yet it will be seen that throughout the whole of the New Testament no instance can be found in which the word signifies any ceremony or sacrament whatever, and still less in which it denotes a secret which is to be kept as a sacred deposit by a priestly caste.

The kingdom of God has its mysteries, but of them our Saviour said, "It is given to you to *know* them." The apostle supposes a man to "*understand* all mysteries, and to be in no wise profited, because he has not love." He would not have the Romans to be ignorant of the mystery which he at once clearly recites, "that blindness in part is happened to Israel until the fulness of the times be come." He speaks of "the revelation of the mystery which was kept secret since the world began, but is now *made manifest*, and by the scriptures of the prophets made known to all nations for the obedience of faith." He *shows* a mystery, and the mystery is that we "shall not all sleep," &c. He preaches among the Gentiles that he may "make all men *see* what is the

[1] 1 Cor. iv. 1.   [2] 2 Tim. iv. 6.

fellowship of the mystery." He entreats the prayers of the Ephesians that *"utterance* may be given him that he may open his mouth boldly to *make known* the mystery of the gospel." He informs the Colossians that "the mystery which has been hid from ages and generations is now *made manifest* to the saints, to whom God would *make known* what is the riches of the glory of this mystery." He warns the Thessalonians against the "mystery of iniquity" which was already working, and whose pernicious activity he is so far from hiding from the Church at Thessalonica, that he describes it as "the son of perdition, who opposeth and exalteth himself above all that is called God, or that is worshipped; so that he as God sitteth in the temple of God, showing himself that he is God." And to Timothy he says, "Great is the mystery of godliness." But even this is a mystery consisting of a glorious series of historic facts. "God was manifest in the flesh, justified in the spirit, seen of angels, preached unto the Gentiles, believed on in the world, received up into glory." In the Book of the Revelation we read of the "mystery of the seven stars" and of "the seven golden candlesticks," but the mysteries are expounded. "The seven stars are the angels of the seven churches, and the seven candlesticks are the seven churches."[1]

But in none of these passages, nor in any other, is there discernible a trace of that species of mystery which consists either of a truth which has been revealed to apostles and which they may conceal from

[1] Rev. i. 20.

others, as if it were their special patrimony and privilege as priests of the most high God, or which they were empowered to invest with mystic efficacy as a means or condition of salvation. They neither performed, administered, applied, consecrated, nor partook of a mystery. They *preached* mysteries, but they never *handled* them. They were stewards, but their stewardship was an embassy in virtue of which they had to deliver and urge a message of reconciliation and love. Whatever truth they had received from heaven touching the nature of man, his moral condition and hopelessness; the eternal purposes of grace; the functions of the Mosaic dispensation; the glorious person of the Son of God; the stupendous fact and meaning of His incarnation, His life, death, resurrection, ascension, and intercession; the obligations of Christian holiness, with the means of its attainment; and the future destiny of the world; they were bound to reveal on peril of a criminal faithlessness to their trust. They had been put in possession of *no* secrets which they were to guard as with the silence of death. As instructors, they might regulate their communications by the capacity of their hearers, giving them milk or meat according as they were able to bear the one or the other. But there was not one ray of light which they had authority to imprison and intercept from the humblest child of God; not one truth in their treasury, new or old, which, as good stewards, they were not to "bring forth;" and, as we have seen, there was no mystery entrusted to them but a mystery of truth which was to become an element of knowledge, and a means of spiritual light, life, purity, and joy.

For the theory which would interpret the word "mysteries" as denoting the rites of baptism and the Lord's Supper, there is not the shadow of a foundation in the New Testament. We speak of them as "sacraments," but even for this name there is no inspired authority as a designation of any Christian ceremony whatever. It was after apostolic days, and concurrently with the growth of sacerdotal ideas in the Church, that both the Greek term $\mu\nu\sigma\tau\acute{\eta}\rho\iota o\nu$, and the Latin terms *mysterium* and *sacramentum* became employed in Christian literature as designations not of truths to be revealed, but to be concealed, and of ceremonies the administration of which was to be reserved exclusively in priestly hands. Indeed, for a considerable period these words admitted of a very loose application. It is hard to say what was not a sacrament in the estimation of some of the Fathers. The Lord's Prayer was a sacrament—dreams sent from God were sacraments—the Trinity was a sacrament—the resurrection of the dead was a sacrament—monogamy was the sacrament of priests and deacons—baptism was the sacrament of washing—the Lord's Supper was the sacrament of thanksgiving. These, however, were not the mysteries of which the apostles were stewards. As Jews, they had known nothing of the application of the term "mysteries" to any rite of the ancient dispensation, rich as it was in the possession of ceremonies of the most pompous and imposing character; and it is certain that they never regarded themselves nor any of their so-called successors as the exclusive administrators of either the rite of baptism or the Lord's Supper. It is not recorded that Peter baptized any one of the three thousand who were converted on the day of Pentecost, nor does it appear that he baptized Cornelius the centurion. Philip had received no commission as a preacher of the Word except that which he had found in the impulse of a fervent love to his Lord; and yet we see him, when driven by persecution from Jerusalem, proclaiming the gospel in Samaria, and baptising the Ethiopian eunuch, and Simon Magus, and others. Of Ananias who baptized Paul we know nothing but that he was a certain disciple, an expression which conveys no intimation of any function whether priestly or diaconal.

And how little Paul regarded baptism as one of the "mysteries" of which he was a steward, we may learn from one fact to which he has given special emphasis himself, and for which he considered he had abundant reasons for thanking God. For one year and six months he was in the city of Corinth, teaching the Word of God, in fulfilment of the Divine command received by night in a vision. "Be not afraid, but speak, and hold not thy peace; for I am with thee, and no man shall set on thee to hurt thee: for I have much people in this city."[1] Now, on the supposition that baptism was one of the mysteries of which the apostle regarded himself as a steward, and especially that it

[1] Acts xviii. 9, 10.

was also a mystery of such transcendent efficacy that he regarded it as the medium or condition of regeneration, it would be but natural to conclude that during those eighteen months he would suffer no occasion to escape him for the impartation of so ineffable a blessing. His ministry was crowned with success. "Many of the Corinthians hearing believed, and were baptized." Who baptized them the narrative in the Acts does not inform us, and apart from a significant asseveration on the part of the apostle, we might not unnaturally conclude that, as the planter of the infant Church in that splendid but corrupt city, Paul himself would have administered this rite.

But the silence of the Acts is more than compensated by the distinct declaration of the First Epistle to the Corinthians, in which he thanks God that he had baptized none of them but Crispus and Gaius, and the household of Stephanas, alleging that Christ sent him "not to baptise, but to preach the gospel."[1] If baptism, however, were the "mystery" it is declared to be by modern sacerdotalists, the alternative indicated by the apostle is strangely inaccurate and misleading. For if without baptism there is no regeneration, no union with Christ, no remission of sins, no hope of eternal life, the complacent self-gratulation of the apostle that he had purposely neglected such an essential condition of salvation sounds like madness. Did the apostle, could the apostle mean, "Christ sent me not to regenerate by the administration of the mystery

---

[1] 1 Cor. i. 15, 16.

of baptism, but to preach the gospel"? Did he understand that the gospel contained a boon more precious than the new birth? If not, why did he bless God that he had regenerated so few? If the new birth is generated by baptism, and according to the theology of sacerdotalism cannot be generated without it, except by an abnormal action of the Holy Spirit, upon which, as it is unrevealed, we are forbidden to presume, the exultant gladness and gratitude which the apostle expresses for his all but absolute neglect of a function so transcendently momentous, baffles our comprehension. If this were one of the "mysteries" of which he was a steward, and if, as he says, "it is required of a steward that he be found faithful," a more astonishing instance of moral defalcation could not be conceived. No further proof is needed than is afforded by such a supposition, coupled with our knowledge of the character of St. Paul, that in his view, and therefore in fact, baptism was not one of the mysteries which pertained to the essence of his office as a steward of Christ. Those conceptions of baptism which demand a special and exclusive order for its administration were a post-apostolic development, rapid indeed, as were other unhealthy growths of both doctrine and practice, but still wholly unsanctioned by inspiration.

And if baptism was not a mystery sacredly confided to the jealous custody of a steward, as little was the Lord's Supper, which was a feast that required for its due observance the presence of neither apostle nor bishop. The incidental references to this rite in the

New Testament show that what is termed, but improperly, its administration, was of a most informal character, and no element could well be more foreign to it than that of mystery. What was the real purport and nature of this ordinance we shall consider at some length in subsequent lectures of this course. In the language of Canon Lightfoot, which will be abundantly sustained as the argument unfolds itself: "The most exalted office in the Church, the highest gift of the Spirit, conveyed no sacerdotal right which was not enjoyed by the humblest member of the Christian community."[1]

[1] "Commentary on the Epistle to the Philippians," p. 184.

LECTURE II.

THE PRIESTHOOD NOT AN ORDER IN THE NEW TESTAMENT (CONTINUED).

LECTURE II.

THE PRIESTHOOD NOT AN ORDER IN THE NEW TESTAMENT (CONTINUED).

IF the course of reasoning presented in the previous lecture is substantially valid, it might seem a work of supererogation to pursue any further the line of argument then sketched; for if in the New Testament, to which alone we appeal as the ultimate source of evidence on the matter in hand, there is discoverable no trace of the priesthood either in name or in office, its alleged apostolicity falls to the ground. But the hardihood and endless repetition with which the claims of a Christian priesthood have been advanced, and the tendency, almost mechanical, which exists in many minds to yield credence to assertions which are repeated with sufficient boldness, will justify my purpose in this lecture still further to strengthen the considerations already adduced, by showing that the sacerdotalism which has allied itself with the gospel is discredited by the qualifications which, according to the New Testament, the ministers of Christ are to possess, and also by the whole genius and aim of the gospel.

III.

The qualifications indispensable to the Christian minister are not necessary for the order and the functions of the priest; while, on the other hand, many of the elements which are consonant, or, at least, not disconsonant, with the validity of the order and functions of the priest, are not only not recognised but disallowed by the gospel. In other words, the names differ, the offices differ, and the qualifications differ. To which we may also add, that the disqualifications differ likewise.

And here it is of some moment that we draw attention to a word we have just used, and which plays the most important part in all Romish and Neo-Catholic writings, touching the orders of the ministry—we mean "validity." This is necessary for the very being of orders, in ecclesiastical phrase, their "esse;" while other things may be important for their well being, in similar phrase, their "bene esse." But these latter elements, however otherwise serviceable and efficacious in the subsidiary functions of the priesthood, and in whatever degree of combination and excellence they may be possessed, never mount so high as to constitute the supreme quality of "validity." There may be faith, reverence, love, chastity, self-denial, knowledge, prudence, zeal, aptness to teach, seraphic devoutness, and every grace in the Christian train; but these are no more than subordinate, and even optional qualifications for the priestly office—invaluable, indeed, to the man who is so happy as to possess them, and to those who may have the good fortune to enjoy the ministrations of a priest so richly endowed, but they are not of the essence of "validity."

All the spiritual excellences possessed by all the saints on earth and in heaven, if combined in one person, would impart to him no authority or power to administer the sacrament of the Eucharist, or to pronounce absolution. While, on the other hand, no ignorance, dissoluteness, infamy, can annul this validity in the case of any priest who, with a due intention, has received holy orders at the hands of a bishop who is himself the inheritor of an untainted commission. I do not hereby affirm that the Church of Rome or any other sacerdotal communion is wholly disregardful of the character of its priests, and that it does not subject them to the exercise of discipline, with its varying degrees of censure and punishment; but I do affirm that in the history of all such Churches there have been instances innumerable in which their priests have exemplified every corruption and crime of which man can be guilty, without any molestation in their sacerdotal functions; and that, according to Tridentine doctrine, the sacraments of the Church have lost none of their virtue in their hands. This conception of validity, as independent of moral and spiritual qualifications, is traceable to a complete inversion of the whole nature and purpose of the gospel, which is thus regarded as predominantly a system of ceremonial efficacy, the priestly manipulator resting his prerogative simply on a pedigree.

But the question we have to consider is, whether we find in the teaching of the New Testament any authority for the doctrine that the ministers of religion can possess a validity of office without the equipment intellectual, moral, and spiritual, which will enable them to expound and exemplify the great truths of the gospel. Can they be clothed with the lofty, the awful function of ambassadors of Christ, by a manual ceremony, which links them to a chronological chain of officials, whose character, however flagitious, cannot neutralise the efficacy of their priestly acts? In the apostolic instructions respecting the qualifications which are to be possessed by the bishop or presbyter, is there any trace of the dogma that there can be authority without fitness, or that there can be fitness without faith, and without that grace which assumes and secures that its possessor will "deny ungodliness and worldly lusts, and live soberly, righteously, and godly in the present world"?

Of the validity of orders, divorced from a competent endowment of intellectual and spiritual powers and sympathies, that apostle, to whose writings we owe our chief directorium on the nature of the Christian ministry and its qualifications, knows nothing. With him, a validity of orders which was but conventional and formal, was a fiction. His validity was not independent of the inner qualifications, but was determined by them. The fitness to preach, or to perform any duty in the Church, preceded the authority, and was its chief warrant, the authority neither creating the fitness nor dispensing with it.

This relation of validity of office to the possession of appropriate qualifications would be recognised at once in any department of life in which reason can play freely without the blinding influence of theological prejudices. There is nothing indeed of which men are growing more impatient than claims of dignity, and authority, and office, which are unsupported by corresponding competence of faculty and character.

Nothing would be more resented in a civilised and enlightened nation than the existence of a caste of physicians or surgeons, whose authority to practise on the constitutions of the people rested on ordination only, while the question of their knowledge anatomical, physiological, chemical, and pathological, was wholly subordinate. The validity of their healing commission, so far as it is formal and recognised, is now made to depend, happily for their patients, on their tested knowledge, of their possession of which both they and the public are assured by the certificates of qualified and incorruptible examiners. What, however, would be the estimation in which a medical lineage would be held whose only validity was grounded on the allegation, even if true, that they had inherited their healing orders from Æsculapius through means of a ritualistic ceremony, which neither communicated, certified, nor implied the existence of the special knowledge which such a caste imperatively requires? And still further, what, if the medicaments employed were alleged to owe their restorative virtue not to any inherent and absolute quality, but to certain words uttered over them, or certain manipulative movements which charged them with their remedial energy? Moreover, what, if so far as the conscious and visible effects were concerned, the medicines were as efficacious without the traditional words or actions as with them? And what if there were to arise an irregular order of practitioners wholly unconnected with the traditional Æsculapian line, who, having diligently studied all forms of disease, and having mastered the virtues of every article in the pharmacopœia, were found to be accomplishing as beneficent a work as those who boast of the validity of their office? And, finally, what if the ceremonies which are most relied upon for producing transcendent effects in the restoration and salvation of the body, were not seen or felt to produce any such effects at all, while the less mysterious agencies applied by the unaccredited physicians assuaged pain, chased fever away, and accomplished every other end for which they were employed?

Would it be possible for any length of time to preserve respect for the order which depended for its public support and reputation solely or mainly upon the unimpeachableness of its genealogical lineage? Would not results be estimated at a higher value than pretensions? and would not qualifications be regarded as essential conditions to the assumption of a valid right to exercise the healing art?

Let a similar law of prescriptive privilege be introduced into the department of education, and let a guild of teachers demand a monopoly of instruction, not because of any practical equipment with the requisite knowledge, but because of their demonstrable succession to some famous pædagogue, and would not the public again insist that validity of office must be determined by qualifications appropriate to the office, and that the only *right* to teach consisted in the *power* to teach? If the aptness of these analogies be assailed on the ground that for the most sacred and awful of the functions of the priesthood the formal validity which ordination ensures is, of itself, the qualification irrespective of the character of the candidates thus consecrated, it is replied that for such *functions as can dispense with godliness the apostles find no room in their conception of a true minister of the cross of Christ.* That a Christian teacher should be, at least, a Christian, one who has passed from death unto life, who has "put off the old man, which is corrupt according to the deceitful lusts," in whom "Christ is formed the hope of glory," is everywhere assumed. That a minister of the gospel who should be able to plead a Divine commission could be less than this, was an idea which no apostle could entertain.

Validity apart from these endowments and experiences would be to them a phantom or a name. Not more revolting would have been a Christian teacher who should have been, at heart, a disbeliever of all the distinctive facts and doctrines of the gospel. A man "given to wine," or "greedy of filthy lucre," or "a brawler," or "a striker," was forbidden to be a bishop; forbidden, not because he could not have been technically and genealogically authorised, but because he was morally, and therefore absolutely and *ipso facto* disqualified; and equally was a man debarred from the exercise of this sacred function if he were not "apt to teach," an expression which clearly implies that one of the essential duties of the presbyter or bishop was that of imparting instruction in the doctrines and obligations connected with the gospel of Christ.

The more than magical potency which is supposed to reside in that validity of orders which it is the exclusive privilege of bishops to confer, was never more arrogantly, I might also say blasphemously, affirmed, than by the late Rev. Henry Melville. With him the validity possessed a transformative energy, which, so far as I am aware, was never claimed for it by any occupant of St. Peter's chair. "If," he said, "whensoever the minister is himself deficient and untaught, so that his sermons exhibit a wrong system of doctrine, you will not allow that Christ's Church may be profited by the ordinance of preaching, you clearly argue that Christ has given up His office, and that He can no longer be styled the minister of the true tabernacle. When everything seems against the true followers of Christ, so that, on a carnal calculation, you would suppose the services of the Church stripped of all efficacy, then, by acting faith in the Head of the ministry, they are instructed and nourished, though in the main *the given lesson be falsehood, and the proffered sustenance be little better than poison*."

This thaumaturgy transcends all the magic of the Egyptians. If it were true, it must be an unspeakable consolation to all the clergy who have received prelatical ordination to know that the regularity of their orders will beneficently neutralise the erroneousness of their teaching. And yet, on this principle, it is impossible to understand the engrossing anxiety of apostles that nothing should be taught but "wholesome" doctrine; or why heretics should have been so rigorously excluded from the Church, when no streak of invalidity attainted their orders. If "validity" can change poison into food, or annihilate its intrinsically fatal qualities, would it not have been wiser to retain the heretics, that this perpetual miracle of transmutation and the evidence it supplies might never be lost from the Church?[1]

Timothy, who must assuredly have been a priest of the sacerdotal type, if such type existed at all in the apostolic Church, was instructed by the Apostle Paul as to the chief matters which were to receive his per-

[1] The following are the words of the late Bishop of Exeter, preached at the consecration of a church at Wall's End :—"This then is the office to which the promise of our Lord was made, that He would be with it always, even unto the end of the world. With it, that is, not so as peculiarly to favour the persons of those that are invested with it, but so as to make the *office* itself effectual to the great purposes for which it was constituted. For them (the ministers) it is very possible that they may be castaways, and yet that they may be humble instruments, in God's hand, to communicate the saving knowledge of His truth to thousands. It is not personal holiness, it is not even zeal for God's honour and for the salvation of men (how much soever it may be the bounden duty of ministers to pray and labour after these graces, and how tremendous soever may be the danger to *ourselves* if we miss obtaining them), yet it is not that holiness or that zeal which, of themselves, can make any *ministerial service of the slightest avail.*"

sonal and assiduous attention, as qualifications for the effective discharge of his ministry; but we search the catalogue in vain for one exhortation or direction from which, except by the most reckless violence, the remotest allusion to sacerdotal functions can be extorted. He was to be an "example of the believers in conversation, in charity, in spirit, in faith, in purity. He was to give attendance to reading, to exhortation, to teaching. He was not to neglect the gift that was in him, which was given him by prophecy with the laying on of the hands of the presbytery. He was to meditate on these things, to give himself wholly to them, that his profiting might appear unto all. He was to take heed unto himself, and unto the doctrine, to continue in them, because, in doing this, he would both save himself and them that heard him. He was to follow after righteousness, godliness, faith, love, patience, meekness. He was to fight the good fight of faith, and lay hold of eternal life. He was to hold fast the form of sound words in faith and love which is in Christ Jesus. He was to commit the things he had heard from Paul to faithful men, who should be able to teach others also. He was to endure hardness as a good soldier of Jesus Christ. He was to study to show himself approved unto God, a workman that needeth not to be ashamed, rightly dividing the word of truth. He was to preach the word, to be instant in season, out of season; to reprove, rebuke, exhort, with all long-suffering and doctrine; to watch in all things, to endure afflictions, to do the work of an evangelist, and to make full proof of his ministry."

That an apostle when formally engaged in giving what seem to be exhaustive instructions and counsels to his son in the faith, both as to his personal and official qualifications, should make no explicit reference to what constituted, on the priestly theory, the most sublime, transcendent, and efficacious prerogatives of his high function, but restrict himself to an urgent, reiterated, impassioned enforcement of duties which pertained to purity of life, earnestness of labour, and the publication and defence of the truth as it is in Jesus, is an enigma which no sacerdotal hypothesis can avail to solve. If the priestly aspects of the Christian ministry are the highest, and cast into the shade every other, why are they here suppressed or forgotten, or at least practically ignored? It were easy to have devoted to them a sentence, and there is not a word even from him who, if he were the apostle of liberty, was also the apostle of order, and who, as we must in all candour avow, knew far better than any of his pretended successors the relative importance of the truths and institutes which are taught and sanctioned in the gospel dispensation. How is it that font, and altar, and priest find no place in these elaborate and comprehensive directions, while the truth and the teacher are vividly conspicuous in them all?

This omission of the sacramental, and therefore of that which is regarded as pre-eminently sacerdotal, becomes all the more startling and significant when we note some of the topics for which the apostle finds room in his two epistles to Timothy. He finds room, for example, for regulations touching the apparel of women, for condemning their undue regard for broidered hair, and gold, and pearls, and costly array; he finds room for directions touching the support from the treasury of the Church of widows, specifying the age and character they must bear before they are entitled to such benevolent alimony; he finds room for dietetic prescriptions to Timothy, whom he recommends to use no longer water, but to take a little wine for his stomach's sake, and for his often infirmities; he finds room to request Timothy to bring the cloak which he left at Troas with Carpus, and the books and the parchments; but he finds no room for directions concerning the administration of the mysteries of baptism and the Eucharist.

The epistles traverse a wide range of topics, enormously varying in intrinsic importance from those which were local, transient, and almost indifferent, to those which possess a universal, abiding, and transcendent value; but neither expressly nor by implication do we find the minister set forth as a priest, or his functions as sacramental. Can this be an accident? Can it be an inadvertent forgetfulness? And if it be neither the one nor the other, in what manner in harmony with the sacerdotal idea shall we explain the silence of the apostle upon those ceremonies whose efficacy is now exalted above that of every other means of grace? What modern bishop of the sacramentarian school, in writing two letters of equal compass to some evangelist entrusted with the commission to put Churches in order, would maintain the like reserve? Would not such epistles be strongly coloured with allusions to fasting, to altars, to priests, to sacrifices, to albs and chasubles, and with strong condemnations of evening celebrations, and as strong injunctions to keep holy the fast days and the feast days?

The letter to Titus, who was discharging in Crete a similar commission to that which had been confided to Timothy, supplies confirmatory evidence of the same truth, that no priestly qualification is specified in connection with those which the elders are to possess. The catalogue is, in fact, all but identical with that which he had drawn up for Timothy, and contains nothing of a priestly complexion.

But only one half of the truth is told when we have proved that the work of the ministry as understood and expounded by the apostle is one which requires no sacerdotal endowment whatever. The other half, and that by no means the less important one in view of the tendencies of the times to the gross superstitions of mediævalism, is that the priest according to his canonical functions may dispense with every qualification which has been specified as constituting the accredited fitness of an ambassador of Christ. He need not be sober, nor apt to teach. He need not possess the common virtues of humanity. They may adorn the man, but they cannot authorise the priest, nor can their absence, or the presence of their counter-vices in their highest degree and virulence, attaint and nullify the validity of his office in the Church of God. False, worldly, debased, corrupt, and the corrupter of others, he has, we are assured, free access to Him "whose eyes are as flames of fire;" can consecrate into saving elements the sacramental bread and wine; and can open the kingdom of heaven, or can shut it against men compared with whose life his is a thing of loathsomeness.

Can any person whose mind is not absolutely blinded by prejudice imagine that such a man would have been accounted qualified for the work of the ministry by the apostles; that knowing him to be the subject of such vices they would have invested him with that validity which is alleged to be created by imposition of hands; or that if such vices had developed themselves after his appointment, they would have championized and shielded the indelibility of his orders as a priest of the Most High God?

The conclusion we draw from these considerations is, that so completely has sacerdotalism in the Christian dispensation obscured and even reversed the true doctrine of the ministry, that the qualifications which are essential to enable the priest to perform his highest and most characteristic functions are not requisite in the preacher of the gospel, and that the characteristics requisite in the minister of the gospel are not essential to the priest; and, further, that elements which would vitiate the right of any man to represent himself as an ambassador of Christ are vauntingly declared so far to coalesce with the sacerdotal office as not to shake its authority, or to impair the energy of its mystic acts and words.

Now, offices which demand different and even disparate qualifications cannot be the same offices; and hence the modern priesthood, and the ministry as it was understood by the Saviour and His apostles, denote two orders of functions which are wholly incompatible with each other. And it is a circumstance to which it is impossible to attach an exaggerated value, that there is not an instance after the outpouring of the Holy Spirit and the full inauguration of the kingdom of Christ in which any Church officer was appointed, or deemed eligible for appointment, who did not possess in the estimation of those by whom he was appointed the grace of God. To say nothing of those who were more specially devoted to the work of the ministry, the first deacons who were primarily selected for the more secular work connected with the Church were to be " men of honest repute, full of the Holy Ghost and of wisdom."[1]

It is not contended that there have not been thousands of men who have filled both the more spiritual and the secular positions in the Church of God who have known nothing of His grace, and that from the lips of sordid hirelings the gospel has been made the savour of life unto life to a multitude which no man can number; but it is maintained that such were never called to that high service by the voice of the Chief Shepherd, who demands as a first condition of the feeding of His sheep and His lambs that the under-shepherd shall love Him. The necessity for

[1] Acts vi. 3.

this supreme qualification was burnt upon the conscience and memory of Peter by the threefold question which formed a significant and pathetic antithesis to the threefold denial, " Lovest thou me ? " And apart from the same gracious and constraining affection, no preacher from the days of Peter until now has ever possessed any authority to minister in the Church of Christ, except such as is human, technical, outward, and subject to revision and reversal by Him whose alone it is to enstamp with validity the orders of any of His servants. The statement that the priest, irrespective of his character, can still impart efficacy to the sacraments, is sufficiently met by another statement, viz., that there is no sacrament in the New Testament which depends in any wise or to any degree for its efficacy on the administrator. Neither his hands nor his words are said to endow either baptism or the Lord's Supper with a regenerative or strengthening energy which they would not receive from the words or hands of any other man. Nor is there the faintest evidence that the administration of either ordinance was restricted to any order of officers in the Christian Church.

In his work on the priesthood the Rev. T. T. Carter, Rector of Clewer, has on this matter fallen into a signal blunder.[1] He supposes that when the Apostle Paul says, "The cup of blessing which we bless," he is referring " to that act of ministry which was his own habitual office." A glance at the Greek would have shown him

[1] "The Doctrine of the Priesthood," p. 80.

that the *we* which he has italicised is not in the original except as it is involved in the verb itself. It is therefore not emphatic, nor is it meant to denote the apostle's own personal and priestly act. And the following verse determines the interpretation of the "we" in its application to the whole Christian community. "For we being many are one body, for we all partake of the one loaf." The blessing of the cup and of the bread is accomplished by the same Church that partakes of them, and that constitutes one body.

To excuse, therefore, the lack of spiritual qualifications in the priest, on the ground that he does not need them for the performance of his most mysterious and thaumaturgic functions, for which it is alleged the validity of orders is sufficient, is on the one hand to disparage and set at nought the apostolic directions as to the indispensable characteristics of the ministry, and on the other to invent alike functions and validity for which there is no apostolic warrant. The priest is created for fictitious work, and work is created for a fictitious priest.

The doctrines of the Church of Rome and of the Church of England are at one touching the non-dependence of the virtue and efficacy of the sacraments on the character of the administrator. The Catechism of the Council of Trent says: "The badness of the minister does not hinder the efficacy of the sacrament. Since the ministers in that sacred function do not act in their own person, but in that of Christ, it follows from this circumstance that whether they be good or bad, provided they use that form and matter which the Catholic Church has preserved according to the institution of Christ, and intend to do in the administration what the Church intends, they do truly consecrate and confer the sacrament." [1]

The same position is embodied in one of the canons of the Council of Trent. "Whosoever shall affirm that a minister who is in mortal sin does not consecrate or confer a sacrament, although he observes everything that is essential to the consecration and bestowment thereof, let him be accursed." [2]

To the same effect is the 26th Article of the Church of England, "on the unworthiness of the ministers, which hinders not the effect of the sacrament."

"Although in the visible Church the evil be ever mingled with the good, and sometimes the evil have chief authority in the ministration of the word and sacraments, yet forasmuch as they do not the same in their own name, but in Christ's, and do minister by His commission and authority, we may use their ministry, both in hearing the Word of God and in receiving of the sacraments. Neither is the effect of Christ's ordinance taken away by their wickedness, nor the grace of God's gifts diminished from such as by faith and rightly do receive the sacraments ministered unto them; which be effectual because of Christ's institution and promise, although they be ministered by evil men. Nevertheless, it appertaineth to the

---

[1] Catechism, quest. 19. On the Sacraments.
[2] Sessio vii. canon 12. *De Sacramentis.*

discipline of the Church that inquiry be made of evil ministers, and that they be accused by those that have knowledge of their offences; and finally being found guilty, by just judgment be deposed."

With the doctrine of the two Churches as to the benefits of the sacraments being conferred on worthy recipients, however unworthy be the administrators, I have no contention. But the agreement on the fact involves the deepest disagreement as to the reasons. They maintain that the sacraments, and especially the Eucharist, though not depending on a good priest for their efficacy, still depend on a priest: I maintain, on the other hand, that their efficacy is wholly unaffected by the administrator, be he who he may, and is due to the subjective condition of the recipient, and to that grace which is never withheld from penitence and faith. They maintain that wicked men do minister in the Church by Christ's "commission and authority," and not simply through the appointment of human officers: I maintain that there is no minister whom Christ has authorized to bear office in His Church who is either wicked or unbelieving; and that an immoral priest or pastor is, at least, as monstrous a spectacle in the Church of Christ as an infidel, unless we are to suppose that the gospel has more tolerance for depravity than for scepticism. Voltaire was a better man than Alexander VI., and if the debaucheries and murders of the latter were regarded as not invalidating his "commission and authority" as a pontifical minister of Christ, what bar could be found to priestly orders in the infidelity of the French philosopher? The prominence which is given to "wickedness" in the 26th Article of the Church of England, and its total silence concerning "unbelief," leave us in doubt as to whether, in its view, a disbeliever even up to the point of absolute Pyrrhonism, but with a conscience sufficiently elastic to seek admission into the Church, would, if successful in his ambition, receive his "commission and authority" from Christ. If he would not, then why should that "commission and authority" be pleaded for wicked men, and vice and crime be treated with an indulgence not extended to a disbelief which may nevertheless be associated with all the moral decencies which have been outraged by priests who have professed a faith which their life belied? Is one who denies the resurrection of Christ from the dead less "commissioned and authorised" by Him than a profligate?

It may be thought that the argument we have now been pursuing encounters a serious difficulty in the person of Judas Iscariot, whose commission as an apostle, in spite of his subsequent peculation and treachery, was as valid as that of St. Peter or St. John. The fact is admitted. His orders were incontestable. They were received directly from the Lord. The election of Judas to the apostolate has ever been one of the profoundest mysteries in the gospel records. It cannot, however, well be doubted that he had to sustain a relation unknown, and for a season unintended by himself, in that great drama which was to culminate in the death of Christ for the salvation of the world. Without being a victim of fate, or accomplishing mechanically a preordained part in the conspiracy which delivered his Lord into the hands of His enemies, he fulfilled, in virtue of the natural outworking of his own character, the prophecy of the betrayal. But he did more than this. For the function of Judas is but imperfectly apprehended if we overlook the striking witness which he bore to the innocence of the Lord. The most convincing testimony of the sinlessness of the Saviour comes from him who would have found a special solace in the hour of his despair and remorse in the memory of any one act of infirmity or sin in his Master. But through those three years, during which he had known Him intimately, he might search in vain for one deed or word which could soothe the tortures of his conscience with the reflection that he had delivered up only an undeserving pretender. Is it inconceivable that the testimony of the traitor, as he flung from his hand the scorching price of blood, was *designed* to be among the most unanswerable proofs of the innocence of the Saviour, and to bar, as if by anticipation, those reckless criticisms which would, in these recent days, find in the blind and doting enthusiasm of His disciples the source of that faultless delineation which the gospel records present?

It is not denied that in Judas we have an apostle without grace, or at least who had lost the grace he once possessed, but we have also an apostle who fulfilled a unique and exceptional function in the history of the unfolding of the great redemptive work. He was one assuredly who was meant to be without successor, and to be a beacon for all time, warning men against the usurpation of gospel commissions without the possession of gospel grace. Betrayal, remorse, and suicide on the part of a man who could plead with justice the validity of his orders, but whose heart was given to covetousness, supply no encouragement to the baseless assumption of orders when divorced from the grace which, since the foundation of the Christian Church, is indispensable to every true minister of Christ. I say, *since the foundation of the Christian Church*, for Judas was not an apostle of that Church, and never received a commission to preach the gospel in that full sense in which it was alone possible to preach it after the death, resurrection, and ascension of our Lord, and after the baptism of the Holy Ghost and of fire. He had not been endued with power from on high, and could therefore possess none of those exalted conceptions, either of the spiritual aims of the kingdom of Christ or of the qualifications demanded in its ministers, which were imparted by the Pentecostal effusion.

And even with reference to the commission which he did possess, how little that was regarded as bestowing on him, or on his fellow-apostles, the exclusive right to go forth and work miracles in the name of Jesus, is seen by the rebuke which the Saviour administered to John, when, in reply to his complaint—" Master, we saw one casting out devils in thy name, and we forbade him, because he followeth not us"—He said, "Forbid him not: for there is no man which shall do a miracle in my name, that can lightly speak evil of me. For he that is not against us is on our part."[1]

The validity of orders can never have afforded an instance so strikingly capable of vindication as this of the apostles of our Lord. The circumstances of their appointment would be fresh in the memory of every one of them. The day and even the hour would not be forgotten. No lapse of time had obscured the lineage. No possible accident could have confused the succession. There was no canonical irregularity, nor was there any deplorable blank in the ecclesiastical record, such as brings disastrous discredit to more recent claims. It was as yet impossible that any pretender could presume to have been appointed along with the rest. They knew each other by name, and they knew their number was only twelve. No authorisation could be more formal, circumstantial, direct, definite, and decisive. That the apostles were by no means insensible to the importance of validity is clear from the jealous remonstrance of such an apostle as John, who, as it would seem, expected that his valiant rebuke of unauthorised agents would obtain the approval of his Master. Now was the time for Him who had set His seal upon these twelve apostles to protect their functions from invasion, and to admonish uncommissioned preachers and workers of miracles that

[1] Mark ix. 38–40.

it was at their peril they either roused consciences or expelled demons without a formal vocation and designation from Him. Did He not owe this to those who were the bearers of His credentials? Did He not owe it to Himself as the sole fountain of authority in His kingdom? Would it have been astonishing if He had confirmed the interdict of John?

The history however is significant in many respects, but most notably in this, that it shows that He who gave validity to the commission of the twelve did not regard it as having an *exclusive* purport. It was a positive authorisation with respect to the twelve, but it was not a *prohibition* with regard to all beyond that narrow circle. And with Him, who surely knew best the relative importance of things connected with His kingdom, the mere ground of circumstantial validity upon which John was standing was unworthy of consideration compared with the actual work of beneficence which was being accomplished in His name by men who had received no formal commission at His hands.

To whose judgment must we defer on the question of a technical and formal warranty—that of the men who, with or without proof, plead it, or that of Him who confers it? We appeal from the narrow officialism of the disciple to the Divine breadth and merciful benevolence of the Master, with whom, we repeat—in that spiritual kingdom which He established after His ascension and the glorious effusion of His Holy Spirit —there is no validity of functions which is not accompanied by the qualifications which the discharge of such functions actually requires; and these functions are such as demand, in the case of the ministers of Christ, faith in Him, renewal of heart, consecration of life, and a power to expound and enforce the truths of the gospel. If these things be already come, the Divine commission is certified by the fact of their existence, and any ordering which may follow can be but a human appointment and regulation. If the fire of Christian zeal be kindled in the soul, its right to burn lies in the fact that it is fire. The behest of heaven to preach the truth rests immovably on him who has felt the grace of heaven, and to whom the gift of utterance has been vouchsafed.

IV.

We are now prepared to enter upon the consideration of the last position which we advanced against the existence of a human official priesthood in the Church of Christ, namely, that it is inconsistent with the genius and purpose of the gospel.

In a letter written to a friend in the year 1836, Dr. Arnold, of Rugby, says: " Every part of the New Testament gives a picture of Christianity, or of some one great feature in it, and every part negatively confutes the priestcraft heresy, because that is to be found nowhere, insomuch that no man yet ever fell or could fall into that heresy by studying the Scriptures: they are a bar to it altogether, and it is only when they are undermined by traditions and the rudiments of men that the heresy begins to make way. And it is making its way fearfully, but it will not take the form that Newman wishes, but the far more natural and consistent form of pure Popery."[1]

In another letter, written to Mr. Justice Coleridge in 1841, he says: "The priest is either Christ or Antichrist; he is either our mediator, or he is like the man of sin in God's temple; the Church system is either our gospel, and St. John's and St. Paul's gospel is superseded by it, or it is a system of blasphemous falsehood such as St. Paul foretold was to come, such as St. John knew to be already in the world."[2]

And again, in another letter, he says: "The kingdom of God is the perfect development of the Church of God, and when priestcraft destroyed the Church, the kingdom of God became an impossibility."[3]

Whatever may be thought of the strength of this language, no one will dispute that it expresses, without any conscious exaggeration, the honest and painful conviction of one of the most profound, learned, sincere, and spiritual men—and they are and have been innumerable—that ever adorned the Church of England. His prophecy, moreover, as to the logical destination to which the Church principles he assailed must conduct, has been signally verified in the history of Newman, Manning, and a host of others who have embraced "pure Popery." His language only expresses in another form the position which has now to be elucidated—that the human priesthood is at variance

---

[1] "Life and Correspondence of Dr. Arnold," vol. ii. p. 60.
[2] Ibid. vol. ii. pp. 261, 262. [3] Ibid. vol. ii. p. 431.

with the whole genius and purpose of the gospel. The adaptation of means to ends which prevails throughout the whole creation, and which, in spite of the teaching of a certain philosophical school, must ever be the most widely influential argument in support of the Being of a God, is not wanting in that last revelation by which He has spoken to us by His Son. Here the design of God has not to be inferred through doubtful and laborious processes of investigation. It is declared in almost every variety of language. The ultimate end which the gospel contemplates with respect to the individual man is the perfection of his nature, the entire and cheerful subordination of his soul to the will of God. That which rendered the gospel a necessity, and without which it would have been impossible, was sin; and the exclamation of John as he saw Jesus coming, assured the world that in Him the necessity was met: " Behold the Lamb of God, that taketh away the sin of the world." The secret of His name was expounded in the fact that " he should save his people from their sins."

It is manifest, indeed, throughout the teaching both of the Saviour and His apostles, that the region within which the truths and spiritual forces that constitute the gospel are designed primarily to work is the heart of man. It is the bitter fountain which springs there that is to be made sweet; it is the tree whose roots are buried there which has to be made good. The Sermon on the Mount was designed, among other purposes, to prepare the way for this conception of the functions and aims of the gospel, by unfolding the spirituality of the law, and leading the Jew into a deeper and more searching interpretation of the seat and quality of sin, both of which had been so grossly misapprehended, that the Saviour said: "Except your righteousness shall exceed the righteousness of the scribes and Pharisees, ye shall in no wise enter into the kingdom of heaven."

The exterior embodiments of sin had come to be regarded as the only symptoms that need occasion the transgressor any alarm, while the subtile *virus* and essence were allowed to rage within. The murder was dreaded, but not the anger from which it sprang. The adultery was branded, but not the look of lust and the impure desire. And this outwardness of interpretation which was put upon sin developed a corresponding outwardness of reliance upon ceremonies of reparation and cleansing.

The scene at the well of Sychar with the woman of Samaria constitutes another stage in the prophetic revelation of that spiritual dispensation which the Saviour had come to establish. In the picture of that future which Christ unfolded, the woman was assured that neither on "this mountain," which to her was consecrated, nor yet at Jerusalem, where was the temple consecrated for the Jew, should men "worship the Father." The age of sacred places, and of the sacrifices connected with them, was coming to an end, and this because "God is a Spirit, and they that worship him must worship him in spirit and in truth." Reverence and awe for what was local in ceremony and service were to break through the limitations which had bound them in an economy which had been but a preparation or scaffolding for what was infinitely higher, and which in fact had " no glory by reason of the glory that excelleth." To say that our Saviour's words only predicted the approaching termination of Judaism, is to charge them with a strange and repulsive shallowness; for the contrast is between the spiritual worship which God requires in the gospel dispensation, and the ritual homage which demands for its due rendering a place and the paraphernalia of a sacrificial service, wherever the place and whatever the service may be. It was not Judaism alone, but every system involving the necessity of place, priests, altars, and victims, that came within the sweep of this prophetic annulment.

The figment of consecration which in the new economy assumes—through the performance of a ceremony—to mark off a space within which souls filled with faith and reverence can have nearer access to God than the same souls with the same faith and reverence can have in any other spot, is of the essence of priestcraft, and ignores the emphatic assurance of our Lord,— "Wherever two or three are gathered together in my name, there am I in the midst of them."

Everywhere, and at all times, men may offer their spiritual sacrifice of prayer and praise. Priests are no more, because temples are no more; and temples are no more, because altars are no more; and altars are no more, because propitiatory sacrifices are no more; and propitiatory sacrifices are no more, because Christ hath offered Himself once for sins for ever. Superstition—usurping the name of Christianity—may rear her temples, which seem like magic creations, their arches intersecting far up in air, like the branches of lofty trees in some forest glade; she may fill the tracery of the windows with colours that vie with those of the rainbow, and which cast their reflected glories through the place; she may to sound of organ and trained voices utter the most touching words in music all but heavenly, that steals from arch to arch in long reverberation, as if shrinking from the silence in which at length it dies away; she may build her high altars, marshal her priests in solemn procession, clothe them with the richest fabrics that skill can make or wealth procure: she may thus charm the imagination, wrap the soul in a sensuous elysium, dissolve it into ecstasies, make it feel even as if that sentimental joy or sorrow were the very godliness which fits for heaven; but, except as the "worship is in spirit and in truth," all this may be nothing more than the fugitive transport of an impressible nature, and all the beauty, and music, and wonder are but a dramatic insult on Him who rent the veil and abolished temples, that He might consecrate the souls of men and dwell in them for ever.[1]

[1] Even M. Renan has caught the spirit of the interview of our Lord with the woman of Samaria, though with a scepticism as to the precise accuracy of all the incidents which is utterly groundless:—

"Le jour où il prononça cette parole, il fut vraiment fils de Dieu.

The same independence of the gospel of all restrictions of place—and therefore of all ceremonialism, the sanctity of which is made dependent on place—is seen in its subsequent development under the eyes of the apostles. Prison and sea-shore, house and synagogue, afforded them all they needed for their ministerial work. They consecrated no water for baptism, no table for the Supper of the Lord. With them, the one circumstance of opportunity or convenience was supreme and sufficient.

The apostles claimed for their prayers no priestly efficacy, but were as dependent on the supplications of the people as the people were dependent on theirs. There is an irresistible pathos in the tones in which the Apostle Paul entreats the Churches to whom he writes to pray for him, that "the word of the Lord may have free course and be glorified." His office clothed him with no power of nearer approach to the throne of grace than was enjoyed by the obscurest saint in the Christian Church.

Il dit pour la première fois le mot sur lequel reposera l'édifice de la religion éternelle. Il fonda le culte pur, sans date, sans patrie, celui que pratiqueront toutes les âmes élevées jusqu' à la fin des temps. Non seulement sa religion, ce jour-là, fut la bonne religion de l'humanité, ce fut la religion absolue ; et, si d'autres planètes ont des habitants doués de raison et de moralité, leur religion ne peut être différente de celle qui Jésus, a proclamée près du puits de Jacob. . . . Le mot de Jésus à été un éclair dans une nuit obscure ; il a fallu dix-huit cents ans pour que les yeux de l'humanité (que dis-je ! d'une portion infiniment petite de l'humanité) s'y soient habitués. Mais l'éclair deviendra le plein jour, et après avoir parcouru tous les cercles d'erreurs, l'humanité reviendra à cet mot-là, comme à l'expression immortelle de sa foi, et de ses espérances."—
" Vie de Jésus," p. 235.

Nor did they assume any priestly function in connection with their work of preaching the gospel. As we have seen, the great purpose of the redemptive economy was to purify man from sin, and to renew within him the image of God. This was the end, and the means were adapted to the end, being moral, as the end itself was moral.

The ignorance of the soul was to be dispelled by the "truth as it is in Jesus;" the hatred of the soul was to be vanquished by the manifestation of the love of God. Not by mechanism, manipulation, magic, incantation, ceremony, but by preaching, teaching, exhorting, persuading, warning, did the apostles seek to accomplish their high commission. They were ambassadors, and they had to expound and enforce a glorious message of reconciliation. "By manifestation of the truth they had to commend themselves to every man's conscience in the sight of God." The workman, who as a minister of Christ was one "that needed not to be ashamed," was one who "*rightly divided the word of truth,*" and not one who discharged with canonical precision and regularity sacerdotal acts. The Apostle Paul reserved his heaviest anathemas for himself, or for an angel from heaven, who should preach any other gospel than that which he had already preached, and not for the man who should be guilty of a ceremonial informality. The gifts which the Saviour was able to bestow on His Church, when He had ascended on high and led captivity captive, were apostles, prophets, evangelists, pastors and teachers, but not a solitary priest.

And in the apocalyptic vision which John beheld, the essential spirit and genius of the New Dispensation was embodied and glorified, not in the form of some pontiff clothed in costly vestments, swinging the golden censer, or offering in high celebration the tremendous oblation of the body and blood of Christ, but in the form of an angel flying in the midst of heaven, having the everlasting gospel to preach unto them that dwell on the earth, and to every nation, and kindred, and people, and tongue; and he was not, with face averted from the world, muttering in tones muffled and inaudible the words of an ineffable mystery, but saying with a loud voice, "Fear God, and give glory to him."[1]

Thus, as we have seen, the conception of a human official priesthood is not only not Christian, but it is anti-Christian. While no place is found for it in name, office, or qualification in the New Testament, it is resented by its entire genius and spirit. Not only is the external ceremonialism of the gospel reduced to a minimum, in direct and purposed contrast with the Jewish dispensation, but the administration even of the sacraments which are appointed is nowhere alleged to constitute the specific and exclusive privilege and duty of the ministry, whatever convenience or order may be supposed to be secured by the custom which has assigned it to them. But of any spiritual grace communicated to any soul through the simple fact that a sacrament is administered by one man rather than by another, we have not a shadow of evidence in the apostolic writings.

[1] Rev. xiv. 6, 7.

And as little proof have we of the efficacy of any sacrament as an *opus operatum* irrespective of the condition of the recipient, while we have demonstration in abundance that, apart from this condition, they convey no sanctifying grace whatever. If, after his baptism by Philip the deacon, the Ethiopian eunuch went on his way rejoicing; Simon Magus, after baptism by the same Philip, sought to purchase the power of imparting the Holy Ghost; which widely contrasted results cannot surely be traced to the common influence of the same sacramental efficacy, but to the spiritual condition of the eunuch and the magician respectively. There is the like absence of all evidence that the elements of the Lord's Supper exert any gracious influence on the communicant in consequence of any priestly ceremony, and apart from the living faith and adoring love of the recipient.

Well does Neander observe: " What Moses expressed as a wish, that the Spirit of God might rest upon all, and all might be prophets, is a prediction of that which was to be realised through Christ. By Him was instituted a fellowship of Divine life, which—proceeding from the *equal* and *equally immediate* relation of all to the one God as the Divine source of life to all—removed those boundaries within which, at the Old Testament position, the development of the higher life was still confined; and hence the fellowship thus derived essentially distinguishes itself from the constitution of all previously existing religious societies. There could be no longer a priestly or prophetic office, constituted to serve as a medium for the propagation and development of the kingdom of God, on which office the religious consciousness of the community was to be dependent. Such a guild of priests as existed in the previous religious systems of religion, empowered to guide other men who remained, as it were, in a state of pupilage, having the exclusive care of providing for their religious wants, and serving as mediators by whom all other men must first be placed in connection with God and Divine things—such a priestly caste could find no place within Christianity. In removing out of the way that which separated men *from God*, in communicating to all the same fellowship *with God*, Christ also removed the barrier which had hitherto divided men *from one another*."[1]

Presuming that the argument against the existence of a human official priesthood in the New Testament need not be pursued further, the question arises in what manner the institution found its way into the gospel dispensation. And this question can find no adequate solution in any one cause. Neither did the priest suddenly obtrude himself upon the Church, nor did the Church suddenly create the priest. Sacerdotalism was a growth traceable to a concurrence of influences and tendencies, some of which were wholly innocent in themselves, and became perilous only in combination. The theory which would compendiously explain the whole phenomenon, by alleging an ambitious conspiracy on the part of the presbyters or

[1] Neander's "Church History," vol. i. (Clarke's Library.)

bishops, is philosophically absurd and historically false. At no period of the Church could any such conspiracy have succeeded in establishing itself in the midst of a reluctant people.

The circumstances which mainly contribute to the existence and power of a priesthood are found in human nature itself. This fact, indeed, has been strongly alleged as no mean support of the caste of the priesthood, as if a general tendency were its own vindication. There are, however, other inveterate and universal proclivities of man, which it is needless to mention, but which, on the same principle, would have been able to defend their folly or their wickedness. Suffice it to say, that the bias of humanity towards a priesthood is no greater nor more general than its bias towards selfishness and sin.

It is incontestable, however, that to this bias towards a priesthood must be traced, in great measure, its intrusion into a Church to whose spirit it is wholly alien, and from which, as we have seen, it was designed to be absolutely excluded. Ill-defined terrors of the future; a fear of God not yet wholly cast out by love; the irksomeness of duties of self-discipline, so needful to the attainment of a higher sanctity of life; the intolerable oppressiveness of a sense of personal responsibility, seeking relief by its transference to others, who were vaguely supposed to be capable of accepting and discharging it; the fatal proneness (alas! too common still, even when most jealously watched) to lift the ritual above the spiritual; and the ingrained associations of priestism, which the converts imported from Judaism and heathenism alike into the circle of the Christian Church, all contributed to prepare the way for a transformation in the type of that religion which, as inherited from the apostles, knew no earthly mediator. The gradual restriction, too, to certain officers, of definite functions and symbolic rites, insensibly clothed these acts and the men who performed them with exceptional sanctity; and the officers themselves, who were not exempt from the common frailties of humanity, were not always strong enough to decline the deference that was offered them, but little by little assumed as rights what the Church had conferred only as prerogatives and privileges, subject to its own will. Concessions begot further encroachments, and encroachments secured further concessions, until at length the laity sank into the most abject spiritual serfdom. Under the influence mainly of men who were converts from heathenism, and whose minds had been saturated with sacerdotalism and with sacred mysteries, sacramentarianism rose into ascendency over the more moral and spiritual aspects of Christianity. Judaism had been abolished and heathenism had been forsaken, but in their stead had grown up a form of Christianity surpassing both in the splendour of its ritual and in the superstitious homage which was paid to priests and priestly acts.

It is a remarkable circumstance, that while neither in the Eastern nor the Roman Church there is any controversy touching the functions of the priest, the question remains undetermined in the English Church down to the present hour. Even the bishops themselves contend with each other as to what it is they confer in ordination, and no wonder the priests debate as to what it is they receive. There is no organisation in our land, or in the world, secular or sacred, in which there reigns such hopeless confusion and conflict as to the range of duties and powers assigned to its various functionaries. Some maintain that the clergyman who pretends to be a priest of the sacrificing order is an impostor; and others, that a clergyman who foregoes the claim is a greater impostor still. Dr. Pusey says "that upon the principle of sacerdotalism hangs the future of England's Church;" while the late Archbishop of Dublin maintained that no such principle was recognised in that Church, but that the term "priest" signifies, and was meant to signify, a "presbyter," to whom was assigned no specifically sacerdotal office whatever. Views thus not only divergent, but fundamentally contradictory, are now dividing the Established Church of our nation, and creating contentions, which for heat and bitterness find no parallel in any political controversies. Opposing camps have been formed, in the shape of societies for the purpose of carrying on this internecine struggle, and a new literature has been created, which bids fair to rifle all the resources of our language of their epithets of violence and objurgation. Neither the mitre nor the crown is sacred from assault when any discourtesy is suspected, or even constructively interpreted against the claims of sacerdotalism. The root of bitterness out of which all this strife has grown is simple. It is this. Does the Church of England recognise a human priest, or does she not? It is for the reader to determine, in presence of the evidence which has been adduced in the two lectures which I now conclude, whether such a priest can bring his credentials from the New Testament.[1]

[1] The following may be regarded as a sample of the Christian amenities which have been engendered by the sacerdotal conflict in the Church of England. The "Church Herald" of July 15, 1874, referring to the Worship Regulation Bill, says: "Mr. Gladstone's opportunity was prepared for him by the strange bunglers whose dense stupidity and owlish blindness would be ballast enough to sink any rational cause. His speech must have been gall and wormwood to the Bishop of Gloucester, who sat smirking and admiring himself in the Peers' Gallery. The clergy have been largely alienated from the Tories by Dr. Tait's odious bill — the blundering, bungling, floundering bill of the purblind archbishop. .... Archbishop Tait lectures and hectors his suffragans with pompous and rude expostulations, scarcely allowing them to maintain that their souls are their own. The cringing, abject, contemptible, slave-spirited manner in which they lick the dust off the feet of this Scotch Erastian and northern adventurer is a sight to make the *devils rejoice and angels weep.*"

The "Church Times" scarcely allows itself to be outdone in this sort of loyal civilities. In its number of January 2, 1874, it says: "The Queen's ostentatious nonconformity, and her scarcely less ostentatious slights to the Church of England, have deprived her example of any religious weight with Churchmen."

And in the same number we read: "When Dr. Ellicott and Dean Law (the bishop and dean of Gloucester) are discrediting their whole faction by dealing with the interests of the Church as if it were a Christmas pantomime, and *they severally clown and pantaloon*, burning their own fingers with the hot poker they intend for the police, we can have little to complain of the way our opponents, religious and irreligious, alike are acting."

LECTURE III.

THE CHRISTIAN PRIESTHOOD—ITS ALLEGED ORDERS AND LINEAGE.

LECTURE III.

THE CHRISTIAN PRIESTHOOD: ITS ALLEGED ORDERS
AND LINEAGE.

IT is no part of my purpose in these lectures to uphold the position that we have in the New Testament a scheme of ecclesiastical organisation and government complete in all its parts, Divine in its authority, and designed for perpetual and universal adoption by all Christian communities. Whatever general resemblance there might be in the polity of the various Churches—a resemblance determined by their spiritual and secular necessities—it is unquestionable that for a considerable period there were diversities of detail, arising from the special circumstances in which each Church was planted.

As they were the offspring of a fervent and adoring love for the Lord who had bought them with His precious blood, the life begotten by this love refused at first to be stereotyped in one inflexible mould. The apostles themselves were contented if this one supreme canon were obeyed—that all things "be done decently and in order,"[1]—and this general principle was con-

---

[1] 1 Cor. xiv. 40. πάντα δὲ εὐσχημόνως καὶ κατὰ τάξιν γινέσθω.

sistent with a large liberty in the details of worship and administration. The passion for a complete mechanical assimilation and uniformity was the development of a later period. A messenger who should have made a missionary visit to all the Churches in existence a quarter of a century after the ascension of our Lord, would have detected numerous departures from any one theoretic ideal. He would have found them differing in their forms of service and in the number of their elders and deacons, though in all there might be men discharging, with the sanction and appointment of the brethren, the ministerial and diaconal functions. It is unquestionable, however, that in the course of the second century substantially the same polity was adopted by all the Churches, and that this polity underwent, in subsequent ages, an almost simultaneous series of changes, determined in great measure by corresponding changes in doctrine, by the growing ambition of the clergy, and by a passion for centralisation, which, little by little, destroyed the original autonomy of each Christian community. At length there grew up a complex and imposing hierarchy, whose claims, both as to the gradation of its orders and as to its pretended lineal descent from the apostles, it shall be our present business to examine.

The Church of Rome has discovered seven orders, all of whom existed "from the beginning of the Church." "Since," it says, "the ministry of so exalted a priesthood is a Divine thing, it was meet, in order to surround it with the greater dignity and veneration, that in the most orderly disposition of the Church (*Ecclesiæ ordinatissima dispositione*) there should be several distinct ranks of ministers, who in virtue of their office should serve the priesthood; and so arranged that, beginning with the clerical tonsure, they may ascend from the lesser to the greater orders. For the sacred Scriptures make clear mention not only of priests but of deacons, and instruct us in very grave language as to the things which are to be specially attended to in their ordination; and from the very beginning of the Church (*ab ipso Ecclesiæ initio*) the names and duties of the following orders are known to have been in use, namely,— sub-deacons (*sub-diaconi*), acolytes (*acolythi*), exorcists (*exorcistæ*), readers (*lectores*), and porters (*ostiarii*); although they are not all of equal rank, for sub-deacons are placed among the greater orders by the Fathers and Holy Councils, in which also we very frequently read of other inferior orders."[1]

And there are the usual canons and maledictions, as follows :—

"Whosoever shall affirm that there is not in the Catholic Church a hierarchy instituted by Divine appointment, and consisting of bishops, presbyters, and ministers, let him be accursed."[2]

"Whosoever shall affirm that bishops are not superior to presbyters; or that they have not the power of confirming and ordaining, or that the power which they have is common to them and presbyters; or that orders conferred by them without the consent or calling

---

[1] Cap. ii. Sess. 23.   [2] Canon 6.

of the people or the secular power are invalid; or that those who are not properly ordained or instituted according to ecclesiastical or canonical power, but derive their ordination from some other source, are lawful ministers of the Word and the sacraments; let him be accursed."[1]

The doctrine of the Church of England touching the orders of the ministry is formally and authoritatively set forth in its preface to the "Form and Manner of Making, Ordaining, and Consecrating of Bishops, Priests, and Deacons."

"It is evident," we are there told, "unto all men diligently reading the holy Scripture and ancient authors, that from the apostles' time there have been these orders of ministers in Christ's Church, bishops, priests, and deacons."

As against the doctrine both of the Church of Rome and the Church of England, it is my purpose to show, with as much brevity as possible, that there is no historic foundation for it in the New Testament, and that there is no one truth touching the government and administration of the Church which is established by more irrefragable evidence, positive and negative, direct and indirect, explicit and implicit, than that there were but two permanent orders of officers in the apostolic Churches, presbyters or bishops, and deacons. The New Testament affords us, on this question, materials for the most complete induction, and the conclusion which such induction authorises is of the most un-

[1] Canon 7.

equivocal character. Ritschl does not exceed the just warranty of the evidence when, in his work on the "Origin of the Old Catholic Church," he declares that "it does not admit even of a doubt that within the New Testament bishop and presbyter are titles of the same office, and that, accordingly, more bishops than one in the first age belonged to a Church; that this fact was not only acknowledged by the interpreters of the ancient Church, but by many of the Catholic authorities of the middle ages."[1] To the same fact deposes, with equal confidence, Rothe, who says that "the identity of the New Testament bishops and presbyters is even now generally acknowledged by unprejudiced Catholic theologians."[2]

And with a candour which marks the whole of his admirable commentaries, Canon Lightfoot states that it is "a fact now generally recognised by theologians of all shades of opinion that in the language of the New Testament the same officer is called indifferently bishop (ἐπίσκοπος) and "elder" or "presbyter" (πρεσβύτερος)."[3] There is in fact an enormous preponderance of modern authority in the most enlightened and dispassionate

---

[1] Es kann keinem Zweifel unterworfen sein, dass innerhalb des Neuen Testamentes ἐπίσκοπος und πρεσβύτερος. Titel desselben Amtes sind, und dass desshalb in der ersten Zeit mehrere ἐπίσκοποι, einer Gemeinde angehört haben. Diese Thatsache ist nicht nur von Exegeten der Alten Kirche, sondern auch von manchen Katholischen Auktoritäten das Mittelalter hindurch anerkannt worden.—" Die Entstehung," &c., p. 399.

[2] Die Identität der Neutestamentlichen, ἐπίσκοποι, und πρεσβύτεροι, wird jetzt auch von unbefangenen Katholischen Theologen immer allgemeiner anerkannt.—" Die Anfänge," p. 176.

[3] "Commentary on Epistle to the Philippians," p. 93.

writers of all Churches against the doctrine of an original distinction between "presbyters" and "bishops," more than enough to overthrow the Tridentine declaration, and to justify some modification in the Anglican preface which has been just cited. For even if it were conceded that towards the close of the life of the Apostle John there seems to be evidence of a nascent episcopacy in the form of a *primus inter pares*, he could have no existence apart from the consent and appointment of his co-presbyters, and could not with accuracy be said to have been one of three orders dating from the time "of the apostles." It is in vain that we seek for such an order in the writings of Paul, or Peter, or James, or Jude. Whether it arose even in its most innocent form before the death of the beloved disciple admits of serious doubt. That it was not known in its diocesan type is as certain as any historic fact in the world. The identity of the name bishop, as employed by many episcopalian writers, with the same name as used by apostles, no more imports the same functionary, than the mayor who was knighted yesterday is after the pattern of a knight of the feudal ages. Both are knights, having no resemblance either in costume, functions, or qualifications. And a like metamorphosis has so transformed the bishop with whom apostles were familiar, that the modern inheritor of the name would suggest scarcely any feature of his ancient prototype. This has been concisely put by Dean Alford when he says, "The ἐπίσκοποι of the New Testament have nothing in common with our bishops."[1] The approximation which such testimonies as have been just cited exhibit towards the views which have been maintained for the last three centuries by the Independents, affords some hope that whatever tendency towards Rome there may be in one section of the Church of England, there is also a counter-tendency in another section to abate an arrogant and unhistoric zeal for the Divine origin of prelatical episcopacy. This will be to all Christian bodies an inestimable gain, even though they should never be comprised within one form of ecclesiastical organisation.

The origin of the term "presbyter," as applied to the more spiritual functionary in the Christian Church, can occasion no difficulty. Presbyters were already well known in the Jewish synagogue, and "it was not unnatural, therefore, when the Christian synagogue took its place by the side of the Jewish, a similar organisation should be adopted, with such modifications as circumstances required; and thus the name, familiar under the old dispensation, was retained in the new."[2] And if the "presbyter" had a Jewish origin, its synonym as a designation of office (*episcopus*) clearly proclaims its Gentile descent; and it is noteworthy that its application is restricted to the officers of the Gentile Churches alone, not however to the exclusion of the designation "presbyters." Thus while in the Church at Jerusalem the "presbyters" are never denominated "bishops," both terms were freely and interchangeably

---

[1] Vol. iii. p. 303. New Testament.
[2] Canon Lightfoot. "Epistle to the Philippians," p. 94.

employed in the Christian communities which were established in heathen cities.

The absolute identity of the two offices is established by such considerations as the following.

1. In no instance are "presbyters *and* bishops" mentioned together, as we find "bishops *and* deacons," in Paul's Epistle to the Philippians.

2. In the directions which are given to Timothy touching the officers of the Church, mention is made only of bishops (ἐπίσκοποι) and deacons (διάκονοι), no allusion being made to "presbyters," clearly because the presbyters and the bishops were the same.

3. In his Epistle to Titus, whom he had left in Crete, to set in order the things that were wanting, and ordain elders (πρεσβυτέρους) in every city, the qualifications for the elders are substantially identical with those which he had specified to Timothy as the qualifications for a bishop. And he adds, "For a bishop must be blameless," &c. Comparing the directions given to Timothy and to Titus, as to the characteristics which are to distinguish "presbyters" or "bishops," nothing but the straits of a controversial exigency could blind any reader to the fact of their absolute identity.

4. In Acts xx. 17, Paul is introduced to us as summoning to Miletus the "elders" or "presbyters" of the Church at Ephesus. And in his farewell address to them he distinctly designates them "overseers," ἐπισκόπους (ver. 28).

5. In the opening verse of the Epistle to the Philippians, the same apostle salutes "the saints in Christ

Jesus which are at Philippi, with the bishops and deacons;" and it is inconceivable that if there had been another order of officers in that Church between bishops and deacons they would have been omitted.

6. The same identity of the two officers is clearly recognised by St. Peter when he exhorts the "elders" (πρεσβύτερους) to "feed the flock of God which is among them, taking the oversight thereof (ἐπισκοποῦντες) not by constraint, but willingly."

7. Of bishops, St. James makes no mention, but speaks of the "elders of the church."

The lines of evidence, accordingly, which are found in the Acts of the Apostles and in those epistles of the New Testament which treat directly or indirectly of the matter now under consideration, all converge to the establishment of this conclusion, that no distinction whatever was known or recognised by the apostles between "presbyters" and "bishops," but that they were different names for the same office.

The endeavours which have been made by some of the defenders of episcopacy to break the force of this conclusion are extraordinary. It has, for example, been affirmed that those officers who were at first designated apostles were afterwards denominated "bishops," a statement which not only is unsustained by any scriptural evidence, but which overlooks the essential distinction between the functions of an apostle, properly so called, and those of a bishop. The apostles were not, in any strict sense of the term, pastors or bishops of any one individual Church.

Their commission was general. They had to plant Churches where they did not exist, and to exercise over them a supervision which could pertain to them alone. To cite the fact that Epaphroditus is termed in the Epistle to the Philippians "an apostle," in proof of the fact that there were three orders of the ministry in that Church, is to take advantage of the equivocal meaning of a word, and to overlook the explicit reason assigned for the use of the term apostle ($ἀπόστολος$) in his particular case, viz., that he was "your messenger ($ὑμῶν ἀπόστολον$) and a minister to my necessity." His apostleship was, therefore, not only one emanating from the appointment of the Church, but restricted to the one special mission of conveying their benefactions to Paul. The word apostle ($ἀπόστολος$) is found in the New Testament above eighty times. It is applied to our Lord Himself as the one sent from God, "the Apostle and High Priest of our profession."[1] It is applied to the original number whom our Saviour appointed to be His ambassadors to the world. It is applied to Paul, as to one born out of due time, and who received an independent commission. It is in one instance applied to Barnabas. It is applied to certain "brethren" who were the companions of Titus when sent by Paul to Corinth, and who are designated the messengers of the Churches ($ἀπόστολοι ἐκκλησιῶν$). It is applied as a general designation to any person who is sent to discharge any function whatever, as where our Saviour says, "The servant is

[1] Heb. iii. 1.

not greater than his lord; neither is he that is sent (οὐδὲ ἀπόστολος) greater than he that sent him."[1] And, as we have seen, it was applied to Epaphroditus as the bearer of the generous contributions of the Philippian Church. But as a term of permanent office, it specifically denotes, except in the case of Matthias, those who were not elected as messengers by the Churches, but who were commissioned by Christ Himself, as His extraordinary ambassadors to the world; and it cannot be doubted that if there had arisen one who should have arrogated the title and the office of apostle in this distinctive sense, he would have been denounced as an impostor, unless he could have produced supernatural credentials of his direct commission from the Lord.

Of the claims of Epaphroditus to be considered a bishop, I have already spoken. Other personages of the New Testament have been appointed, by certain episcopalian writers, to the same prelatical office; but, as has been most triumphantly demonstrated, on the most precarious grounds.[2]

"The first of these individuals is noticed in the Epistle to the Colossians, i. 7 and iv. 12, 13 : 'As ye also learned of Epaphras, our dear fellow-servant, who is for you a faithful minister of Christ.' 'Epaphras, who is one of you, a servant of Christ, saluteth you, always labouring fervently for you in prayers, that ye may stand perfect and complete in all the will of God.

[1] John xiii. 16.
[2] See Dr. Davidson's "Ecclesiastical Polity," pp. 162–164.

For I bear him record, that he hath a great zeal for you, and them that are in Laodicea, and them in Hierapolis.'

"Those who can infer from these words that Epaphras was diocesan bishop of Colosse must be very perspicacious. The weaker advocates of episcopacy alone adduce them as proof of a position incapable of legitimate demonstration. And why are they not consistent? Why do they not deduce the conclusion from the same passages that Epaphras enjoyed the bishoprics of Laodicea and Hierapolis, as well as that of Colosse?

"That Archippus was bishop of Colosse or Laodicea has been inferred by Dodwell from the Epistle to the Colossians, iv. 17, and from the second verse of the Epistle to Philemon. 'And say to Archippus, Take heed to the ministry which thou hast received in the Lord, that thou fulfil it.' 'And to our beloved Apphia, and Archippus our fellow-soldier.' The Apostolic Constitutions assign him the bishopric of Laodicea. He appears to have filled some office in the Church of Colosse, although the nature of it cannot be discovered at the present day. Many think that he was a *deacon*, perhaps because the word translated ministry is τὴν διακονίαν. It is more probable, we think, that he was a *bishop*, not, however, a *prelate* or *diocesan* bishop.

"A comparatively late tradition makes Sosthenes bishop of Colophon. The Sosthenes mentioned in 1 Cor. i. 1 was probably a different person from the ruler of the synagogue in Acts xviii. 17. All that can be gathered from the New Testament respecting him is, that he was a Christian well known to the Corinthians, and associated in the gospel with the apostle Paul.

"Crescens was also an assistant of Paul in preaching the gospel, but this is all the information concerning him furnished by the New Testament. The traditions respecting him in the Apostolic Constitutions and the writings of the Fathers rest on no foundation. Apollos was a preacher, chiefly at Corinth, but there is not a shadow of proof that he was a diocesan bishop.

"We know nothing of Diotrephes except what is stated in the Third Epistle of John. He seems to have been one of the members of the Church, and ambitious to have the pre-eminence.

"Timothy was probably an *evangelist*. He was requested, at least, to do the work of an evangelist (2 Tim. iv. 5). He attended Paul for a considerable time, assisting him in his labours, and sharing his dangers. Whitby admits that he did not hold an office identical with that of a modern prelate.

"Titus is not called an *evangelist*, but it is probable he was so, because the directions given to him by Paul closely resemble those given to Timothy. He was left in Crete to ordain elders in every city, and to set in order the things that were wanting. Having finished the work for which he had been left in the island, he was sent for the next year to Nicopolis (Titus iii. 12).

"Thus Timothy and Titus were employed by the Apostle Paul to perform certain ecclesiastical duties, for which doubtless they were well qualified by the Holy Spirit; but it cannot be proved that they were located at Ephesus and Crete as *stated* office-bearers presiding over dioceses, and having the kind of episcopal jurisdiction which a prelate legally exercises. They were required to set in order the things that were wanting, and to ordain elders in every city (Titus i. 5); but, in so doing, they acted under the express direction of an inspired apostle, for Paul says, 'As I had appointed thee.' 'Evangelists,' says Stillingfleet, 'were sent sometimes into this country, to put the Churches in order there, sometimes into another; but wherever they were, they acted as evangelists, and not as fixed officers. And such were Timothy and Titus, notwithstanding all the opposition made against it, as will appear to any that will take an impartial survey of the arguments on both sides.'[1]

"Whenever *an apostle* shall appoint *an evangelist* or *any other* to do a work similar to that entrusted to Timothy and Titus, we shall render all due honour to men *so* called and equipped for their ecclesiastical employment. Perhaps we might even concede to them the title and

[1] Dean Stanley, in his "Sermons and Essays on the Apostolic Age," admits that it is not necessary to prove at length the wholly temporary character of the office, if it may be called an office, which Timotheus and Titus held respectively at Ephesus and Crete, of whom the first was governor of the Church only in Paul's absence (1 Tim. iv. 13; i. 3), and left it altogether before Paul's death (2 Tim. iv. 9); and the second was to leave the island that very winter (2 Tim. iv. 10; Tit. iii. 12).—pp. 46, 47.

jurisdiction of a diocesan bishop. But we cannot metamorphose modern prelates into Timothys and Tituses without a scriptural warrant. There is an essential difference between them as to the mode of their appointment, the authority by which they are sent, the affairs committed to their care, and the power which they rightfully possess or ambitiously usurp.

" James is said to have been bishop of Jerusalem. He who has been so styled was probably James the Less, one of the apostles, and there is nothing in the New Testament to show that he was superior to the other apostles, or to justify Baur's extravagant assertions respecting him, as if he were *the bishop of all bishops, more than an apostle, the representative of Jesus Himself.* Like all the apostles, he had the care of the Churches, although he seems to have chiefly resided in Jerusalem, and watched over the disciples in that city. In the apostolic council he does not occupy such pre-eminence as the archbishop of the metropolis would naturally possess in virtue of his office. On the contrary, some of the other apostles are as prominent as he. Paul and Barnabas were sent as a deputation from the Antiochian Church, a second time, to *the apostles and elders.* The whole narrative, in short, contained in the fifteenth chapter of the Acts of the Apostles, plainly shows that the body of the disciples was present at the consultation of the apostles and elders. Hence the letter containing the decision was sent forth in the name of the apostles, elders, and brethren. Neither James nor any other of the apostles assumed ecclesiastical authority over the Church. They cherished no ambitious designs, although they might have successfully executed many had they been so disposed. Theirs was a nobler, because a humbler, spirit. Their tempers and characters were too deeply imbued with holiness to allow self to usurp that place in their desires which belonged to the *Great Master* whom they faithfully served." [1]

A strong support for the episcopal office as distinct from that of presbyter has been sought in the angels of the Churches mentioned in the Apocalypse, but with no unanimity on the part even of episcopalian interpreters themselves. In any case we should decline to respect any argument in favour of any form of Church government which rested mainly or largely on the language of the most symbolic and obscure of all the books of the New Testament; and assuredly no evidence derived exclusively from such a source could countervail the evidence supplied by the acts of the Apostles and their instructions to the Churches they had planted.

Dean Stanley expressly denies "that any ecclesiastical institution can be deduced from the mention of the angels of the seven Churches, in the total absence of any proof for such an application of the word in the apostolic age, and against the uniform use of it in all other parts of the Apocalypse in its usual sense of a heavenly messenger, which seems to be required especially in this place by the obviously figurative and

[1] Davidson's "Ecclesiastical Polity," pp. 162–167.

prophetical style of the whole address in which the term occurs."

Canon Lightfoot, with equal emphasis, denies that the angels of the Apocalypse are bishops. Speaking of the Book of the Revelation, he says: "Its sublime imagery seems to be seriously impaired by this interpretation. On the other hand, St, John's own language gives the true key to the symbolism. 'The seven stars,' so it is explained, 'are the seven angels of the seven Churches, and the seven candlesticks are the seven Churches.' This contrast between the heavenly and the earthly fires—the star shining steadily by its own inherent eternal light, and the lamp flickering and uncertain, requiring to be fed with fuel and tended with care—cannot be devoid of meaning. The star is the suprasensual counterpart, the heavenly representative; the lamp, the earthly realisation, the outward embodiment. Whether the angel is here conceived as an actual person, the celestial guardian, or only as a personification, the idea or spirit of the Church, it is unnecessary for my present purpose to consider. But, whatever may be the exact conception, he is identified with and made responsible for it to a degree wholly unsuited to any human officer. Nothing is predicated of him which may not be predicated of it. To him are imputed all its hopes, its fears, its graces, its shortcomings. He is punished with it, and he is rewarded with it. In one passage especially the language applied to the angel seems to exclude the common interpretation. In the message to Thyatira the angel is blamed because he suffers himself to be led astray by 'his wife Jezebel.' In this image of Ahab's idolatrous queen some dangerous and immoral teaching must be personified, for it does violence alike to the general tenour and to the individual expressions in the passage to suppose that an actual woman is meant. Thus the symbolism of the passage is entirely in keeping. Nor, again, is this mode of representation new. The 'princes,' in the prophecy of Daniel, present a very near, if not an exact parallel to the angels of the Revelation. Here, as elsewhere, St. John seems to adopt the imagery of this earliest apocalyptic book.

"Indeed if, with most recent writers, we adopt the early date of the Apocalypse of St. John, it is scarcely possible that the episcopal organisation should have been so mature when it was written. In this case probably not more than two or three years have elapsed from the date of the pastoral epistles, and this interval seems quite insufficient to account for so great a change in the administration of the Asiatic Churches." [1]

The limits within which episcopacy, but not of the diocesan type, began to make its appearance, may be determined with considerable accuracy, but it is not so easy to ascertain the exact period within these limits. Indeed, all the elements needful for the solution of this problem are not in our hands, and it

[1] Philippians, pp. 197-199.

is all but certain that they never will be. It is enough to know that the New Testament affords no indications of the existence of "presbyters" and "bishops" as two distinct orders. At the latest period at which, during the life-time of the apostles, there is any explicit mention of them, they are indistinguishably one and the same. To this conclusion we are impelled in spite of the anathema of Rome and the preface to the "Form and Manner of Making, Ordaining, and Consecrating of Bishops, Priests, and Deacons, according to the order of the United Church of England and Ireland."

As to the only other permanent office in the Church, that of the deacons, I see no reason to search for its origin beyond the record given in the Acts of the Apostles (chap. vi.), according to which it had its birth in a secular exigency—viz., a murmuring among the Grecians, that in the distribution of money, in the Church at Jerusalem, their widows were neglected, while those of the Hebrews were treated with partiality and favour. This complaint coming to the ears of the apostles, led them to decide on the election of men who should serve tables, while they determined to devote themselves to the Word of God and to prayer. And, accordingly, seven men were selected by the people themselves out of their own number, and were appointed over this business. Attention to this secular element of the Church constituted the differentiating feature of the deacon. Not that he was restricted to it, for, as we have seen in a previous lecture, Philip the deacon preaches the gospel, and not only he, but *all* who were scattered abroad by the persecution which arose in Jerusalem. This they did without appointment or ordination, animated solely by the love they bore to Him who had redeemed them by His blood. From the fact that in his salutation to the Church at Philippi, the apostle distinctly specifies bishops and deacons, and from the instructions he gives to Timothy touching the various qualifications of a deacon, it may be fairly concluded that the twofold order of officers was deemed at least expedient, if not necessary, for the complete organisation and the healthy working of the Christian communities.[1]

From the consideration of the hierarchy of the Churches which allege, against all evidence, the apostolicity of the distinction between "bishops" and "presbyters," we now proceed to the consideration of its lineage, which claims to be that of an apostolic succession.

The key-stone of the arch of sacerdotalism was instinctively recognised by the Oxford Tractarians when, in their first publication, they thus formulated the tenet of apostolic succession, perversely interpreting of the priesthood language by which the Saviour desig-

---

[1] I agree with Professor Lightfoot that there is "no reason for connecting it (the diaconal office) with any prototype existing in the Jewish community. The narrative offers no hint that it was either a continuation of the order of the Levites, or an adaptation of an office in the synagogue. The philanthropic purpose for which it was established presents no direct point of contact with the known duties of either."—Philippians, p. 187.

nated the whole Church of God. "We have been born not of blood, nor of the will of the flesh, nor of the will of man, but of God. The Lord Jesus Christ gave His spirit to the apostles; they in turn laid their hands on those who should succeed them, and these again on others; and so the sacred gift has been handed down to our present bishops, who have appointed us as their assistants, and in some sort representatives."

"I know," continues the same writer, "that the grace of ordination is contained in the laying on of hands, not in any form of words, yet in our own case (as has ever been used in the Church) words of blessing have accompanied the act. Thus we have confessed before God our belief that through the bishop who ordained us we received the Holy Ghost, the power to bind and loose, to administer the sacraments and to preach. Now—how is he able to give these great gifts? whence is his right? Has he any right except as having received the power from those who consecrated him to be a bishop? He could not give what he had never received. It is plain then that he but *transmits*, and that the Christian ministry is a succession. Enlighten the people on this matter. Exalt our holy fathers the bishops as the representatives of the apostles and the angels of the Churches, and magnify your office as being ordained by them to take part in their ministry" (Tract No. 1).

Again: "Why should we not seriously endeavour to impress our people with the plain truth, that by separating themselves from our communion they separate themselves not only from a decent, orderly, useful society, but from the only Church in this realm which has a right to be quite sure that she has the Lord's body to give to His people" (Tract No. 4).

Again: "As to the *fact* of the apostolic succession, *i.e.*, that our present bishops are the heirs and representatives of the apostles by successive transmission of the prerogative of being so—this is too notorious to require proof. Every link in the chain is known from St. Peter to our present metropolitans" (Tract No. 7).

The late Dean of Chichester, for greater security, preferred to have an alternative source for the order of the English Church, and hence he says:—" There is an unbroken spiritual descent from St. Peter *or St. Paul*, which bishops, priests, and deacons can trace." These words surely suggest a disastrous divarication in the genealogical line which professes to secure for each priest an indisputable succession from the apostles.

The boldness of the language which has just been cited might impose on many. It is difficult to believe that this was not the effect contemplated. There is a convincing force to the minds of large multitudes in round and unqualified asseverations, and it is the common manœuvre of men who are conscious that they are walking in a vain show, and urging unsupported pretensions to trumpet their claims the more loudly, the more conscious they are of their utter baselessness. There is, however, an occasional access of suspicion in some of these writers that the historic evidence may of itself fail to carry conviction, and hence, with a delicious candour, one of them says: " I readily allow that this view of our calling has something in it too high and mysterious to be fully understood by the unlearned Christians. But the learned, surely, are just as unequal to it. It is part of that ineffable mystery called in our creed the communion of saints, and, with all other Christian mysteries, is above the understanding of all alike, yet practically alike within reach of all who are willing to embrace it by true faith" (Tract No. 4).

Doubtless, if the dogma may thus be relegated among the mysteries of the gospel as being incapable of comprehension, it will be safe enough in that awful enclosure from critical examination. But we must endeavour to arrest it on its way thither, and to show that it has no title to the shelter of such a sanctuary. It has no authority in Scripture, and it has none in history.

I.

We shall proceed now to examine its alleged scriptural foundation.

Great stress is laid on our Lord's commission to His apostles, as found in John xx. 21 : " As my Father hath sent me, even so send I you." The relevance of this passage to the tenet we are examining is by no means clear. It is, in fact, intensely obscure. Whatever else it means, it cannot, without exegetical torture, be made to utter a whisper in favour of this ecclesiastical pretension. What are the points of comparison intended by the words " as " and " so "? Will any one venture to affirm that they declare an analogy in the nature of the work which Christ, as the sent of the Father, had come to accomplish, to the nature of the work which Christ was here empowering them to execute? The Saviour did not delegate them to repeat the work which was finished on the cross. They were not to bear the sins of many, to suffer the just for the unjust, to open a new and living way, to reconcile by their life and death, man to God. The words *as* and *so* cannot define the nature of the two missions. They affirm the authority under which the missions were respectively constituted, that of Christ being grounded on the authority of the Father, and that of the apostles being grounded on the authority of Christ; and it would be far more reasonable to conclude, from the teaching of this passage alone, that the apostles were successors to Christ, and were to repeat the awful drama of His redemptive sorrow and death and resurrection, than that the apostles were themselves to have successors endowed with their manifold authority as planters of the Church. Their commission is here distinctly given. So far as the words go, it is *their* commission only. No mention is made of any others; and to bring within the compass of the words all the prelates of the Anglican or of any other Church, is to invest them wantonly with an elasticity which they do not and cannot possess. The mission of Christ was special, and the mission of the apostles was special; and as it would be an unwarrantable usurpation on the part of an apostle to assume a parity of position and office with Christ, so it is an unwarrantable usurpation on the part of ministers of Christ, under what name soever, to take their place side by side with the apostles. "Even so send I you," were the words of the Lord, and they must be held as rigidly applying to the apostles, until it can be shown that others were expressly included in them.

In the next verse we are told that "when he had said this He breathed on them, and saith unto them, Receive ye the Holy Ghost: whose soever sins ye remit, they are remitted unto them; and whose soever sins ye retain, they are retained."

It is not needful to enter here into a consideration of the meaning of the words which set forth the high powers committed to the apostles: whether the sins they were to remit and retain were spiritual sins, or ecclesiastical ones, or both. The question before us is, be the function here referred to what it may, to whom was it accorded, and by whom was it meant to be exercised? Almost every word in the passage has been a battle-field. Men differ as to the meaning of the gift of the Holy Ghost. Does it here denote the extraordinary powers of a miraculous nature by which the apostles were to authenticate their Divine mission, gifts of tongues and healing, and the discernment of spirits? or does it denote endowments of a mere intellectual and spiritual kind? And whatever the endowments might be, were they bestowed then and there? Or were they, as some suppose, reserved until the day of Pentecost? Or was a measure of the Spirit vouchsafed when the Saviour breathed on His apostles, as an earnest of that fuller baptism which awaited them? The discussion of these points, however interesting in itself, would seduce us much too far from the point now before us, which is that, be the gift of the Spirit what it may, and be the sins forgiven and retained what they may, were that gift and that forgiving and retaining power for the apostles in special, or were they in the general for all prelatical bishops and such priests as they might successively ordain? For the latter assumption there is not a tittle of evidence. There is no proof that the apostles ever employed the formula, "Receive ye the Holy Ghost." Neither in the Acts of the Apostles nor in any of their epistles do we meet with it. They laid their hands on men both in office and out of office, and the Holy Ghost was imparted, but the impartation was avouched and demonstrated by the effects that were seen. But this formula, with all its awfulness of claim, is employed in the service of the ordering of priests in the Episcopal Church of our country. The bishop, as if standing in the place of Christ; as if possessing the Spirit in infinite measure, and capable of bestowing or withholding it at will; as if he had access to the very springs and secret places of the soul of the candidates; as if his prerogative of vouchsafing this unutterable gift were as absolute, though at first derived from another, as the very prerogative of Christ Himself, pronounces over the deacon, then *in transitu* to the priestly office, these solemn words: "Receive ye the Holy Ghost for the office and work of a priest in the

Church of God, now committed unto thee by the imposition of our hands. Whose sins thou dost forgive, they are forgiven ; and whose sins thou dost retain, they are retained."

And it will be observed that these words are not in the form of a prayer, but of an authoritative communication, and cannot, in my judgment, escape the imputation of serious blasphemy, especially when it is remembered that no evidence whatever is given that the words, as used in the ordination of the priest, have, either in themselves or together with the imposition of hands, conferred any spiritual blessing. It lacks, at least, all palpable attestation. It is followed by no gift of tongues, no miracle of healing, no discerning of spirits, no illumination of the intellect, no enlargement of knowledge, no purification of the heart. For long centuries the Church shrank from employing Christ's language in its service of ordination. Fifteen ancient rituals have not a vestige of it, and it was only when the Church had reached its darkest and corruptest stage that it crept into such profane use. The opinion of Dean Alford on the passage we have just considered is creditable to his candour, and worthy of grave attention. He considers the gift of the Spirit to have been twofold — miraculous and ordinary. The miraculous element was temporary; the ordinary state abides in the Church. In so far as it is in the ministers of Christ, he says it is "not *by successive delegation from the apostles, of which fiction I find in the New Testament no trace.*"

Nor is the other passage usually cited in favour of

apostolic succession more serviceable to the cause for which it is adduced. I refer to the final commission of our Lord: "Go ye therefore, and teach all nations, baptising them in the name of the Father, and of the Son, and of the Holy Ghost: teaching them to observe all things whatsoever I have commanded you, and, lo! I am with you alway, even unto the end of the world."

The argument reared on these words assumes the following form. Here is a Divine commission given by our Lord to the apostles. But this commission contemplates the diffusion of the gospel even to the ends of the earth, and to the end of the world. Those, however, to whom he gave the commission would necessarily die before this vast purpose could reach its accomplishment. They must therefore be prepared to appoint successors who should perpetuate and extend the work of evangelisation; and as these must perforce also die, other successors must take up their office and functions, and so on to the termination of the Christian dispensation.

Now the conclusion, which is not so much drawn as assumed, is that these successors of the apostles must be bishops, and bishops, too, of the diocesan type. And this, as we have shown, is an inference as groundless as inference can well be.

From the nature of the case the apostles *could* have no successors. A definite work was assigned to them, for which they possessed definite and related qualifications. An apostle must be one who had seen the

Lord. So essential was this, that Paul laid special stress upon it when vindicating his apostolic prerogative: "Last of all he was seen of me also, as of one born out of due time." And so little did the apostles contemplate the idea of their being succeeded by others possessing the same office and functions with themselves, that when James was killed by Herod, no successor was appointed; and though both Paul and Peter refer to their approaching death, not one word was said by either concerning the necessity of electing others who should fulfil the duties which they had received by special commission from their Lord. The stupendous fabric of the apostolic succession is, so far as the authority of Scripture goes, a fantastic, ethereal structure, reared by that pride which puffeth up, in violation of truth and of that charity which buildeth up. The more narrowly we examine the passages upon which it seeks to establish itself, the more we see that they decline to yield the tumid imposture their support. The voice of the New Testament is clear as the sound of the trumpet on the point of the extraordinary nature of the apostolic office and of its necessarily temporary duration; and equally clear is it on the point fatal to High Church pretensions, that there are but two orders of officers in the Christian Church—bishops or presbyters, and deacons.

II.

We shall now look at the dogma in the light of history. This part of our subject might have been properly foregone, for if the chain fails to have any firm point of attachment to the apostles themselves, it is utterly valueless. It is like an electric wire, which, however complete in itself, transmits nothing if disconnected from the battery. It is, however, of some importance to look at the quality of the chain, especially as the echo of the late Bishop of Oxford's words has scarcely yet faded from our ears: "The bishops of the Church of England are by unbroken succession the descendants and representatives of the original twelve."

Many, conceding that the office of the first apostles was peculiar, and incapable, from its very nature, of transmission, claim for the prelates of the Church of Rome and of the Church of England, and for the subordinate ministers whom they have ordained, a succession, in the sense that a chain of regular consecrations runs up from them to the apostles—a chain which has lost no link, and every link of which unbroken chain contains the mystic grace which at once authorises and empowers its receiver to administer the ordinances and to preach the Word. If any one link of this chain be broken, then the whole spiritual electricity escapes, and sacramental grace is lost to him who vainly depended on that link. Now, let us grant for a moment that all that is claimed in this theory were true. Let us grant that every bishop and priest in the Churches of England and Rome has received his commission in direct and undisrupted line from the apostles. Let us grant that a register has been kept from the beginning more faithfully than any register in a royal or ducal house, and that every clergyman can trace his spiritual pedigree with unfailing certainty. Let us not contest the rigid strictness of the descent. What have we, then, as a result? This: that each priest has been ordained by the laying on of hands by men who themselves were similarly ordained by men who received a corresponding ordination from others, and so on, until you reach the apostles, who received the Holy Ghost from the inspiration of our Divine Lord. You have, that is, the fact of a concatenated ordination. Have you, of necessity, anything else which can authenticate and demonstrate its existence by any evidence whatever? I claim to know what it is. A prelate or a priest brings me the certificate of his ordination, which I am supposing is immaculate on the point of regularity, and I ask what it means, and what it secures. Has the man's intellect been strengthened? No. Has he obtained any wonderful illumination? No. Has he acquired any increased purity of heart? No. Can he show anything he has received? Nothing. It reminds one of what has been well said of the "indelible" character imparted in the unreiterable sacraments of the Romish Church. "As to the *ubi* of the character, there was no less variety of sentiment; some placing it in the essence of the soul, others in the understanding; some in the will, and others, more plausibly, in the imagination. . . . . So that the whole of what they agreed upon amounted to this, that in the unreiterable sacraments, as they call them, *something*, they know not *what*, is imprinted, they know not *how*, on something in the soul of the recipient, they know not *where*, which can never be deleted."

But, further, the question demands consideration whether this mysterious something which is supposed to be communicated in ordination cannot be neutralised and destroyed. Is there nothing that can invalidate orders? Is there no non-conductor through which the alleged grace cannot pass? What if the bishops be immoral? can they still impart it? Or what if they be heretical? Or what if they be both immoral and heretical? Will neither vice nor fundamental error intercept the flow of the mysterious influence, and leave all unblessed who have had the misfortune to be ordained by such profligates and heretics? Now the defenders of apostolic succession are, strange to say, by no means agreed among themselves as to whether error in fundamentals on the part of a bishop will or will not rob him of ordaining grace. Some hold that it will not, others that it will. This is a dismal uncertainty, surely, when the validity of ministerial orders is at stake. But to the purpose of my present argument it matters not what answer is returned. There is a dilemma which must impale on its horns both parties, whether they affirm or deny the disqualifying power of heresy. If it be said, Let the bishops be as heretical as they may, still does the mystic grace pass to the man whom they ordain; we reply that the orders of the Church of Rome are as valid as those of the Church of England; and the orders of the

Greek Church as valid as either; and the orders of the Arians were as valid as those of the Athanasians; and the orders of the most heretical as valid as those of the most orthodox; and the orders of those who preach damnable—because damning—doctrine as valid as those of the men who preach saving truths. If it be said, on the other hand, heresy on the part of ordaining bishops does intercept and nullify the ordaining grace, then what a disastrous uncertainty befalls modern episcopal orders in our country, when we remember the enormous number of heretical prelates through whose hands they have come! Now, as I shall proceed to show, many of the archbishops and bishops of England had their ordinations, not only in the Church of Rome, but in Rome itself, and they transmitted the orders they had thus and there received; and another dilemma at once arises out of this incontestable circumstance, a dilemma well put by Mr. Henry Rogers in his admirable article on Anglicanism in the "Edinburgh Review" for 1843. "If," says he to the defenders of apostolic succession in the Church of England, "if error in essentials is sufficient to invalidate orders, we ask, Had the Romish Church so erred when you separated from her? If she had, her own orders were invalid, and she could not transmit yours. If she had not, then, as you all affirm that nothing but heresy in fundamentals can justify *separation*, you are schismatics, and your *own* orders are invalid."

Now it is a somewhat curious circumstance that

while the late Bishop of Oxford was asserting the reality of personal apostolic succession, Archbishop Whately, who was assuredly not his inferior either in logic or candour, denounces the assumption as having no trustworthy foundation whatever. What can be thought of a claim affirmed by a bishop and repudiated by an archbishop? Oxford says, "I can trace my pedigree right up to the apostles in an unbroken chain." Dublin retorts, "There is not a minister in all Christendom who is able to trace up with any approach to certainty his own spiritual pedigree" ("Kingdom of Christ," p. 175). And when it is considered that it is as much the interest of an archbishop as of a bishop, and even more, to vindicate where possible the continuity of those orders which it is his high prerogative to confer, this confession of Archbishop Whately is the more significant and convincing.

His whole reasoning upon this matter is so clear and conclusive that I will quote it, presuming that it will obtain from some a deference that might not be paid to any similar remarks proceeding from a Nonconformist. "If," says the archbishop, "a man consider it as highly *probable* that the particular minister at whose hands he received the sacred ordinances is really thus apostolically descended, *this* is the very utmost point to which he can with any semblance of reason attain; and the more he reflects and inquires, the more cause for hesitation he will find. There is not a minister in all Christendom who is able to trace up with any approach to certainty his own spiritual pedigree. The sacramental virtue . . . dependent on the imposition of hands, with a due observance of apostolic usages, by a bishop, himself duly consecrated, after having been in like manner baptised into the Church and ordained deacon and priest—this sacramental virtue, if a single link of the chain be faulty, must, on the above principles, be utterly nullified ever after in respect of all the links that hang on that one. For if a bishop has not been duly consecrated, or has not been previously rightly ordained, his ordinations are null, and so are the ministrations of those ordained by him; and these ordinations of others; . . . and so on without end. The poisonous taint of informality, if it once creep in undetected, will spread the infection of nullity to an indefinite and irremediable extent.

"And who can undertake to pronounce that during that long period usually designated as the dark ages, no such taint ever was introduced? Irregularities could not have been wholly excluded without a perpetual miracle, and that no such miraculous interference existed, we have even historical proof. Amidst the numerous corruptions of doctrine and of practice, and gross superstitions that crept in during those ages, we find recorded descriptions, not only of the profound ignorance and profligacy of life of many of the clergy, but also of the grossest irregularities in respect of discipline and form. We read of bishops consecrated when mere children; of men officiating who barely knew their letters; of prelates expelled and others put into their place by violence; of illiterate and profligate laymen and habitual drunkards admitted to holy orders; and, in short, of the prevalence of every kind of disorder, and reckless disregard of the decency which the apostle enjoins.

"It is inconceivable that any one *even moderately acquainted with history* can feel a certainty, or any approach to certainty, that amidst all this confusion and corruption every requisite form was, in every instance, strictly adhered to by men, many of them openly profane and secular, and unrestrained by public opinion through the gross ignorance of the population among which they lived, and that no one not duly consecrated or ordained was admitted to sacred offices. . . . Even in the memory of persons now living there existed a bishop concerning whom there was so much mystery and uncertainty prevailing as to when, where, or by whom he had been ordained, that doubts existed in the minds of some persons whether he had ever been ordained at all. I do not say that there was good ground for the suspicion; but the existence, actual or even possible, of such a suspicion—the actual or even conceivable concurrence of circumstances such as to manifest the possibility of such an irregularity —is sufficient with a view to the present argument."

Bishop Hoadley, who was successively bishop of four sees and of Winchester for upwards of twenty-five years, expressly writes :—" I am fully satisfied that till a consummate stupidity can be happily established and spread over the land, there is nothing that tends so much to destroy all respect to the clergy as the demand of more than can be due to them; and nothing has so effectually thrown contempt upon a regular succession of the ministry as the calling of no succession regular but what was uninterrupted, and the making the eternal salvation of Christians to depend upon that uninterrupted succession, of which the *most learned men must have the least assurance, and the unlearned can have no notion but through ignorance and credulity.*"

Lord Macaulay, in his review of Gladstone's book on " Church and State," writes thus :—

" Since the first century, not less, in all probability, than a hundred thousand persons have exercised the functions of bishops. That many of these have not been bishops by apostolical succession is quite certain. Hooker admits that deviations from the general rule have been frequent, and with a boldness worthy of his high and statesmanlike intellect, pronounces them to have been often justifiable. 'There may be,' says he, 'sometimes very just and sufficient reason to allow ordination made without a bishop. Where the Church must needs have some ordained, and neither hath, nor can have possibly, a bishop to ordain, in case of such necessity the ordinary institution of God hath given (yielded) oftentimes, and may give place. And, therefore, we are not simply and without exception to urge a lineal descent of power from the apostles by continued succession of bishops in every effectual ordination.' "[1]

[1] See Appendix B.

Again, Lord Macaulay says:—" The transmission of orders from the apostles to an English clergyman of the present day must have been through a very great number of intermediate persons. Now, it is probable that no clergyman of the Church of England can trace up his spiritual genealogy from bishop to bishop so far back as the time of the Conquest. There remain many centuries during which the history of the transmission of his orders is buried in utter darkness, &c.

"We do not know whether the spiritual ancestors of any of our contemporaries were Spanish or Armenian, Arian or orthodox. . . . . It is surely impolitic to rest the doctrines of the English Church on an historical theory, which, to ninety-nine Protestants out of a hundred, would seem much more questionable than any of those doctrines. Nor is this all. Extreme obscurity hangs over the history of the middle ages, and the facts which are discernible through that obscurity prove that the Church was exceedingly ill regulated. We read of sees of the highest dignity openly sold, transferred backwards and forwards by popular tumult, bestowed sometimes by a profligate woman on her paramour, sometimes by a warlike baron on a kinsman still a stripling. We read of bishops ten years old, of bishops five years old, of many popes who were mere boys, and who rivalled the frantic dissoluteness of Caligula. . . . .

"We are therefore at a loss to conceive how any clergyman can feel confident that his orders have come down correctly. Whether he be really a successor of the apostles depends on an immense number of contingencies such as these; whether, under King Ethelwolf, a stupid priest might not, while baptising several scores of Danish prisoners who had just made their option between the font and the gallows, inadvertently omit to perform the rite on one of these graceless proselytes; whether, in the seventh century, an impostor, who had never received consecration, might not have passed himself off as a bishop on a rude tribe of Scots; whether a lad of twelve did really, by a ceremony huddled over when he was too drunk to know what he was about, convey the episcopal character to a lad of ten."

Now it is not unnatural for men to ask whether those who so unblushingly affirm the doctrine of apostolic succession do not favour the public with a catalogue of the names of those bishops who are alleged to have been in the line of this descent? They do; and it is in some respects one of the most arrant pieces of convicted imposture in the world. Many of the names are those of persons who have no historic existence whatsoever. They are found in the catalogue, but nowhere else under heaven. When they were born, and where; when baptised, where, and by whom; when they were ordained, and where, and by whom; where they laboured, and how long: on all these matters there is not a beam of light. They are Romish inventions, and they are nothing more. It is worthy of observation that in the fourth century, Eusebius, the ecclesiastical historian, endeavoured to complete the chain of bishops which had existed from his time up to that of the apostles. He was the first to engage in this enterprise, which one might naturally imagine was not at that time one of insuperable difficulty. But what does he say? He confesses that he feels like one "attempting" a desert and untrodden path, and that he was utterly unable to find even the "bare" traces of those who had gone before him, save here and there some slight marks discernible like signals from afar. And though he expresses his hope to be able to preserve the successions, if not of all, yet of the most eminent of the apostles, he confesses afterwards that he knows nothing of the persons who laboured with Peter and Paul, except what he learned from St. Paul's epistles. This is acknowledged by Eusebius, who lived in the fourth century, and yet the late Bishop of Oxford, who lived in the nineteenth century, could affirm that his pedigree, and that of his ministerial brethren, is quite clear and unbroken right up to the apostles.

Now in order to show the uncertainty of this whole matter, and how little the bishop held himself amenable to historic facts when he uttered so bold a statement, the very first links are unsettled. It remains undetermined even to the present day whether Peter, who is supposed to have been first bishop of Rome, ever saw Rome. The first link is rotten, and what of the second? Several of the bishops say Clement was Peter's successor; but these are contradicted by Irenæus, and Eusebius, and Jerome, and Augustine, who affirm that Linus succeeded Peter. Bishop

Pearson proves that Linus died before Peter, and that therefore Linus could not succeed him. Cabassute, the Popish historian of the councils, says: "It is a very doubtful question concerning Linus, Cletus, and Clemens, as to which of them succeeded Peter." Dr. Comber, a very learned divine of the English Episcopal Church, says: "Upon the whole matter there is no certainty who was bishop of Rome next to the apostles."

But what about the third successor of the apostles? Here confusion is worse confounded. Cletus is the third name accepted by Romanists and High Churchmen. Now what says Dr. Comber about Cletus? "The like blunder there is about the next pope (or bishop of Rome). The fabulous pontifical makes Cletus succeed Linus, and gives us several lives of Cletus and Anacletus, making them of several nations, and to have been popes (that is, bishops of Rome) at different times, putting Clement between them. Yet the aforesaid Bishop of Chester (Pearson) proves that these were only *two* names of the same person. . . . . And every one may see the folly of the Romish Church, which venerates two several saints on two several days, one of which never had a *real* being, for Cletus is but the abbreviation of Anacletus's name." (Dr. Comber, part i. chap. 1.) Bishop Stillingfleet says: "The succession is as muddy as the Tiber itself; for here Tertullian and Rufinus and several others place Clement next to Peter; Irenæus and Eusebius set Anacletus before him; Epiphanius and Optatus both

Anacletus and Cletus; Augustine and Damasus, with others, Anacletus, Cletus, and Linus, all to precede him. What way shall we find to extricate ourselves out of this labyrinth?" ("Irenicon," part ii. chap. 6, p. 322.) And yet the Bishop of Oxford pleased himself with the phantom of an undoubted succession all the way, and unbroken down from the apostles to the present bishops of the *Church of England!* Here I might close, but as this assumption has played, and is still playing, so important a part in that movement which is rapidly betraying our English Church into the hands of Rome, it may not be entirely a work of supererogation to adduce still further evidence.

The defenders of apostolic succession, as I have hinted, are by no means in accord among themselves as to the manner in which their claim is to be made good. Some of the bolder spirits among them, having a sublime disdain for the verities of history, endeavour to run a new line of succession, without calling at Rome. Conscious that Romanism is and has been the hot-bed of heresy and corruption, and that its bishops, chief and subordinate, have frequently been the most cruel, besotted, and lecherous men on earth, they have been solicitous to travel by a cleaner way. This expedient, however, has been disowned by many learned writers in connection with the Church of England, who have felt that, however desirable the cleaner way might be, it cannot be found, and that if the Episcopal Church of our country has any apostolical orders at all, they must be held with all the taint of the Romish medium through which they have descended; and that to disown this medium is to leave the house without foundation, or to endeavour to hang a chain on nothing. But a few plain facts, accessible to every student of history, and as incontestable as they are accessible, will suffice to show that if Romish orders vitiate the apostolic succession of the bishops and priests and deacons of a Protestant Church, then is the apostolic succession of the Bishop of Oxford and his brethren hopelessly corrupted.

In the year 668 *Theodore* was Archbishop of Canterbury. He was a prelate for twenty-two years, and was consecrated in Rome by Pope Vitalian. *Northelm* was Archbishop of Canterbury in 735, and he was consecrated by Pope Gregory III. at Rome. *Lambert* was Archbishop of Canterbury in 763, was consecrated at Rome by Pope Paul I., and himself ordained for the space of twenty-seven years. *Plegmund* was Archbishop of Canterbury in 891, exercised his prelatical authority for twenty-six years, and was consecrated at Rome by Pope Formosus. Now this Pope Formosus was succeeded by Stephen VI., who declared his ordinations to be null and void; and yet Plegmund, the Archbishop of Canterbury, whose ordination was declared null and void by Pope Stephen, spread his abortive consecrations throughout England for the space of twenty-six years. And not to specify all that might be mentioned, Agelnoth, Theobald, Richard, Stephen Langton, and Boniface, successively archbishops of Canterbury over the space of ninety-six years, had all Romish ordinations, and in their turn, as necessity arose, consecrated the bishops of the English Church. And Henry Chichley, Archbishop of Canterbury in 1414, received his episcopal orders from Pope Gregory XII., and exercised his ordaining functions for twenty-nine years. And who was this Pope Gregory XII.? He was one of *three* pretenders to the papal chair, and it was needful to call the Council of Constance in order to adjudicate upon these conflicting claims, and the result was that Gregory XII., who consecrated *Chichley*, was deposed, and was declared to be neither a pope nor a bishop; and yet Chichley for the space of nearly thirty years, though ordained, according to the Council of Constance, by one who was neither pope nor bishop, continued to communicate his hollow and fallacious orders. So far for the *see of Canterbury*.

But it may perhaps be supposed that the see of York can present a cleaner lineage. Not a whit. From the year 1119 to the year 1342, a period of two hundred and twenty-three years, there were twelve archbishops of *York*, whose episcopal functions extended over the space of *one hundred and ninety years*, and every one of them had been consecrated, directly or indirectly, by popes. In the see of Durham we meet with nine bishops from 1133 to 1345, consecrated *directly* or *indirectly* by popes; and those bishops, with this papal consecration, ordained priests and deacons in the diocese of Durham for *one hundred and fifty-seven years*. How, in the face of facts like these, which are detailed and authenticated in Bishop Godwin's " Lives of the English Bishops," any man can console himself with the hope that his orders flow to him in a channel free from the seething and contaminating corruptions of Rome, beggars any ordinary imagination to conceive; and I am constrained to pronounce the attempt to palm such a notion upon the public either as one of the most signal instances of ignorance anywhere to be found, or as a gross and shameless historic fraud. There is no demonstration, save that which is purely mathematical, which is more overwhelmingly complete and stringent than that which explodes the doctrine of apostolical succession, both in the Church of England and in the Church of Rome. There is scarcely one way in which that succession can be conceived as broken, in which it has not been broken. Does it nullify orders if a man be consecrated who is under age? Instances of this nature appear in abundance. Does it nullify orders if a bishop obtain his see by purchase? Who does not know that for some centuries such simony was the all but constant practice? Does heresy nullify orders? Then who shall count for us the heretical popes and bishops? Does it nullify orders if a bishop be elected by force? What shall we say then of the election of Ambrose, Bishop of Milan, who ran away under the shelter of night, in order to escape the unwelcome office? And what shall we say of Synesius, Bishop of Cyrene, who tells us that "he would rather have died a hundred deaths than become a bishop; that he lamented the loss of his hunting establishment and pursuits; that he was a sceptic on some points of the Christian religion; and claims the prerogative of deceiving the people on the ground that, as darkness is good for those afflicted with disease of the eyes, so a falsehood is advantageous to the mob, while truth may be noxious"? In ten distinct ways, at least, we learn from the canon jurists, orders may be made null and void, and in every one of these ways have the orders of the Anglican clergy been hopelessly vitiated; so that we may conclude, in the language of the immortal Chillingworth, when speaking of the impossibility of any priest establishing his lineal descent from the apostles. "To know this one thing," he says, "you must first know ten thousand others, whereof not any one is a thing that can be known, there being no necessity that it should be true; . . . that of ten thousand probables, no one should be false; that of ten thousand requisites, whereof any one may fail, not one should be wanting. This to me is extremely improbable, and even cousin-german to impossible. So that the assurance hereof is like a machine composed of an innumerable multitude of pieces, of which it is strangely unlike but some will be out of order, and yet if any one be so the whole fabric will of necessity fall to the ground. And he that shall put them together, and maturely consider all the ways of lapsing and nullifying a priesthood in the Church, I believe will be very inclinable to think that it is a hundred to one that amongst a hundred seeming priests there is not one true one."

This *Chillingworth* wrote of Rome: it is equally true,

as we have seen, of England. But what if the claim of the late Bishop of Oxford were true? What if every clergyman in England, from the Archbishop of Canterbury down to the last ordained deacon, could show the chain of succession without a flaw? What if the mystic grace flowing from apostolic hands was so persistent and indefeasible that it would run clear and untainted through simony, drunkenness, murder, and every other sin in those through whose hands it has demonstrably descended, if it have descended at all: what, I say, in that case is it worth? Here comes one on whose head the hands of the bishop have just rested, establishing as they rested there the connection of the neophyte with the wondrous chain. Let us venture to question the young man, who not unnaturally thrills with the excitement of his new orders. "You have been ordained to-day?" "I have." "You have by your ordination been constituted a successor of the apostles?" "I have." "Can you speak with tongues that you have never learned?" "I cannot." "The apostles wrought miracles: can you imitate them in this respect?" "I cannot." "When the hands of the bishop were on your head, were you conscious of any special illumination?" "None." "Your passions, have they been subdued by the act?" "I fear not." "You are not sensible of any increase of holiness?" "I am not." "In fact, so far as the testimony of your consciousness goes, you cannot depose to any intellectual or moral bestowment which the bishop's hands have left upon you as a sign and proof of apostolical succession?" "I am not aware that I can." "Did you ever hear of any who had received as valid an ordination as you have, and yet who erred fatally from the truth?" "I have." "In your own Church, Samuel Clarke was an Arian?" "He was." "And Dr. Whitby also?" "He was." "And many others?" "Yes." "And in recent days Bishop Colenso is as true a successor of the apostles as the Bishop of Oxford?" "I am afraid I must grant it." "And he can ordain in Natal others like-minded with himself?" "So it appears." "Then this gift you receive by episcopal ordination does not preserve from heresy?" "I fear not." "Have you ever known drunken priests in your Church?" "A few." "Once, I believe, there were not a few?" "So I have read." "And these all were in the line of succession?" "They were." "So that it would seem that your ordination neither secures orthodoxy nor morality?" "Neither." "And yet you regard your ordination in the apostolic line as a blessing unspeakable?" "I do." Truly unspeakable it is, and also inconceivable.

In a work written by the late Frederick Myers, M.A., perpetual curate of St. John's, Keswick, and distinguished alike by its philosophical calmness and its reverence for the teaching of the Divine Word, he candidly declares that "this assertion that there is and needs be on earth an unbroken succession of ministers, who have continuously received and transmitted an invisible latent gift of grace, is one which not only has no proof, but cannot have any. For, observe: it is not the mere fact of regular succession which thus is required to be proved before the legitimacy of any minister's commission can be made out, but it is the validity of the ordination of each one of the succession; and this against the presumption to the contrary, which an apparent absence of any gift of grace would seem to imply. If we should know without dispute the names of all the persons who have filled any particular see from the apostles' time to our own, and the names of the persons by whom they were consecrated, this would go but a little way to the proof that any apostolic gift had been duly transmitted through the medium of this succession. For that some scheme of means is essential to the conferring of such a gift by one man to another will be admitted. Then what the essential means are must first be indisputably determined, and then, whether these means have been in each case strictly observed. The only proof which could be received as satisfactory in a case where such tremendous results depend upon the alternative, must be one which shall afford a reasonable probability that, in every one of the distinct terms of the series of ordinations between the apostles' times and our own, this scheme has been observed uniformly in all essential particulars. Now, the evidence which is necessary to the establishing of this is of too complex and subtle a character to be conveyed through the ordinary channels of human testimony.

"Never in any religion in the world was there heard

of anything so difficult of reception as this theory of the transmission of an invisible latent gift of grace for nearly two thousand years being essential to the validity of priestly acts.

"There was nothing like it that we know of in the world before Christianity; nothing in any of the manifold forms of heathen priesthood; nothing in the Jewish dispensation, though there certain ceremonial omissions invalidated the acts of the priest. All that was required to prove the legitimacy of their priestly succession was the historical evidence of an ordinary genealogical descent, irrespective of all gifts or graces whatsoever. Such evidence is intelligible and reasonable; but on invisible evidence nothing can be believed, or, if anything, everything. And thus, though there were manifold causes of uncertainty with respect to a Jew's satisfaction in making his offering through a priest (such as those pertaining to the performance of all his due lustrations), yet with the Jew there was no doubt who was or who was not a priest.

"This was not a matter dependent upon a man's possession of an imperceptible gift, but simply on that of a legitimate ascertainable pedigree. The matter for inquiry was only whether he was or was not of the family of Aaron, and the genealogical tables of the Jews were all most carefully and publicly preserved. And, moreover, God at sundry times and in divers manners interposed with His miraculous signs to testify His approbation of the sacrifices of the people. Up to such times, then, there was proof that all was right, and that the priests as well as the offerings were acceptable in His sight. There was then, here, no room for doubt about the validity of the priest's commission. His credentials were almost palpable, and no doubt for centuries seems to have arisen. And when after the captivity such doubt did arise, we read that those who could not trace their descent by publicly authenticated documents were put away from the priesthood till a priest should arise with Urim and Thummim, that is, with a Divine oracle which should compensate for the chasm in the records of their genealogy. The introduction, therefore, of the hypothesis of a priesthood of apostolical representatives, with no apostolic evidences of their mission, puts us into a worse condition spiritually, with regard to freedom of access to God, than was known to Judaism. The exclusive theory here, as elsewhere throughout, is a stepping backwards. For besides all the bondage which the notion of a mediatorial order introduces, the supposition that the transmission of a gift of grace—a gift of which there is necessarily no evidence—is necessary for the validity of the ministerial commission must ever cause to the private worshipper all that uneasiness of mind which must follow from the conscious inability—nay, the acknowledged impossibility—of proving what it is of the greatest importance to believe; and, in fact, all the inconveniences which are justly represented as arising from the supposition that the personal qualifications of the minister affect the validity of his formal acts, attend likewise the supposition that any official qualifications are necessary besides his being the acknowledged minister of the Church of which we are members. Wherefore, to contend against this idea of apostolical succession must ever appear to many no necessary evidence or even presumption of irreverence, but rather only a legitimate assertion of Christian liberty."[1]

By no writer of modern times, conformist or nonconformist, has such deserved but withering exposure been given of the worshippers of the idol of apostolic succession, and the exclusive claims of episcopacy, as by the late Archdeacon Hare, with whose words we close this lecture.

"This friendly relation between our Church and the Protestant Churches on the continent subsisted during the whole of the last century, and was continually manifested in the writings of our divines, and in the manner in which we repeatedly selected our missionaries from those Churches, ordaining them to the ministry in our own Church. At length, however, on a sudden, some twenty years ago, when difficulties were assailing our Church on every side, a knot of men took it into their heads that they should get a knock-down argument against the Dissenters if they were to assert that episcopacy is an absolutely indispensable condition of Christ's Church; so that without it faith is nothing, the sacraments are of no effect, and they who have grown up feeding on the word of truth, and living by trust in the Saviour, are still aliens from

"Catholic Thoughts," &c., pp. 102-105.

the inheritance of grace, and are left to the uncovenanted mercies of God. One might have thought, indeed, that the heart and mind of the Church, that the Christian spirit of the English nation, would have revolted from such a notion, and would have spewed it out into the abyss where the spirits of evil fatten on the refuse of folly. But alas! no. The notion pampered our pride. We who were raised above the Church of Rome by the possession of a pure faith and worship, if we were in like manner raised above other Protestant bodies by the possession of that form of government which is indispensable to the Church, to what a pinnacle of glory should we be exalted! What a feather in our cap would it be if we were the only pure branch of Christ's Church upon earth; for the other branches that might claim equal purity were so small in comparison, that they might almost be left out of the account, or at the utmost would only form a cluster of satellites around us. And then what a convenient summary mode of getting over every difficulty, of pushing aside every knotty argument with the Dissenters, to tell them off-hand, *You have no part in Christ: you are not members of His Church: your sacraments are nought:* you are no better off than the heathens; nay, *worse, because you have rejected the privileges which have never been offered to them.* Owing to these two congenial motives, to that selfish arrogance which leads people to exalt all the circumstances and accidents of their own condition, till they are firmly persuaded that it is the normal state of mankind, and to the desire of depressing and triumphing over the Dissenters, the notion of the indispensable necessity of episcopacy has found acceptance with many of the members of our Church. Many of them have adopted it inconsiderately, without reflecting on the consequences it entailed with regard to the foreign branches of the Church. Others, when these consequences are pointed out to them, exclaim, *What are these consequences to us? Let those whom they concern see to them! The rules of the Church must stand, though hundreds of millions are doomed to perdition thereby.* Yet they who prate thus have gone through no laborious research in investigating the grounds of their terrific opinions. One might have thought that nothing less than absolute necessity, nothing less than the plainest, most explicit, most cogent, most irrefragable testimony of God's Word, would have induced a sober-minded Christian to admit such a doctrine into his mind. But where are the texts by which the maintainers of that doctrine have deemed themselves constrained to adopt it? They cannot produce one, not a single one, which, unless it be grossly wrested awry, will lend them any support. They will indeed refer to some half a dozen verses which they have picked up in some blundering manual of ecclesiastical history; but not one of these, when rightly interpreted, will be found to bear out their proposition, and the chief part will probably attest little else than the ignorance of those who cite them for such a purpose. To these misquoted texts of

Scripture, add a dozen exaggerated sayings culled out, without any critical discrimination, from this Father and from that, and you have the whole ragged, crippled troop which our episcopolaters are wont to muster for maintaining their position, that episcopacy is indispensable to the Church, and for repelling every one who presumes to approach the Church without bearing the episcopal flag. Among the numberless follies of our age, hardly anything is so sad as to see men, otherwise amiable and kindly disposed, grasping at a thunderbolt to crush the fly that is buzzing in their ears, and ready to hurl the thunderbolt, though millions of creatures should be overwhelmed by the blow which they aimed at the fly.

"This monstrous error, however, which would restrict the power of Christ's mediatorial sacrifice and the efficacy of His sacraments within the limits of Episcopal Churches, is still confined, I trust, in the main to some of our weaker brethren, who, in the want of logical and plastic power, stake themselves up with positive, peremptory assertions. But a modification of the same error is not uncommon, even among the better writers of our day, who have lately become squeamish in the application of the term *Church* to any branch of the Church except such as are subject to an episcopal government; who call the Lutheran Church, for instance, the *Lutheran Body* or the *Lutheran Communion;* and who think to evade recognising the Scotch Church by terming it *the Kirk*. Such silliness might make one laugh, unless the miserable evils which absurdities of this kind produce turn one's laugh into a groan. Notwithstanding my sincere regard and respect for several persons who have adopted these practices, I feel bound in duty to Christ's Church, and especially to all the reformed branches of it, to declare that I cannot view this distinction in any other light than as a piece of coxcombical affectation and of uncharitable, unchristian presumption." [1]

[1] "Mission of the Comforter," vol. ii. pp. 1007-1010.

LECTURE IV.

*THE PRIESTHOOD: ITS FUNCTIONS—
AT THE ALTAR.*

LECTURE IV.

THE PRIESTHOOD: ITS FUNCTIONS—AT THE ALTAR.

AFTER having considered the priesthood in the light of the New Testament, and seen that there it finds no place in name, office, or qualification, but that it is resented by the whole spirit and genius of the Christian dispensation; and after having shown that its vaunted hierarchy and lineage are equally discredited both by apostolical authority and the facts of history, I now proceed to the examination of some of those functions which the Christian priesthood, falsely so called, assume to possess the exclusive prerogative of discharging. I say "some of those functions," for aught approaching to an exhaustive discussion of all the duties and powers which are supposed to pertain to the priestly office would extend this work to unmanageable proportions. I shall omit all consideration of the sacrament of Baptism, partly because I have devoted to it already a treatise, whose special aim was the examination of its alleged regenerative power,[1] and partly because the validity of this sacrament does not depend, either in the Romish

[1] "Baptismal Regeneration." *Ecclesia.* Second series.

or English Church, on its administration by a priest. If the matter and the form be duly combined; in other words, if water be applied " in the name of the Father, the Son, and the Holy Ghost," by any person, be he clerical or lay, orthodox or heretic, the rite lacks none of its essential qualifications or effects.

The case, however, is different with respect to the sacraments of the Eucharist and of Penance. According to the sacerdotal conception, these cannot be devolved. They pertain so absolutely to the priest, that in the hands of any other they become abortive ceremonies, administered by an unauthorised and sacrilegious usurper. It is to the consideration of the priest as a sacrificer and a confessor that we shall devote the five lectures that follow, believing, as we do, that it is in this double function that the priest inflicts the most signal dishonour upon the character of God and the sufficiency of the Saviour's work, and propagates an influence which has demoralised every people among whom it has had unrestricted sway. As the authority of the Scriptures is boldly alleged in support of these stupendous claims, it will be necessary to examine carefully the nature of that authority. This is the more needful with respect to the eucharistic sacrifice, inasmuch as while upon almost every other distinctively Romish dogma or practice tradition plays the chief part, the doctrine of the Mass is confidently grounded upon the express and unequivocal declaration of the Divine Word.

One of the chief advantages (indeed, the chief one)

which have been pleaded in favour of the Romish doctrine of Transubstantiation, and of the Lutheran and Ritualistic doctrine of Consubstantiation, is that they have for their warrant and vindication the literal rendering of our Saviour's language on the occasion of the institution of the Lord's Supper; while it is alleged as against every other theory, that it is in a greater or less degree a figurative interpretation.

The great Reformer, in his controversy with Carlostadt, was as impassioned in his appeal to the very words of our Lord as were the most strenuous defenders of the dogma of Transubstantiation, though he seemed to be wholly unconscious of the fact that his own doctrine was far less consonant with these words than that of the Church from which he had seceded. The formula, "Here is my body," is the only one which can be regarded as strictly expressing the theory of Consubstantiation; while the Lateran definition has the merit of embodying with more of *apparent* exactness the language of institution. Given the stupendous assumption that the Transubstantiation has been effected, and no words could more emphatically express it than "This is my body." But whatever may be urged in the general in favour of a literal interpretation, and however true it may be that any departure from such interpretation requires to be vindicated from caprice and wantonness, this is a principle which has to be accepted with very obvious and even extensive limitations. There are, for example, whole departments of literature in which the adoption of the principle of the literal interpretation would create the greatest havoc, such as that of poetry. The intrusion of this bare, rigid, literalistic method of exposition into such a domain, would be as desolating as an untimely blast of winter amid gardens blooming with the flowers and blossoms of June. It would be little short of insanity to bring to Spenser and Shakespeare and Milton the same spirit of literalism which would be serviceable and safe enough in the reading of a book of travels, history, or geography. And before we can determine with any certainty what is the principle of interpretation which we must apply to any language, it is necessary to ascertain what are the general characteristics of the writer or speaker, the extent of play which he allows to his imagination in the use of illustrations, and the general variety and depth of colouring which his style may derive from the glow and fervency of an earnest and impassioned nature. The reader who disregards these considerations will miss as frequently as he will hit the mark, and will certainly fail to realise the highest truths which the writer seeks to teach, treasuring up the shells and husks, while the kernel and the seed are neglected.

1. Is it any exaggeration, then, if touching the language of our Lord as recorded in the Gospels, we say that the literal interpretation of it is that which is least capable of unfolding its meaning? Was there ever so large a proportion of instructions couched in language that absolutely demands a figurative exposition? What becomes even of the Sermon on the Mount, if every

word is to be pressed to the full extent of its literal
signification? And do we not find it explicitly stated
that the parable was His ordinary method of teaching?
And where there is no parable, is not His language often
marked by its tropical colouring, its paradoxes, and its
condensed and pregnant apophthegms, which must
utterly bewilder and mislead the man whose only critical instrument is the literal method of interpretation?
It is, unquestionably, one of the most obtrusive facts
connected with the Gospels, that our Saviour's disciples,
whether within the inner or outer circle, were perpetually misunderstanding and resenting His meaning, because of the perverse application of this barren and
superficial principle. It was the literal interpreters
that revolted from Him at Capernaum, when they
supposed that He spoke of giving His flesh to eat; it
was the literal interpreters who imagined Him to speak
of the temple at Jerusalem, when He spoke of the
temple of His body; it was the literal interpreters
who thought that when he said, "Take heed, and beware of the leaven of the Pharisees and the Sadducees,"
it was because they had taken no bread with them;
it was a literal interpreter who regarded Him as
inculcating the necessity of a second natural birth,
because He had spoken of a birth from above. While,
therefore, it is true that the literal rendering is the one
most applicable to the words and writings of men who
are avowedly narrating facts or expounding a philosophy, it is inept and worthless when it affects to
deal with the language of One whose teaching was al-

most wholly of a metaphorical character. I hold that in such a case it is not the figurative interpretation which is put on its defence, but the literal; and that, therefore, when the Catholic assumes that his doctrine of Transubstantiation is effectually shielded by the literal sense of our Lord's words, he has to show cause why he has adopted in this individual instance a principle of interpretation so exceptional, that if it were applied to the general teaching of our Lord it would utterly pervert its meaning, and in many passages convict it of the most extravagant absurdity. The Romish allegation, therefore, against the Protestant doctrine of the Eucharist, that it departs from the literal meaning, is a high testimony to its probability, because it affirms its harmony with the whole tone and manner of the Saviour's instructions; for it would be a novel canon of hermeneutics that that is the most unquestionable signification which violates most the acknowledged style of a writer or speaker. He who could say, "I am the true vine," and "I am the door," and "I am the good shepherd," could also say, "This is my body;" for in each case He was setting forth in His own figurative and characteristic way the relation He sustained to His own followers; and the attempt to place the expression He employed at the Last Supper in a category distinct from the rest, as if (unlike them) it was meant to embody a literal fact, is not only to assume the whole point in dispute, but to disregard the pervading spirit and form of our Saviour's ministry.

This, however, is not all. Not only do the Romish

and Ritualistic theories ground their claims on a principle of interpretation which is inapplicable to the main proportion of the teachings of our Lord, but they are in demonstrable incongruity with the very principle which they invoke. While vaunting their adherence to the letter, they violate the letter, and that too without conforming to any species of figure which can be clearly construed either by the reason or the imagination. The charge which has been uttered with such confidence and constancy against almost every Protestant variety of opinion touching our Lord's words, viz., that it shirks the *literal* meaning, recoils with even greater force upon those who prefer it; for the literal meaning is that which the Protestants avowedly reject, while it is, in fact, inconsistently sacrificed by the Sacramentarians, who claim to preserve it. The difference, accordingly, between the Tridentine exposition of the language in which the Saviour instituted the Supper, and others, is a difference not between the literal and the figurative, but between different forms of the figurative. This proposition I now proceed to establish.

In his account of the Last Supper St. Matthew tells us that "as they were eating, Jesus took bread, and blessed it, and brake it, and gave it to the disciples, and said, Take, eat, this is my body" (Matt. xxvi. 26).

Now, what was to the apostles, or what is to any man the meaning of *body* as applied to the human frame? Its literal signification embraces a variety of conceptions, such as size, form, organisation, reciprocal relations of parts, diversity of functions and susceptibilities. Of any body of man, and, therefore, of the body of Christ, except as thus constituted and endowed, they knew nothing and could understand nothing. The expression "my body" they would interpret (if they interpreted it literally) as meaning that very body which alone they had known as the body of their Lord, the body in which He had been their companion, in which He had sat on the Mount, walked through the corn-fields, slept in the vessel, trodden the waves, rested, thirsty and weary, on Jacob's well, and in which He then spoke to them at supper. But to imagine that, as they gazed on that which He held in His hand, and which wore the semblance of bread, they understood His declaration in its literal sense, is to believe that they suddenly surrendered all their conceptions of what a human body means, as to bulk, form, organs, and faculties; that they did this while in fact they heard Him speaking in a human body, with all those properties as conspicuously connected with it as they had ever been : in other words, it is to believe that the apostles did not interpret the word "body" in its literal and accepted sense, and that they did not regard that morsel which they ate as having the dimensions, to say nothing of other qualities belonging to the body of their Lord.

The perplexities into which the Church of Rome has fallen by its declaration of a doctrine which is discredited by every sense of man, whether separately or in combination, is clearly seen in the Catechism of the

Council of Trent, where it is difficult to say whether is the more conspicuous, its devotion to the letter, or its anxiety to explain it away. For example, in the thirty-first question it enjoins that "pastors must explain that in this sacrament are contained not only the true body of Christ, and whatsoever appertains to the character of a true body, such as bones and nerves, but also Christ whole and entire." And then in the forty-second question we read; "They must next teach that our Lord is not present in this sacrament as in a *place*, for place regards things themselves inasmuch as they possess any magnitude: and we do not say that Christ our Lord is in the sacrament, inasmuch as He is great or small, terms which appertain to quantity, but inasmuch as He is a *substance*. For the substance of the bread is changed into the substance of Christ, not into His magnitude or quantity; and substance, no one will doubt, is contained in a small as well as in a large space. The substance of the air, and its entire nature, for example, whether in a large or small quantity, and that of water, whether confined in a small vessel or flowing in a river, must necessarily be the same. As then, to the substance of bread succeeds the body of our Lord, we must needs confess it to be in the sacrament after exactly the same manner as was the substance of the bread before consecration, but whether it was present in great or small quantity was altogether a matter of indifference."

To an ordinary reader, what is here given with one hand is taken back with the other. The expressions, "true body of Christ," "whatsoever appertains to the character of a true body," "bones and nerves," would seem to necessitate the conception of the "very body" of our Lord with which the disciples were familiar; unless indeed that was not His true body, and that from the day that He called His disciples to the evening of the Paschal meal, and even to the moment of His consecration of the bread, He had never been known to them in His own body, but had been a deceptive phantom. "Nerves and bones," as they existed in Him, would also seem to suggest, inevitably, certain dimensions. The apostles, at least when our Saviour corrected their misapprehensions as to His being a spirit, by reminding them that a spirit had not flesh and bones as they saw Him have, would think of these essential constituents of His bodily frame as occupying a certain amount of space. The "true body of Christ," which is the Romish phrase, must have had in their eyes a definite magnitude, no more and no less, so that had they met in the streets of Jerusalem a man a cubit higher or lower in stature, they would not have looked at him a second time under any suspicion that he might possibly be the Christ. They would not have mistaken for "his true body" that of a child, nor that of one of the sons of the Anakim.

But after thus, by language of the most definite character, calling up the idea of a certain magnitude, it is necessary to soften the shock created by it when confronted with the diminutive size of the consecrated wafer. The sense of incongruity which instantaneously arises between the bones and nerves of an ordinary human body, and the host, which can be placed on the tongue, has to be appeased by the help of a metaphysical distinction, which informs us that "Christ our Lord is not in the sacrament in so far forth as He is great or small, terms which appertain to quantity, but inasmuch as He is a substance. For the substance of the bread is changed into the substance of Christ, not into His magnitude or quantity."

Here the common and established conceptions of a "true human body," and of "nerves and bones," as occupying space, are rudely set aside by an unliteral and fantastic interpretation in favour of a conception which eliminates from them all fixed spatial relations; for while there is but one whole Christ in each whole wafer, there is also one whole Christ in each particle of it when separated, even though it should be but of microscopic minuteness. The illustration by which the catechism seeks to support this extraordinary dogma leads one to wonder that a Church which can *command* should ever commit its interests to the precarious method of reasoning, for the analogy which it adduces fails wholly to reach the point it was meant to sustain. "The substance of the air," it says, "and its entire nature, for instance, whether in a large or a small quantity, and that of water, whether confined in a small vessel or flowing in a river, must necessarily be the same; and in like manner the whole nature of water is of necessity not less in a small vessel than in the river." By the "whole nature," *tota natura*, the

Church of Rome must mean the substance, or its illustration is wide of the mark; but it would have shown a more exact appreciation of the matter in dispute if the Council of Trent had proved that there was both the same amount of substance in the small vessel of water as there was in the river from which it was taken, and that the substance in the vessel was not only *like*, but numerically the *same* as the substance in the river. Both of these conditions must be fulfilled in order that the analogy may have any pertinence whatsoever. It would be also needful to establish another assumption which neither science nor philosophy has as yet succeeded in proving — viz., that the substance of any human body—whether that of our Saviour or that of any other man—has not a definite extension in space, and that extension exactly corresponding with the magnitude and form by which the body becomes cognisable to the senses of sight and touch. It remains to be demonstrated that there is a single point of the bones and nerves — things absolutely unknown to us except under spatial relations—at which substance is not present, and present also in such manner that the substance at one point is numerically distinct from the substance at any other point. In other words it remains to be demonstrated, and we must wait long for the proof, that there is any accident or species which has not a substance strictly coextensive with it, whether it be an atom or a mountain, a twig or a tree, a cell or the sum-total of such cells as constitute the organism and bulk of a human body. If the substance of the bread before the alleged transubstantiation occupied space, then it must have occupied it as *magnitude* greater or smaller; and as the body of our Lord is said by the Church of Rome to be in the sacrament "*after exactly the same manner* as was the substance of the bread before consecration," it must have occupied space as magnitude greater or smaller. This conclusion can only be evaded by denying that it is the manner of the substance of bread to occupy space, which is a proposition upon which the Infallible Church has not, so far as I know, as yet set its seal.

To allege that what the apostles ate at the Last Supper was in a *mysterious* sense the real body of Christ, is to surrender the whole question, and to confess that the literal sense of body must be relinquished. Of all the distinctions which have been elaborated in subsequent ages, and especially by the schoolmen, for the purpose of supporting the Romish doctrine, the apostles knew nothing. They were as ignorant as the table at which they sat of the subtleties which fill the pages of Aquinas and Scotus; and had the Saviour employed language embodying such distinctions, it would have been by a violent and unexplained departure from what He knew the apostles could only interpret in a wholly different sense.

The Church of Rome seems to be in great perplexity as to the manner in which the doctrine of Transubstantiation shall be commended to the acceptance of mankind. At one time it aims to bring it as far as possible within the apprehension of the reason, by argument and analogy; and at another, as if conscious of the utter miscarriage of this process, it appeals to a blind and unquestioning faith. It coquets with logic, but with timorous misgivings. It is, however, most at home when it invokes the authority of tradition. It would fain explain the *modus* of the change of the elements, or the nature of the presence in many places at the same time of the body of our Lord, and then with a delicious simplicity confesses it can with difficulty express it (*exprimere vix possumus*).[1] It has, however, a final resource left in the word *sacramentaliter*, sacramentally, which it uses as a talismanic wand in every logical strait, as if indeed the word did not conceal the mystery which it is meant to elucidate. We desire to know what the change and presence *are*, and we are informed what they are *denominated*. In the Catechism of the Council of Trent the holy Fathers inform us that "if after consecration the body of Christ is really and truly present under the species of bread and wine, not having been there before, it must have become so by change of place, by creation, or by the change of another thing into it." These are the three possible predicaments upon which the catechism then proceeds to adjudicate as follows. "Now, that the body of Christ cannot be rendered present by change of place, is evident, as it would then cease to be in heaven; for whatever is moved must necessarily cease to occupy the

[1] "Concilii Tridentini, De Eucharistia," p. 92.

place from which it is moved. Still less can we suppose that the body of Christ is rendered present by creation, an idea which cannot even be conceived in thought. It remains, therefore, that the body of the Lord be contained in the sacrament because the bread is changed into it, and therefore it necessarily follows that none of the substance of the bread remains."

It appears from this that the creational mode of the presence is disallowed solely on the ground that it cannot be "conceived even in thought," and that the appeal is made to the decision of the human faculties. Did it not, however, occur to the sacred council that the same human faculties pronounce with equal certainty and confidence against their third predicament, namely, that "the bread is *changed* into the body"? For it is absolutely inconceivable that when two bodies coexist in time the one can be changed into the other without a change in both, and yet the Church of Rome, while affirming the change of the bread, denies the change in the body of Christ! It has therefore, with a curious fatuity, rejected one proposition because it is inconceivable, and accepted another, though equally inconceivable.

2. The so-called literal interpretation is irreconcilable with the fact that the *bread* is termed *bread*, and the wine "the fruit of the vine," after consecration; and, therefore, when according to one theory the substances of both had disappeared, and according to another existed co-ordinately under the same species with the body and the blood of Christ. This designation by

their ordinary names of the elements commanded to be used in the sacrament of the Lord's Supper must embarrass every theory which involves a substantial change. For whether, according to the Romish view, the substance of the bread had been changed into the substance of the body of Christ; or whether, according to the Neo-Catholic view, the substance of the body took its place under the same accidents with the substance of the bread, the accidents could have no value or significance compared with that sacred Person whom they are supposed to veil, and of whom they are but the appointed medium and vehicle to the soul. When our Saviour is said to have taken bread, it is not pretended that He took simply certain properties which had no relation to, or inherence in any substance whatsoever. He took the bread, which was of the same kind as that which had been just used at the Paschal meal, and which it is admitted was bread in substance as well as in species. It is called bread before He consecrated it, He calls it bread after it is consecrated, and when, according to the Romish theory, it was not bread, except in those external phenomena by which it became discernible to the senses. That is, its name not only did not denote what it was, but did denote what it was not, circumstances which violate every principle by which appropriate terminology should be guided. If a change so miraculous as that under consideration had been effected, and if it were not only important but necessary to salvation that such change should be believed, nothing would seem to have been more essential than to relinquish and even forbid the use of the terms bread and wine from the moment of the alleged consecration. The inveterate force of association which leads all men to denominate bread that which has all the properties of bread, and which was as strong in the disciples of our Lord as in us, required not only that no additional strength should be given to the association, but that it should be finally dissolved by a marked and invariable substitution, after consecration, of the words body and blood for bread and wine. If such substitution had been made and uniformly observed, then, though even this would not have warranted the inference that a real transelementation had been accomplished, it might not unfitly have been pleaded by the Romanists as affording a significant support to their theory. It does not avail, in answer to what has now been advanced, to say that though the substance is changed the name of the old substance is retained by the new, because the appearances and properties are the same, and things are named from what they seem to be; for not only does this assume the point in dispute, viz., that a change has really transpired, but it was of pre-eminent and even vital moment to guard the apostles and all Christians against what would have been in this case the powerful illusions of the senses; and the more certain this mystic transformation is assumed to have been, the more needful it was by a corresponding nomenclature to render a misapprehension impossible. So far, however, from any precaution having been taken by our Saviour for this purpose, He described the contents of the cup, which after consecration He had given to the disciples, as "this fruit of the vine," an expression which would have been in the highest degree untrue if the whole substance of that fruit had, according to the Romish theory, vanished; and misleading if, according to the Ritualistic theory, the "fruit of the vine" had been only the least important element in the cup.

Moreover, as so much emphasis has been laid on the "*this*" in the words of consecration, with the view of supporting the sacramental theories now under consideration, it should not be forgotten that the same word brings all its weight, whatever it be, to prove that what the wine was before consecration it was also after, for Jesus said, "*This* fruit of the vine;" and the Apostle Paul, in his comments on the Lord's Supper, showed that in his view the consecration had made no difference in the substance of the bread, for he says, "As often as ye eat *this* bread and drink this cup, ye do show the Lord's death till he come." It is clear that if after the consecrating act so miraculous a transformation had been effected that the common substances of bread and wine had been replaced by the body and the blood of Christ, and that it was of transcendent moment that this change should be accepted as matter of undoubting faith, nothing would have been easier than to have used exclusively the terms which were alone appropriate to the awful elements of which the disciples were commanded to partake.

It is granted by Cardinal Wiseman and other

champions of Transubstantiation, that had our Saviour said, "This bread is my body," instead of "This is my body," the Romish doctrine would have lost the support of the words of institution; but this very combination of the demonstrative pronoun with the noun, which he admits to be so fatal, appears in the language of the apostle, "As often as ye eat this bread," from which, unless the authority of the apostle is to be set aside, it is manifest that the consecration left the bread unchanged. Either the solitary "this" of our Lord was identical in meaning with the "this bread" of the apostle, or it was not. If it were, then the term *bread* defines the substance after consecration, and the term *this* cannot denote *body*. If it were not, then there must have been a difference between the effect of consecration as accomplished by our Lord and as accomplished subsequently by the presiding officers in the Churches; a difference so great, that what was *body* in the former case was only *bread* in the latter, and if in the latter, in every subsequent celebration of the Eucharist throughout the world.

3. The so-called literal sense is strikingly disproved by the language of our Lord touching the meaning of "*the cup.*" It is impossible to read the writings of Roman Catholic theologians without observing the significant manner in which they bend their main strength to the exposition of His words in connection with the bread; for, as we shall see, the formula in which the import of the wine is expounded by our Lord is to

them hopelessly intractable. The consecration of the bread, with its "*Hoc est corpus meum*," has largely overshadowed the consecration of the wine, but it must be remembered that both were coessential factors in the Last Supper, the latter completing the former. What were the precise words uttered by our Lord in consecrating the cup, it is impossible for us to ascertain, and no Church on earth can give an authoritative ruling on this point. According to St. Matthew, He said, "Drink ye all of it; for this is my blood of the covenant, which is shed for many for the remission of sins:" according to St. Mark, He said, "This is my blood of the covenant, which is shed for many;" according to St. Luke, He said, "This is the new covenant in my blood;" and according to St. Paul, He said, "This cup is the new covenant in my blood." Of these four authorities (if indeed St. Paul may be held as constituting an original and independent one), two represent our Saviour as declaring that the cup was, not His blood, but "the new covenant in his blood;" one as declaring that "this is my blood of the covenant;" and one as declaring, "This is the blood of the new covenant." If the exact expression employed by our Lord is to be determined by the numerical value of testimony, then, according to St. Luke and St. Paul, He said, "This cup is the new covenant in my blood;" and, on the supposition that this was the case, what becomes of the doctrine of Transubstantiation, or the literal interpretation which it so confidently invokes? It is scarcely too much to say that this portion of the original rite (assuming for the moment that we have the exact words of Christ) works irreparable disaster to the Romish theory. Take, for instance, the first word "this." What is its reference? Nothing has been mentioned but the cup (ποτήριον)—the vessel itself—and to the vessel which may contain any liquid it must on the literal theory be strictly confined; for if it be said that the cup metaphorically denotes its contents, we must suggest that metaphor is a dangerous and even an illicit intruder in a region where the letter is to be not only supreme but exclusive. Waiving, however, this objection, and allowing the word cup to denote metaphorically its contents, we have still to deal with the fatal combination, "this cup." For this combination is one, the non-occurrence of which in connection with the consecration of the bread seems to have been the chief circumstance which, in the opinion of Cardinal Wiseman, establishes the doctrine of Transubstantiation. Here we have another illustration, added to thousands more, of the inexpediency and danger of inventing a general principle for the purpose of meeting a special case; for, as I have now to show, the general principle is hopelessly refuted by another special case of precisely the like character. The Cardinal, as has been already stated, admitted that "had our Saviour said, 'This bread is my body,' 'This wine is my blood,' there would have been a contradiction. The apostles might have said, 'Wine cannot be His blood,' 'Bread cannot be His body;' but when our Saviour uses this indefinite word we arrive at its meaning only at the conclusion of the sentence." But how fares this astounding canon of criticism when applied to the words of our Lord with reference to the cup? Here we have not the indefinite "this," which affords such consolation to the Cardinal, but the definite, because defined, "this cup;" and are we therefore to say, because we have not the indefinite "this," but the definite "this cup," there is here "some contradiction"? On such a theory his Eminence carries his ill-managed subtlety to irreverence. It would seem that the use of a noun after the demonstrative may make all the difference between a literal fact and a contradiction. If some one should take the Magna Charta in hand, and say, "This is the shield of English liberty," it would be a literal fact that the document would be a shield, all appearances to the contrary notwithstanding; but if he should say, "This document is the shield of English liberty," it would be a contradiction. But was it ever acknowledged as a law of language that a combination of demonstrative and noun could play such havoc as to convert a literal truth into a contradiction? It boots nothing to allege that the words, "This is my body," must not be classed with such illustrations as the one which has just been given; for Cardinal Wiseman's expedient is either a general principle of language, which will stand good as an ordinary law of interpretation, or it is an exceptional device, invented to meet a special case. If it be the former, then it would be seen to be valid in the instance of any similar formula, whatever might be its subject-matter. If it be the latter, then it is simply a bold and reckless assumption of the very point which it behoved him to prove. He had to prove that the solitary "this" was wholly different in meaning from "this" accompanied with its substantive, and he invented or adopted a canon which has no other illustration than that which the canon was created to meet. He had to defend an interpretation of a disputed passage. For this purpose he formulates a law. The authority for the law is demanded, and he cites the disputed passage. A more palpable and vicious circle was never devised, even by his Eminence himself.

And it is incompetent for any one who accepts his reasoning to suggest that possibly our Lord did not say "this cup," but "this;" for in the first place we have two testimonies to the fact that He did say "this cup." In the second place, if He said "this," and not "this cup," it is evident from the two testimonies to the contrary that the one expression is equivalent to the other, and there is no contradiction in either. In the third place, the Apostle Paul calls it "this cup," after consecration. In the fourth place, our Saviour also denominates it "this fruit of the vine;" and in the fifth place, St. Luke and St. Paul testify that our Lord said, "This cup is the new covenant in my blood," a statement which is perfectly in harmony with "this is my blood of the new covenant," on the principle of a figurative interpretation, but on no other. For, literally speaking, "this cup" could never be a "new covenant;" and just as little could "this cup" be "blood." It is only necessary to add further here that the language of our Lord touching the cup throws a flood of light upon the "this" which occurs in His declaration concerning the bread. For as it has been shown that the "this" of one Evangelist is explained by another as being "this cup," so as our Lord did only take bread and the cup, the "this" in the expression "this is my body" could refer only to the bread; and as the contents of the cup still remained after consecration "this fruit of the vine," so must the bread have remained "this bread."

4. The so-called literal interpretation is flagrantly violated by the Romish doctrine, which enlarges arbitrarily and wantonly the exposition which our Saviour Himself gave of the bread and the cup. This strange amplification is defended upon the principle of inference and concomitance, but our contention is that the inference and the concomitance are in the direct teeth of the language upon which they are professedly grounded. Indeed, it will not be difficult to show that the Tridentine doctrine is not only manifold, but also inconsistent with itself. It expounds differently at different times the sacramental elements, and the expositions refute each other.

The first canon of the Council of Trent declares that "if any one shall deny that in the most holy sacrament of the Eucharist there are contained truly, really, and substantially the body and blood, together with the soul and divinity, of our Lord Jesus Christ, and therefore the whole Christ, or say that He is in it only as in a sign or figure, or by His influence, let him be accursed."

In the third canon we read : " If any one denies that in the adorable sacrament of the Eucharist, a separation being made, a whole Christ is contained under each species, and under every part of every species, let him be accursed."

In the presence of these canons the literal interpretation seems to have faded wholly out of view. Our Saviour never said of the bread, " This is my blood," nor of the cup, " This is my body ; " and with neither the one nor the other did He associate His soul and divinity. But the Church of Rome, as if to show how bravely it can trample on the letter while professing to reverence it, makes each species, and every portion of each, being separated, a whole Christ. It would appear strange, if the bread through transformation had become the whole body and blood, soul and divinity of Christ, that the cup was needed at all ; and equally strange, if the blood was indeed as much under the form of the bread as the body, that our Saviour did not say, " This is my body and blood." The homage which the Church of Rome pays to the letter is further curiously illustrated by the manner in which it observes the command of Christ, " Drink ye all of it." This injunction, according to the Council of Trent, may mean, " Drink ye none of it," and hence the cup is withheld from the laity. Our Saviour made the drinking of the cup as essential a part of the ordinance as the eating of the bread, and the apostolic Churches without exception both ate the bread and drank the wine; but the Church of Rome, as if wiser than the Lord and His apostles, rules that it is sufficient to administer half the original feast. And with an effrontery which would be astounding were it not of a piece with so much of its ecclesiastical legislation, after assuring the laity that when they eat the host they do in fact both eat and drink, not only the body and blood, but the soul and divinity of our Lord, its priests, not content with the portion they have given to the laity, both drink the cup and eat the host; thus suggesting the question whether, if the laity who eat the wafer have a full and perfect, the priests who both eat the wafer and drink the cup have not two full and perfect sacraments. If they have not, it would be interesting to see how the conclusion is avoided; and if they have, and derive any benefit from such a pleonastic sacrament, why does a Church which cherishes such love for its children withhold from them all a blessing which it could so easily confer, and which was the incontestable privilege of Christians for centuries? If the sacrament in one kind is sufficient for the people, it is sufficient for the priest; if it be insufficient for the priest, it is insufficient for the people; and if it be beneficial for the priest, it would be beneficial for the people. The truth is, that all the reasons which have been assigned by the Romanists for their mutilation of the sacrament bear the appearance of weak and palpable evasions. To allege the danger of the cup being spilled, is to overlook the fact that such a contingency must have been *foreseen* as clearly by the Saviour as it is *seen* by them, and yet that such prevision did not lead Him to interdict the cup to any of His followers; and it is to ignore the precept and practice of a thousand years. An express Divine command, as clear as was ever uttered, is set aside on grounds which are too frivolous to merit serious consideration. The Papal Church, on this matter, and on many others, vaunts its prerogative to erect its own decisions into laws that abrogate Divine prescriptions. It has banished the cup from lay communion, and it might with equal propriety have banished the bread in its stead; and may now, with as much of decency and deference to the authority of Christ, banish it in addition. Its appeal to the words of institution, and to their literal signification, can be regarded in no other light than a daring hypocrisy, when we see not only how it can supplement the words "body and blood" with soul and divinity, but how it can sever the ordinance in twain, depriving the vast majority of its votaries of that which the Saviour left them as their legitimate and inalienable heritage.

The endeavour to support this arbitrary innovation upon a practice enjoined by our Lord, and scrupulously respected for centuries in the Christian Church, by an appeal to Scripture, affords another curious illustration of the perverted exegesis of the Romish theologians. Appeal is made to the language of St. Paul in 1 Cor. xi. 27. "Wherefore whosoever shall eat this bread, OR drink this cup of the Lord, unworthily, shall be guilty of the body and blood of the Lord." The disjunctive conjunction *or* may be fairly conceded to be the approved reading, instead of *and*, as in our Authorised Version; and whatever advantage this admission may yield to the Romish cause, it is fully entitled to enjoy. But what is this advantage? Does it justify the inference that communion in one kind is sufficient? So far from this, the language distinctly declares that the unworthy participation of either one or other of the sacramental symbols involves the gravest sin. If a father enjoins upon his son two duties, with the warning that the careless discharge of either the one or the other will be visited with sure and heavy penalty, is it therefore to be inferred that the right fulfilment of either releases him from the other? This, however, is the characteristic logic of the Vatican theologians, and that, too, in the face of the fact that in the immediate neighbourhood of the text so violently pressed into service, the apostle emphatically and repeatedly enjoins the eating *and* the drinking as co-essential factors of the ordinance. "For as often as ye eat this bread, *and* drink this cup, ye do show the Lord's death till he come." "But let a man examine himself, *and* so let him eat of the bread, *and* drink of the cup. For he that eateth *and* drinketh (unworthily), eateth *and* drinketh judgment to himself, not discerning the Lord's body."

Cardinal Manning, who certainly cannot be suspected of lacking the courage of his opinions, has come to the rescue of his Church on the question of the mutilated communion, though it is impossible to compliment either his logic or his temper in his recent controversy with Lord Redesdale.[1] There is abundant dexterity of fence, such as we might expect to find in a man whose natural subtlety has been sharpened in the schools of Ultramontane casuistry to an almost preternatural acumen. His candour, however, is less conspicuous, and the forms of his answers to the questions of Lord Redesdale reveal a greater anxiety for victory than for the truth. What ingenuousness, for example, can we discover in the Cardinal's admission, with its limiting caveat — "Our Lord ordained that the holy sacrament should be consecrated and received by His apostles in both kinds; *but He did not ordain that it should be received by all Christians in both kinds*"? How far such a method of interpretation would carry him, it is difficult to see. It would, at least, limit the obligations of obedience on the part of all Christians, except the apostles, to such injunctions as could be proved to be directly addressed to them. One would have imagined that the obvious inference, apart from any restrictive clause, would have been that what apostles were to do "in remembrance of Christ," was to be done by every faithful disciple, in like "remembrance" of Him; and that cause requires to be shown for tampering with the integrity of the institution. Moreover, one would have thought that the logic of the Cardinal would not have timidly and inconsistently halted at one half of the

[1] "Daily Telegraph," Oct. 16, 1873, and following numbers.

conclusion which its premises authorise. For as the Cardinal alleges our Lord "did not ordain that it should be received by all Christians in both kinds," so neither, upon his method of inference, did He ordain that it should be received by *any* Christian (except the apostles) in *either* kind. If we are to regard the transactions of the upper room as having no relation to any but the immediate apostles of our Lord, it is obvious that there is no obligation resting upon the Church in subsequent ages to observe the service of the Eucharist. But, on the other hand, if we are to regard them as having a prospective reference, not merely to the apostles, but to the Church in all future time, any *selection* from the constituent elements of the original feast must be treason to the rest, and to the Divine authority, which equally commanded *one* and *all*. The Cardinal, therefore, must be pleased courageously to face the dilemma which his extraordinary manœuvre has created. If because our Saviour "did not ordain that the sacrament should be received by all Christians in both kinds," it is to be inferred that the cup may be denied to the laity, so also it is to be inferred, and on the same ground, that "the bread" may be denied to the laity, and that the sacrament may be abolished altogether. If the sacrament be obligatory at all, it is obligatory as a whole; if it be not obligatory as a whole, it is not obligatory at all. But the conclusion authorised and necessitated by the Cardinal's premises is wider still. It is not the laity alone that lack their Saviour's injunction to observe the "Lord's Supper:" the clergy are equally destitute of the same Divine warrant, no word having been uttered at the original appointment of the feast which commanded its observance in future ages either by priest or layman. It wears, therefore, the unworthy aspect of a subterfuge, when, in order to shelter the Romish dogma and practice of a mutilated sacrament, an inference is drawn from the silence of our Lord; which, if applied with equal-handed fairness, annihilates the obligatory character of the whole ordinance, but which also is arbitrarily and illogically restrained to such moiety of the ordinance as the Cardinal and his Church choose to perpetuate. In short, this is the alternative which the Cardinal has persistently evaded when considering the language of institution; either both bread and wine are commanded, or neither. If both, the Church of Rome has despotically divided the sacrament; if neither, she has despotically established a sacrament of salvation without a Divine authorisation.

But what was the exact nature of our Lord's intention with respect to the perpetual wholeness of the Sacrament, as consisting of both bread and wine, is left neither to the decision of the Church of Rome, nor of its valiant champion, Cardinal Manning. The Apostle Paul, writing a generation after the ascension of our Lord, informs the Corinthians that he had received from Him an account of the Supper, which he forthwith proceeds to expound, and from which it is clear that the Saviour Himself intended that the sacrament should be participated in both kinds. Now, as the apostle is writing to laymen, all his instructions and injunctions on this matter are designed for laymen, and one of the precepts which he had received from the Lord was, that after the bread had been eaten, the cup should be taken and drunk. The statement, therefore, of Cardinal Manning, that our Lord "did not ordain that it (the sacrament) should be received by all Christians in both kinds," is in explicit contradiction to the testimony of the Apostle Paul that this was the ordination of Christ, and that such was the assurance that he had received from the Saviour Himself. In any question of competition of authorities, his Eminence will not assuredly claim to carry it over an inspired apostle, and if he did, such claim would be steadfastly resisted. The matter, therefore, stands thus. On the evening on which the sacrament of the Lord's Supper was instituted, His disciples were commanded to eat the bread and to drink the cup; in his recapitulation of the nature of the ordinance, St. Paul declares that he had received from the Lord instructions enjoining upon the Churches communion in both kinds; and we have no instance in which any apostle either forbids the loaf or the cup, or declares either of them to be sufficient apart from the other. When Cardinal Manning affirms that "communion in both kinds was in use for centuries, and is in use in some places at this day," and adds, "but not as a necessary obligation by Divine commandment;" it is for the reader to judge what can be a "necessary obligation" and what a "Divine commandment," if the authority of inspiration cannot constitute the one, and a precept of inspiration cannot constitute the other.

Further, a conclusive refutation of this theory of mutilation has been suicidally provided by the Church of Rome itself, in consequence of its determination to suborn the sixth chapter of St. John as a witness to the doctrine of Transubstantiation. Our Saviour said, "Verily, verily, I say unto you, Except ye eat the flesh of the Son of man, and drink his blood, ye have no life in you. Whoso eateth my flesh, and drinketh my blood, hath eternal life; and I will raise him up at the last day. For my flesh is meat indeed, and my blood is drink indeed. He that eateth my flesh, and drinketh my blood, dwelleth in me, and I in him." Here, on the Romish hypothesis that this portion of the chapter refers to the sacrament of the Lord's Supper, the two separate acts of eating and drinking are specified with all the emphasis of repetition as alike indispensable to life, to a glorious resurrection at the last day, and to the reciprocal indwelling of Christ and His disciples. Nothing is said of the eating of the blood, or of the drinking of the flesh, the former being presumed to be performed by the layman, and the latter by the priest; but the eating of the flesh of the Son of man, and the drinking of His blood, as *distinct acts of physical participation*, are pronounced to be indispensable to salvation. And since, to a Church which insists upon the literal meaning of terms, the *mode* of participation must be as important as the *substance* participated, the *drinking* must be as necessary as the *eating*, and therefore salvation in the Church of Rome must be restricted to the priests. To discount from the teaching of Christ the words " eat " and " drink," as modal terms enjoining modal operations, and to treat them as if they were absolutely synonymous, is to relinquish the literal interpretation, and to sacrifice the whole structure reared upon it. A further inference from this Tridentine rendering of the language of our Lord is this : that as the eating of the flesh of the Son of man, and the drinking of His blood, infallibly secure eternal life, so there is no corruption, no infamy, no blasphemy on the part of the sacerdotal caste that can be a bar to their salvation when once they have partaken of the host and the contents of the chalice. Almost every conceivable liberty, therefore, has been taken with the literal meaning by the Church which vaunts this as the impenetrable shield of its dogma of Transubstantiation. It has invented a definition of body unsanctioned by common usage, and unknown to the apostolic age ; it has made each emblem not merely to represent but to include the other, both without warrant, and in express contravention of the marked separateness assigned to them in the words of institution ; and it has, on the same principle of concomitance, enlarged the connotation of both " the body " and " the blood," by comprising within each of them the soul and the divinity of our Lord.

5. The so-called literal interpretation involves an anachronism, inasmuch as it antedates the death of our

Lord upon the cross. Some sense of this discrepancy is apparent in the service of the Mass, where we find that the language used in the "consecration of the wine" employs the future tense: "This is the chalice of my blood of the new and eternal testament, the mystery of faith which *shall be* shed for you and for many unto the remission of sins."

These are alleged in the Romish office to be the words of our Lord, and this, too, against the evidence of all the Gospels, which say nothing of the "eternal testament," or of the "mystery of faith," terms which have been invented, and for which the authority of Christ has been unwarrantably claimed. The change of tense is equally unsupported, and imputes to our Saviour language which He certainly did not utter; and so far from alleviating the difficulties which oppress the Romish theory, seems rather to aggravate them, for if the shedding of the blood was still future, the disciples could eat and drink only by anticipation of what had not yet happened. If the blood was not yet shed they could not drink of the "shed blood;" and yet the literal interpretation of our Lord's words compels the belief that the great propitiation was made before it was made, that He was dead before He died, and that the Mass was eaten before the sacrifice was slain. While we should not rashly limit the omnipotence of God by measuring it according to the line of our limited capacities, we cannot allow contradictions to be consecrated and sheltered under the name of mysteries; and it is a contradiction to suppose that

that had already happened which was not to happen till the following day.

6. The literal interpretation is inconsistent with the plea of miracle which has been usually urged in its defence, for there is no definition of a miracle, which keeps in view the primary object of a miracle, that can cover the stupendous change which is alleged to have followed the words of consecration.

All the miracles with which we are acquainted appeal to the sense or senses of man. It is only as thus apprehended that they are known to exist at all. If they are supposed to have transpired in a sphere utterly beyond the cognizance of man, to whatever other creatures they may be manifestations of power, they cannot be so to him. God may be working miracles every day in some portion of His illimitable universe, kindling new suns, or creating new forms of life; but if they are observed by no eye but His own they are not miracles of evidence, and are not meant either to inspire faith or to support it. The miracles which our Saviour performed were such as made their appeals to the senses. This property marks every one of them. They consisted of changes, but they were changes which reported themselves to one sense at least, and some of them to more senses than one. They were wrought on purpose that they might be recognised, and (what it is of supreme moment to consider) the species or accidents were changed that they might be recognised, a fact which is absolutely reversed in the pretended miracle of Transubstantiation. If Jesus cured the blind man, he saw, and others knew that he saw. If He healed the dumb man, he spake, and others heard him speak. If He restored the paralytic, he walked, and others saw him walk. If He cleansed the leper, his flesh became clean, and others saw that it was clean. If he raised the dead, the dead did in fact rise, and others saw that he had risen. The senses were the only tribunal to which Christ appealed in attestation of His own resurrection. His disciples saw Him, and when Thomas, who was absent on our Saviour's first appearance to His disciples, doubted, and demanded both visible and palpable evidence, he was invited to test in the most sensible manner the certainty of the fact that He was indeed risen.

But what condition of a miracle does this professed change in the elements fulfil? To what sense does it appeal? When the water was turned into wine, the change was indubitably attested by one sense at least, the sense of taste. It is more than probable that it had simultaneous confirmation from the senses of smell and sight. We know that the effect it produced on the palate, and possibly on the whole frame, was such that the governor of the feast said, "Thou hast kept the good wine until now."

Here was a miracle avouched by the testimony of those who drank the wine. It was not a miracle lacking all confirmation: on the other hand, it had all the proof of which it was susceptible. If, as in the case of the wafer and the sacramental wine of the Romanist, the liquid at the marriage of Cana had retained the colour, the fragrance, the taste, the chemical and physiological properties, that is, all the accidents of water, and the guests had observed none of the accidents of wine, they would not have seen a miracle, but an imposition, to which they would have been but ill reconciled by the metaphysical figment that the substance was changed while the accidents remained. They would have said, "We know of no wine except by its accidents, its effects upon the outward senses, and the inward sensations." When our Saviour spoke of His miracles He spoke of them as works which challenged the observation of men. When He sent back to John the disciples whom John had commissioned to inquire whether Christ were He that should come, or they should look for another, He said, "Go and tell John the things that ye do see and hear." But where is the proof of the miracle of Transubstantiation? Let there be one sense at least that will certify the wonder. Which shall it be? The smell declares it is bread, the taste declares it is bread, the touch declares it is bread. There is no experiment to which the most advanced and subtle science can subject it which does not terminate in the same instantaneous verdict—it is bread. We have every part of the man competent to form a judgment on the matter pronouncing that no change has taken place; that bread it was, and bread it is; and denying that any miracle whatever has been wrought, because the evidence which miracle always brings with it is not forthcoming. If we are to discredit all our senses when they combine in one testimony and affirm the same truth, then it is far easier and wiser, assuredly, to discredit only one sense, and that the sense of sight by which we read the sentence, " This is my body."

What indeed is our authority for believing that the Church of Rome holds the doctrine of Transubstantiation? We have no sensible proof of the fact but the hearing and the sight. The smell, the taste, and the touch decline their testimony on the matter, and we have, therefore, less proof that that Church holds the doctrine, than we have that the bread and the wine are unchanged by the words of consecration.

7. The literal interpretation (so called) of our Lord's language is inconsistent with His own teaching as found in the sixth chapter of St. John. This chapter has been made to play a somewhat extraordinary part in the sacramental controversy, partly on account of the occurrence in it of language which seems to support the Romish theory, and partly because it contains other language which is fatal to that theory. Leading theologians in the Papal communion have held the most opposite views as to whether the discourse of our Lord at Capernaum had any reference to the Last Supper whatsoever, and this because on the supposition of such reference it appears to afford the completest refutation of the doctrine and practice of communion in one kind. The deposition it brings into court is somewhat unmanageable, and hence it has become necessary, since the Church of Rome resolved to avail itself of some of its evidence, to draw an

arbitrary line of demarcation between one portion of it and another. Albertinus, in his exhaustive work, "*De Eucharistia*," cites two popes, four cardinals, five bishops, and several doctors, professors, and preachers who deny that the chapter bears any direct relation to the Eucharist. The extent to which it has been pressed into service, not only by the Romanists, but by some Anglican divines, will justify and even demand a somewhat extended consideration of the whole chapter. Our Saviour had performed the miracle of the multiplication of the loaves and fishes, on the other side of the sea of Tiberias, and had then returned to Capernaum. The multitude whom he had fed, having learned that He had crossed the lake, followed Him. The predominant motive which impelled them was the carnal one of enjoying the benefits of a similar miracle. " Ye seek me, not because ye saw the miracles, but because ye did eat of the loaves and were filled." Seeing that their hearts were set on the mere material and perishable blessings of His ministry, He reminded them that there was another hunger and another thirst, which required a nourishment that should endure unto eternal life, and for this they must labour. Their curiosity being roused as to what that labour could be which should put them in possession of this ineffable aliment, He said, " This is the work of God, that ye should believe on him whom he hath sent ; " a clear intimation, which is more expressly confirmed in the subsequent part of the chapter, that the bread which is to engender and sustain eternal life is appropriated by faith. His hearers no sooner caught the word "faith," than they demanded a sign which might warrant it, and pleaded the fact that manna was given to their fathers from heaven. Upon which the Saviour replied, "Verily, I say unto you, Moses gave you not that bread from heaven; for the bread of God is he which cometh down from heaven, and giveth life unto the world."

The literal interpreters who stood around Him at once fell into the same mistake as the woman of Samaria had done with respect to the water which was to quench the thirst for ever, and supposing that our Saviour referred to bread which could be manducated in the ordinary manner, they said, "Evermore give us this bread." They thought the bread was literal bread, the eating, literal eating, and the eternal life a physical life exempted from all decay. But this misapprehension was promptly met by our Lord, who said, "I am the bread of life; he that cometh unto me shall never hunger, and he that believeth on me shall never thirst." Here He employed terms which are confessedly synonymous in Scripture. Eating, drinking, coming, believing, are interchangeable. The mention of the fact that He was the bread of life that came down from heaven started another perplexity in their minds, for as yet they had no conception of His divinity, and knew him only as a man. But the perplexity only led Him to asseverate his previous statement with increased emphasis. "Verily, verily, I say unto you, He that believeth on me hath everlasting life. I am that bread of life. Your fathers did eat manna in the wilderness, and are dead.

This is the bread which cometh down from heaven. If any man eat of this bread he shall live for ever: and the bread which I shall give is my flesh, which I will give for the life of the world."

The mention of flesh again revolted the natural interpreters, who supposed Him to mean that they could live only as they ate of His natural body, and drank of His natural blood; and Christ, seeing their recoil, promptly reminded them that their literal interpretation was fallacious; "that the flesh profiteth nothing;" and that "the words he spake unto them, they were spirit and life." Now this interpretation, in which the profitableness of the flesh is so absolutely denied, conflicts so violently with the Romish interpretation, which insists upon the indispensableness of the presence of the flesh, and bones, and sinews, and nerves, that we cannot hesitate to denounce this latter exposition as an arbitrary travesty of the words of our Lord. The flesh cannot both be necessary and unprofitable; and let it be observed that our Lord affirms both that except we eat His flesh we have no life in us, and that the flesh profiteth nothing—statements which defy all reconciliation, except upon the principle that "by his flesh which giveth life," He means the blessed truths embodied in the gospel, which He came not merely to announce but to be, and the Spirit by which these truths are applied to the soul. And whatever carnal interpretation the Capernaites put upon His language, it is clear that Peter comprehended it in its spiritual import; for when, in allusion to the angry retirement of some of the disciples, the Saviour said, "Will ye also go away?" Peter immediately answered, "Lord, to whom shall we go? thou hast the words of eternal life;" evidently adopting the sentiment that Christ had just uttered, "The words I speak unto you, they are spirit and life."

Thus a consideration of the whole chapter seems to us to establish the following conclusions.

(a) That it is marked by its perfect unity of subject, and that the division which has been made by Romanists and certain Anglicans, for the purpose of extracting from it support for sacramentarian ideas, is wholly gratuitous and arbitrary. Even Cardinal Wiseman himself wavers as to the exact position where the line of demarcation shall be drawn. He speaks of the "signification of His discourse as far as the forty-eighth or fifty-first verse," thus acknowledging the uncertainty of his critical faculty, and enjoying the option of fixing the one boundary or the other, as the exigencies of the controversy may require. But where is the transition? Is there any sign of it in the forty-eighth verse, "I am the bread of life"? This is the identical theme which has been treated from the twenty-seventh verse, and only repeats what had been already affirmed in the thirty-fifth verse, "I am the bread of life." Is there any sign of it in the forty-ninth verse, "Your fathers did eat manna in the wilderness, and are dead"? Substantially the same truth had been affirmed in the thirty-first verse by some of the disciples, "Our fathers did eat manna in the wilderness," and hence our Saviour continues the same theme. But is there any sign of transition in the fiftieth verse, "This is the bread which cometh down from heaven, that a man may eat thereof and not die"? But had He not already in the thirty-second verse said, "My Father giveth you the true bread from heaven;" and what sign is there here of the line of separation which his Eminence drew with such a hesitating finger? He seems to attach great importance to the fact that in the earlier part of the discourse Christ did not "suffer the idea of *eating Him* to escape His lips;" but surely this is nothing better than solemn trifling, for as He spoke of Himself under the emblem of bread, the correlative operation of eating is necessitated by the laws of thought and language, for how can bread nourish except by being eaten? Moreover, it is in the former portion of the chapter that He contrasts Himself as the true bread with the manna which the fathers *ate;* and that there might be no misapprehension, in the fifty-eighth verse, and therefore in that portion of the chapter which the Cardinal isolated from the rest for the purpose of supporting his sacramental theory, our Lord says, "This is that bread which came down from heaven: not as your fathers did eat manna, in the wilderness, and are dead: he that eateth of this bread shall live for ever." The figure, therefore, of bread with which our Saviour began His discourse He resumes at the end, and the theory which requires the bisection of the chapter into two unequal parts is an expedient which rudely breaks the unity of treatment, and yields, as we have seen, no real strength to the Romish cause.

(*b*) We see further that the literal interpretation of our Lord's words—" Except ye eat the flesh of the Son of man, *and* drink his blood, ye have no life in you"—condemns by anticipation the practice of communion in one kind, for the flesh requires to be eaten, and the blood to be drunk. If the letter, therefore, is to rule, the Church of Rome is now condemning the whole body of the laity to destruction, for they are not drinking the blood in any sense which can satisfy the literal meaning of the word " drink."

(*c*) It follows from the literal interpretation of our Saviour's words—" Whosoever eateth my flesh, and drinketh my blood, hath eternal life "—that the participation of the Mass under both species absolutely insures the salvation of all such communicants, and that no wickedness can avail in any degree to endanger it. The Church of Rome insists that it is physical manducation which is here invested with saving power; and, therefore, to import any elements into the conditions which are here specified, such as faith, contrition, holiness of life, is to expand the literal meaning so far as to destroy it. The ideas suggested by flesh and blood are definite, and so are the ideas of eating and drinking. No spiritual qualification whatever is suggested, and for the literalist to insist on such a qualification, is to disallow the precision and completeness of the letter. If, after consecration, the wafer and the wine are absolutely, and not relatively;

really, and not figuratively; objectively, and not subjectively, the body and the blood of Christ, then they are verily, and indeed, eaten and drunk by the vilest priest that ever disgraced humanity: but if any spiritual or moral condition whatever is requisite, in order that to him the consecrated elements may become the flesh and the blood of our Lord, then the consecration has effected only a precarious and relative transformation of the elements, the faith of the recipient being indispensable to turn the bread and the wine into the flesh and blood of Christ. This, however, is a dogma which the Church of Rome condemns. Hence, while the letter destroys the laity, however good, because they do not drink "the blood," it saves the priests, however bad, because they both eat the flesh and drink the blood.

(*d*) But the arbitrary division into two parts of this chapter, together with the literal interpretation of that portion which has been pressed, though illicitly, into the service of the Romish Church, seems to draw after it a consequence much more grave, if possible, than any which has been mentioned. It, in fact, reduces to absolute nullity all the teaching of our Lord prior to the fifty-first verse. For if He is treating of things altogether distinct from each other, and He means in the latter portion of the chapter to teach that eternal life depends on the eating of His flesh and the drinking of His blood in the Eucharist, and that this eating and drinking are not emblematic statements of the same truth which He has inculcated in the earlier portion of the chapter, then we have eternal life promised without the sacrament in the first instance, and the next moment declared to be inseparable from it. For in the forty-seventh verse, a verse which Cardinal Wiseman allows has no reference to the sacrament, our Saviour says, "He that believeth on me hath everlasting life." The life, therefore, is independent of the sacrament, or if not, then the teaching of our Lord is convicted of contradiction. This is a conclusion which, while inevitable on the literalistic principle of exposition, is so irreverent, that no opinion of cardinal, canon of council, or decree of pope can give it authority; and it is a conclusion which results from the forced interpretation of a chapter which throughout teaches, now in emblem and now without it, the same glorious truth, that Christ in His person, life, work, death, and resurrection, is the one fountain of everlasting blessedness.

To develop in detail all the absurdities which are involved in the dogma of Transubstantiation would require a separate and lengthy treatise. The following are samples of a hundred more which spontaneously suggest themselves. We are required to believe that there can be accidents which are the accidents of nothing—that there can be substance without accidents—that there can be accidents which are exactly the same, and yet which are accidents of substances wholly different.

Aristotle affirms that an accident cannot exist except in its substance. Ammonius, Alexander,

Themistius, Philoponus, and Averroes, all affirm the same. Boethius, the great Latin commentator of Aristotle, defends the doctrine of his master; and Athanasius, Gregory of Nazianzum, Gregory of Nyssa, Epiphanius, Basil, Augustine, Cyril of Alexandria, consent with one voice to the same doctrine, that "accidents must inhere in substances." We are required to believe that that which seemed one loaf of bread when held in the hands of our Saviour was His own one and only body, that it became when broken in each of its separate parts the same one and only body, so that each disciple partook of the whole, and that all partook of the same. We are required to believe that the part is equal to the whole. We are required to believe that the body of the Saviour which is in heaven has not the properties of bread, and that the body of Christ which lies on the altar has the properties of bread, and that these two bodies with different properties are one and the same. We are required to believe that this body has no definite dimensions, inasmuch as it is in every wafer, and also in each of its separated particles, and that it has definite dimensions, and sitteth at the right hand of God, where it is the shrine and manifestation of the incarnate Deity, whom saints and angels adore with ceaseless praise. We are required to believe that every communicant of the Church of Rome has eaten the body of Christ whole and entire at every sacrament of the Eucharist, and that if he has consumed a hundred hosts he has but partaken of one whole Christ in all, and yet has partaken of one at each separate communion, and we are required to believe that one substance is converted into another substance which coexisted with it, and yet was distinct from it. These, and a thousand other contradictions we are required to believe, if we would accept the doctrine of Transubstantiation. There is no one error, (to use no harsher name) which has given birth to a more revolting brood of absurdities by which reason and Scripture alike have been outraged and dishonoured, but which will, we are confident, at some day, be it distant or be it near, contribute to the overthrow of that system of spiritual and ecclesiastical despotism which for so many centuries has overshadowed and blighted some of the fairest countries in the world.

LECTURE V.

*THE PRIEST AT THE ALTAR (CONTINUED): THE
LORD'S SUPPER—CONSECRATION AND THE
REAL PRESENCE.*

LECTURE V.

THE PRIEST AT THE ALTAR (CONTINUED): THE LORD'S SUPPER—CONSECRATION AND THE REAL PRESENCE.

IT will be impossible rightly to understand the ground on which sacerdotalism invests with such a mysterious and awful sanctity the sacrament of the Lord's Supper, except as we realise the meaning of what is technically denominated *consecration*, a term which has no warrant or equivalent in the New Testament in the sense attached to it by the Romanists and Ritualists. When it first makes its appearance with a definite ceremonial signification, it intimates that the priestly leaven is already beginning to work in the Church of Christ, transforming an ordinance of commemoration and fellowship into a dreadful mystery. By degrees, the table is converted into an altar, and the consecrated bread and wine become nothing less than the stupendous oblation of the body and blood of our Lord offered by a sacrificing priest.[1] Into this ceremony of consecration, for which such thaumaturgic influence is claimed, it is my purpose now to inquire. The late Archdeacon Wilberforce, whose Anglicanism at length

[1] See Appendix D.

developed into full-blown Romanism, heads his first chapter in his work on "The Doctrine of the Holy Eucharist," "*Consecration, the essential characteristic of the Holy Eucharist*," and his first sentence thus sounds a key-note, with which, however, the subsequent course of his reasoning is in striking dissonance. "An inquiry into the nature of the Holy Eucharist must be founded upon Scripture, and upon that passage of Scripture by which this solemn rite was authorised as well as explained." What then is the nature of that transcendent consecration which transmutes the common into the sacred, and which renders the perishable creatures of bread and wine at once the tabernacle and vehicle of the incarnate Son of God? Upon what act or words of the priest does this change depend? There should be no obscurity nor ambiguity as to the precise conditions which determine the accomplishment of a miracle the most astounding and the most multiform that was ever performed; a miracle including in the same indivisible act and moment an annihilation, a creation, and a substitution, which avouch themselves to no sense of man, and which every test of every sense separately and in combination absolutely discredits. Whether such a miracle, the only one, if admitted, in the Divine Word which is susceptible of no verification either by sense or consciousness, can be proposed as an object of faith, the reader may judge by what has already been advanced. We have now to do with the act of consecration, which is alleged to be the essential characteristic of the Holy

Eucharist. After quoting the words of institution, Mr. Wilberforce says, "The emphatic words of this declaration consist in each case of three parts. 'This is my body,' 'This is my blood.' We have here, to speak logically, a subject, a predicate, and a copula. There is something spoken of, 'this,' which was taken by our Lord—there is the affirmation itself, ' It *is* my body'—there is '*my body*,' '*my blood*,' which in each case is the predicate, or thing affirmed concerning the subject. . . . . To begin with the first—the *subject*—our Lord's words respecting it involve this main truth, that Consecration is the essential characteristic of the Holy Eucharist; for our Lord does not speak of bread at large, or wine in general, but of *this, i.e.*, of that which was consecrated or set apart. No doubt His words had a further application; their ultimate reference was to the 'inward part or thing signified,' which was the real object under consideration, but they had also an *indirect* relation to the 'outward and visible sign.' Now, viewing the thing in reference to this last, it was the bread which He had blessed, over which He had given thanks, and which He had broken, and the cup over which He had given thanks, which were the subject-matter of the declaration. The consecration, therefore, by which these elements were separated from all co-ordinate specimens of the same material, is that circumstance which gives them the peculiar character which His words express."[1]

We have now, therefore, to inquire in what that act

[1] "The Doctrine of the Holy Eucharist," p. 7. (Third edition.)

of consecration consists, and this inquiry must, as Mr. Wilberforce alleges, be "founded upon Scripture, and upon that passage of Scripture by which this solemn rite was authorised as well as explained." In the outset it must be noted that no consecration is mentioned by the Evangelists, except such as is conveyed by the words εὐλογήσας or εὐχαριστήσας. Any other consecration than what is embodied in these words is an assumption "not founded on Scripture." We have therefore to consider what is the import of these words. When our Saviour took bread and blessed, He performed an act which was common among the Jews, and which was observed in that very meal of the Passover upon which the Lord's Supper was engrafted, and from which it derives the most striking elucidation. The father of the household took the bread and blessed, and also the wine and blessed, and the words in which the latter benediction was offered show that not the earthly substance, but the heavenly Giver, was the object of it. "Blessed art thou, O Lord our God, King of the universe, who hast created the fruit of the vine. Blessed art thou, O Lord our God, who hast chosen us above all nations, and exalted us above all peoples, and hast sanctified us with Thy commandments. Thou hast given us, O Lord our God, appointed seasons for joy, festivals and holy days for rejoicing, such as the feast of unleavened bread, the time of our liberation, for holy convocation, to commemorate our exodus from Egypt. Blessed art thou, O Lord, who hast sanctified Israel and the festivals. Blessed art thou, O Lord our God,

King of the universe, who hast preserved us, and kept us, and hast safely brought us to this time." This was the blessing uttered by the master of the feast, and it is clear that its object was God alone. In other words it was, in the strictest sense of the term εὐχαριστια, a thanksgiving to the Source of all good. That the blessing of the Saviour was more than this, save as the bread and wine were associated with the ideas of the New Dispensation, we have no proof whatever beyond that which may be found in the practices and language of post-apostolic times, a species of evidence which is inadmissible when we are considering the scriptural account of the institution of the Lord's Supper.

Further, we remark that the words εὐλογήσας and εὐχαριστήσας are used indifferently and interchangeably. Mark says that with the bread in His hands our Lord εὐλογήσας, Luke says εὐχαριστήσας, and Paul also employs the latter expression. Now, if the act of our Lord in relation to the elements which He held successively in His hands is adequately represented, as it must be by the word εὐχαριστήσας, it is manifest that the blessing was wholly a thanksgiving to God; for in no scriptural writer whatever does εὐχαριστέω denote a blessing directed on a material object. It expresses thanksgiving, and that exclusively. Its object is a person, and not a thing. It may be man or God, but an insensate creature it cannot be. Too much emphasis cannot be laid on this fact, for it explodes the sacramentarian and sacerdotal idea of consecrating the bread and wine. Two words are employed, not, let it be remembered, as exact equivalents in all cases, but as expressing the same act on this occasion. One word (εὐλογήσας) has the wider meaning, the other word (εὐχαριστήσας) has the narrower import, and *never any other*. It can never signify more than "giving thanks," and therefore nothing more than "giving thanks" was done by our Lord when He took the bread and the wine. It is a just principle of interpretation of language in general, and not less so of the language of our Lord in connection with the Last Supper, that where two words are employed interchangeably, one of them with a wider and another with a narrower meaning, the narrower one must be considered as defining the act to which both refer. If, for example, it were said that our Saviour entered Jerusalem, and also that He rode into Jerusalem, the riding must define the mode of His entrance, for modes of entrance are manifold, but riding excludes all but one. And so, while the participle εὐλογήσας leaves it uncertain for the moment which of several meanings, possible to it in general, it actually does possess in the particular case before us, that meaning is strictly and conclusively defined when another word takes its place which has no signification but one. The word εὐχαριστήσας never means, nor can mean, anything but "having given thanks;" and hence εὐλογήσας when employed as its substitute can have no other import. To assign to either of them a special, and hitherto unknown sacramental signification, of which no notification is given, is to adopt an arbitrary procedure, which not only assumes the very point to be proved, but renders language a mere instrument of caprice.[1]

The same two words appear elsewhere in the Gospels, and perform precisely the same interchangeable function. In the narrative of the feeding of the multitude, as given by St. Mark (viii. 6, 7), we encounter them both in such close connection, and with such marked identity of signification, as to debar the assumption that εὐλογήσας could possess a mystic meaning beyond that which is expressed in the phrase "having given thanks." With respect to the loaves, we are told that "having taken the seven loaves and given thanks" (εὐχαριστήσας), "he brake them." With regard to the fishes, we are told that "having blessed" (εὐλογήσας), "he commanded to set them also before them." It would be an unscholarly refinement which should either, on the one hand, seek to establish a distinction here between the act denoted by εὐχαριστήσας and that denoted by εὐλογήσας, or which should on the other impart to εὐχαριστήσας a meaning which it never possesses; while we must further maintain

---

[1] This reasoning is not affected by the expression of St. Paul (1 Cor. x. 16), "The cup of blessing which we bless, is it not the communion of the blood of Christ?" for it was a common form of speech among the Jews that meat and wine were blessed when thanksgiving had been offered to God on their account; and Ambrose says, "The apostle calls it the cup of blessing, because when we have it in our hands we praise Him with admiration of the inestimable gift, blessing Him that He shed His blood for us" (Ep. i. ad Corin. Hom. 27). Of any objective change produced on the cup the apostle says not a word, but implicitly forbids any such supposition, by the fact that he immediately designates the bread over which thanks had been offered, "the bread which we break."

that if these words, as used in the Lord's Supper, are supposed to confer any special consecration on the elements, and to imbue them with certain powers which they did not previously possess, they must be regarded as having conferred the same consecration and the same powers in the miracle of the loaves and fishes, a conclusion which, we apprehend, no sacramentarian would be prepared to accept.

Nor can we concede the distinction which it has been attempted to set up, that εὐλογεῖν denotes the blessing in its material influence on the bread and wine, and εὐχαριστεῖν denotes the blessing in its heavenward aspect as directed towards God. The assumption which has been made in order to secure the consecration theory, that our Saviour both blessed with the εὐλογεῖν and the εὐχαριστεῖν, is oppressed with difficulties which no critical dexterity can escape. For it is not said, either in regard to the bread or the wine, that He εὐχαριστήσας καὶ εὐλογήσας, or we should have been compelled to admit the possibility of a distinction, whether we might be able sharply to define it or not. In no passage are the words used together as *complementary* of each other, as two constituent factors of one whole; and we are therefore driven to the conclusion that if εὐχαριστήσας does adequately express all that our Saviour did, it was a thanksgiving, and could be nothing more. And this inference derives further corroboration from the fact that the prayers in use among the Jews show that the form in which bread was blessed, whether in their ordinary or sacred meals, was wholly one of thanksgiving and praise to God.

Though my sole reliance as to the meaning of the act of benediction (εὐλογία) or thanksgiving (εὐχαριστία) is based on the words of Scripture to which Mr. Wilberforce made his appeal, it is noteworthy that the account given by Justin Martyr of the Lord's Supper affords striking confirmation of this interpretation. "There is then brought to the president of the brethren (τῷ προεστῶτι τῶν ἀδελφῶν) bread and a cup of wine mingled with water; and he, taking them, gives praise and glory to the Father of the universe, through the name of the Son and the Holy Ghost, and offers thanks at considerable length for our being counted worthy to receive these things at His hands. And when he has concluded his prayers and thanksgiving, all the people present express their assent by saying *Amen*. This word answers in the Hebrew language to γένοιτο. And when the president has given thanks, and all the people have expressed their consent, those who are called by us deacons give to each of those present to partake of the bread and wine mixed with water, over which the thanksgiving was pronounced. And this food is called amongst us εὐχαριστία" (1st Apology, 65, 66).

The only consecration, therefore, of which we read in the New Testament, is that of "giving thanks," followed by the designation of the elements of bread and wine as the emblems of His body and His blood. In what precise words this eucharistic consecration was effected we know not, as neither the Church of Rome nor that of the East has embodied them in its other traditions or fabrications. The prayer of our Lord on the occasion is unrecorded, and for centuries after the death of the apostles no other prayer was composed and enforced on the various religious communities. St. Gregory, though without any authority, says that it "was the custom of the apostles to consecrate the host by offering the Lord's prayer alone;" and Basil demands, "Which of the saints left us in writing the words of invocation in the oblation of the bread and wine of the Eucharist?" while, as we have just seen, Justin Martyr informs us that the president "offered thanks at considerable length," without giving us any word of the prayer itself, and clearly intimates that it was the thanksgiving, and that alone, which determined the designation of the Supper as the "Eucharist." This was the only consecration known in the apostolic Churches, and for a considerable period afterwards. By degrees, however, a mystic meaning began to be attached to the declarative words, "This is my body," and "This is my blood of the new covenant," until at length, and notably after the time of Cardinal Cajetan, and in consequence, probably, of his powerful influence, the chief, or indeed the whole of the consecrating virtue was alleged to inhere in the utterance of these words. This opinion met with strong resistance from learned doctors of the Church, who maintained that the words in question were not operative, but declarative, and that the consecration was restricted to the prayer of our Lord. The opinion, however, of Cajetan grew in favour, until at length the whole question received its final settlement at the Council of Trent, which invested the declarative words with the sole consecrating power, a decision which is in open violation of the language of institution.

But this decision opened the way for more questions than it had settled, and even to this day the Church of Rome has given no authoritative ruling as to the precise import of the several terms of the expression, "This is my body." Learnedly (if, indeed, so reputable a word may be applied to such disputations) have the writers of that Church, both before and since the Council of Trent, discussed concerning the subject *hoc* (this), the copula *est* (is), the predicate *corpus* (body), and even concerning the meaning of the whole expression. Their divergences of opinion have been caustically likened by Albertinus to the foxes which Samson bound, which, though united at their tails, were wide apart in their bodies, and widest of all at their heads. And further he says, "Not only do they disagree, but bitterly quarrel, their opinions reciprocally destroying each other, after the fashion of the confusion of Babel." Vasquez, one of the most learned writers of that Church, says that with respect to the pronoun *hoc* there is such a diversity of opinions, that it would be irksome even to mention them in detail. Christopher de Capite Fontium says: "I would that the scholastic doctors who fight so much concerning the pronoun *hoc* would conform their opinions to the words of a council, and thus put a happy termination to their labours and strifes." And Catharinus says: "Let the reader consider the labour and pains, I had almost said even to the death itself, of nearly all writers, when being asked what signifieth that pronoun *hoc*, they write such heaps of contradictory things as to drive mad any man who considers them too minutely. The blessed Thomas Aquinas recounts all their answers, and blames them all. He then gives one which Scotus and Petrus Aureolus censure, and then each of them in turn gives his own; and Scotus, indeed, pours out so many words, and draws so many conclusions, that I should greatly wonder at the patience of any man who could read him; and, after all, he so trembles in giving his own opinion, that he shows himself by no means sure of it."

Albertinus then classifies the chief interpretations of the meaning of *hoc*, omitting many which are too shadowy to be distinctly grasped. It means in the first place *nothing*, and this is the opinion of Pope Innocent III., of Durandus, of Catharinus, and several others. The second opinion makes *hoc* denote something, but this something is not substance, but only the accidents of the bread. The third makes *hoc* denote the bread, but with a threefold variation, for it may mean the bread both in its substance and accidents together, as was held by Bonaventura and others; or it may mean the bread in its substance, not as it is in itself, but as it is converted into the body of Christ; or it may mean the substance of the bread, not so far forth as it is bread, but as it is substance *in general*, so that our Lord meant, " This substance is my body." The fourth opinion which was espoused by Scotus represents *hoc* as signifying the individual existence which at length becomes the body of Christ. The fifth makes *hoc* mean that which is contained under the accidents of bread, whatever that may be, for it was left undeterminate and vague. And the last opinion is that which maintains that *hoc* denotes not only the bread, but the bread and the body of Christ lying hidden in the bread.

And the subtlety of the Romish theologians was by no means exhausted in their refinements upon the signification of the pronoun. The copula *est* (is) was another bone of contention, about which they wrangled with the same interminable but fruitless ingenuity and fierceness. In the first place, there were those who taught that it means "becomes," " passes into," "is changed into," " is transubstantiated into." In the second place there were those who with Occam took *est* as meaning *erit* (will be). In the third place some held that it meant *contains*; and, in the fourth place, others took *est* as denoting the simple substantive verb *is*, and as thus expressing the exact identity between the subject and the predicate.

And the predicate was not less an attractive battle-ground than the subject and copula. By some, *corpus* (body) was regarded as denoting the *materia prima* of which the humanity of Christ consists, and not something compounded of matter and accidents; by others, as denoting something compounded of matter and form. Others, as Cardinal Cajetan, held that it denoted "body" according to the common notion of "body" as such, but not according to the particular notion of a living man; others, that it signified something composed of matter and a certain form which they call *corporeity*, and which they say was prior to the rational soul in man; and others (though even still the list of variations is not exhausted), that it comprises the bones, flesh, nerves, and cartilages, and may be used indifferently, when speaking of a living or of a dead body.

These are samples of a brood of extravagant and revolting fantasies, all of which have been born out of a fundamental error, viz., that of supposing that our Saviour could mean, in the words of institution, to outrage every sense of man, when He employed in the inauguration of the Supper, language, which when interpreted as figurative, finds its analogies not only, as we have seen, in other expressions of our Lord, but in every nation and kindred and people and tongue. For we hold that in no language which is entitled to the name is any form of expression more natural, common, graphic, and inevitable, than that which employs the verb "to be" for the verb "to signify," or "to represent." This usage begins with childhood, is heard in their games every day, and could not be dispensed with in life or literature without a grievous and irreparable loss of one of the most striking, vivid, and picturesque figures of speech.

We shall now proceed to consider yet further the

real nature of the institution of the Lord's Supper, so far as that nature can be determined by an appeal to the words which our Saviour Himself employed on that night when He was betrayed. By these words the essential object and purpose of the ordinance must be determined. What the meal was on the evening of its appointment, it must have been designed to continue in the Church, until the commemoration of the death of Christ should be superseded by the vision of His face and the celebration of the marriage supper of the Lamb. It cannot be supposed that in the inauguration of this institution our Saviour would omit its prominent and characteristic purpose, or leave it to be obscurely inferred and doubtfully supplied in the future development of the Church. That which is not found as an essential feature of the original Supper should not have place as an essential feature in any of its pretended imitations; while it is equally clear that no adventitious practice introduced by the Church under the plea of order, or any other plea, should be allowed to overshadow the main, if not indeed the only design of our Lord. It is almost impossible to elaborate that which is simple without obscuring it. The human accretions smother that which they were designed to embellish, and divide with it, or rob it wholly of, the reverence which is due to it alone.

The extent to which this mischief has been committed in connection with the Lord's Supper has been partially illustrated already, and will receive fuller elucidation in the course of the present lecture. The

Supper has become an elaborate ritual—the elaborate ritual a drama, enacting, with the accompaniments of incense, vestments, and genuflexions, the sacrifice of the Son of God. Hence the spectacle of a high celebration, as seen in the Romish Church, and as imitated with hardy courage in an increasing number of Anglican churches, suggests in the feeblest manner that it is intended to represent the Lord's Supper; and this very name, by which among others it was anciently known, has sunk into comparative disuse, because of its felt disconformity with the scenic pomp and magnificence and sacrificial symbolism by which its simple meaning has been both obscured and perverted. The very last suggestion which the service of the Mass would awaken in any mind, familiar only with the Evangelic narratives, would be that it is the Lord's Supper, and hence its most common designations are the Holy Eucharist, the Holy Sacrament, and the Holy Sacrifice of the Mass.

Now, in any serious endeavour to understand the original purport of the Lord's Supper, it is necessary to disabuse the mind of the influence of misleading names, especially when they have come to embody conceptions wholly foreign to the primitive institution which they professedly denote. Names ensnare the mind even unconsciously, and hence the suffrage of the convictions or feelings is illicitly bespoken and forestalled by sundry ecclesiastical terms which are themselves objectionable. It is not contended that our terminology is always to be restricted to that which is employed in the Word of God; but it is contended that when it varies it shall be sacredly controlled by the Divine idea, and that it shall not suffer any unwarrantable enlargement or diminution. A neglect of this salutary precaution has been one of the most disastrous banes to theological science, to the peace of the Church, and to the practical influence of the gospel among men. The relation of thought to language—a relation so close and almost indissoluble as to have suggested to one school of philosophers the doctrine that language is a necessity to thought— enforces the importance of watching the introduction of words into any region of human speculation, and chiefly into that which concerns the religious interests of mankind. Hence we have not now to inquire what is the nature of the Holy Eucharist, or the Holy Sacrament, or the Holy Sacrifice of the Mass, all of which terms come to us weighted with the traditional practices and associations of centuries; but what was the nature of that meal which was designated by an apostle the Lord's Supper, and which received its first, authoritative, and sufficient exposition from the lips of our Lord Himself? What it was then it was to be in all subsequent ages of the Church; and if in any community it be now essentially more or less, it may wear impressive names, and be celebrated with overpowering pomp by the priest and with abject and trembling awe by the people, but it is not the Lord's Supper.

The proposition, then, which seems to embody all the

essential elements of the ordinance in question, and which it will be now my endeavour to illustrate and defend, is "*that the Lord's Supper is a simple meal, appointed by our Lord Himself, and enjoined upon His disciples as a monumental assurance and seal, on His part, of His infinite love, as shown in His sacrificial death; and as a commemoration, on their part, of that same death through the participation of the emblems of bread and wine.*"

This definition may by some be regarded as too wide, and by others as too narrow. It may be deemed sufficient to condemn it that it seems little more than a restatement of the doctrine of Zwinglius, the great Helvetian reformer. I am, however, less concerned to know that it can be branded by a certain name than to believe that it comprehends and expresses all that can be fairly considered as essential in the words of institution. It does not presume to deny the existence of other and most important truths, which are inevitably suggested by such a meal, such as the unity of the Church, the necessity of mutual love, the obligations of a holy life; but it regards these not so much as essentially involved in the definition of the Lord's Supper, but as natural inferences from its great central truth.

It has been already hinted in the preceding lecture that the Lord's Supper, while a new institution, was in its forms grafted upon the Paschal meal, and was not an abrupt and violent innovation. In this respect, as in so many others, the Old Dispensation faded away in the dawning light of the New. The transition was less one of sudden shock than of gentle inosculation, as may be seen in the practice observed by the apostles, even after the ascension of our Lord, of worshipping in the temple. With them the foliage of Judaism fell because thrust forth by the verdure of an economy which was pre-eminently one of spirit and life.

No intelligent view can be formed of the Lord's Supper if it be forgotten that it arose out of another feast, and employed, in fact, the materials which had been provided for that feast, and that both the one and the other were feasts of commemoration. It would be strange indeed, this being the case, if the older ordinance reflected no light on the new. I must venture to assume that the feast, at the close of which the Lord's Supper was instituted, was that of the Passover, omitting all discussion of the alleged discrepancy between the Synoptists and St. John as to whether the Saviour and His disciples partook of the Passover at the usual time. The question is one embarrassed with difficulties, but while, after due consideration, convinced that the discordance is more in semblance than reality, it must be enough for my present purpose to proceed on the supposition that "Jesus ate the Passover with His disciples." And what was that Passover? It was a feast of commemoration, not originated by the Jews, but commanded by God, and designed to be in after ages to them and their children a witness of that glorious historic deliverance which God had accomplished on their behalf. But it was wholly an emblematical feast, and was never assumed to be any other.

The materials employed, whether such as were originally prescribed—the lamb, the bitter herbs, and unleavened bread—or such as were afterwards adopted without express Divine authority, were symbolic, and nothing more. There was no rehearsal or dramatic representation of the actual Passover itself. The feast was called by the name of the act of deliverance, but it was neither the act itself nor even the historic exhibition of it. Nor was the lamb the sacrificial lamb whose blood warded off the death that sent mourning into the homes of the Egyptians.

It is of the highest moment to bear these facts in mind, as they cast a very significant light upon the incidents of the Lord's Supper, a feast designed to commemorate a still more glorious deliverance. On the same night on which the angel of death slew the firstborn of the Egyptians and saved the firstborn of the Israelites, the feast of the Passover was eaten; and on the same night in which Jesus was betrayed and condemned to death, the feast of the Lord's Supper was eaten; and as God said to the Israelites, "And ye shall eat it in haste, it is the Lord's passover," though it was not the literal passover, but its sign or symbol, so Christ said, "This is my body broken for you," though it was not His body, which was not yet broken, but was a sign or symbol of it. For my own part, I find it impossible to treat these circumstances as insignificant coincidences. They wear the appearance of designed correspondence and coadaptation. And the phrase, "It is the Lord's passover," is no more figurative than the phrase, "This is my body," and requires or disclaims equally with the latter the interpretation which supposes an actual transubstantiation. The expression, "It is the Lord's Passover," is as definite and as emphatic as the expression, "This is my body;" and the imagination is as competent to realise the Paschal feast as being transformed into the "passing over of the angel of God," as to realise that a morsel of bread is changed into the body and blood, soul and divinity, of our Lord Jesus Christ. As competent, I have said, and I may add as incompetent; for with regard to the dogma of Transubstantiation, the Church of Rome has withdrawn it alike from the realm of reason and imagination, and relegated it to that of mystery, to the sacred shelter of whose impenetrable darkness it is no more entitled than the Paschal feast which was transubstantiated, with equal certainty, into the veritable Passover itself by the words of the Lord, "It is the Lord's passover." For can any reasonable man pretend to affirm that there is such a momentous difference between the personal pronoun "it" and the demonstrative "this," that had it been recorded that our Saviour said, "*It* is my body," the evidence for transubstantiation would have been undermined? Both pronouns would have denoted with equal precision that which He held in His hand, and hence the true key of the language, "This is my body," is to be found in the expression, "It is the Lord's Passover;" both being equally literal and equally figurative, the latter, however, being regarded as figurative only, by every branch of the Christian Church. To seek for an explanation of the form and meaning of our Saviour's words beyond the limits of that ancient feast of commemoration which He had just been administering, is to renounce the near and obvious for the distant and obscure, and to create difficulties alike for reason and for faith where no difficulties exist.

I have defined the Lord's Supper as a "*feast of commemoration*," and so far forth the definition is in harmony with that of every Church, Greek, Roman, Protestant, Evangelical, and Socinian. On this one point there is no dissentient voice, nor could it well exist so long as any respect was paid to the words of our Lord, "Do this in remembrance of me." But concerning the elements of that commemoration, the conceptions which it includes, the emotions which it presupposes, the faith which it pledges, there is the widest divergence; for the commemoration cannot be the same to those who differ either as to the nature of the death of Christ, or as to the sense in which the words body and blood are to be accepted. And, as will be seen, the commemoration has been so interpreted in some theories of the Supper, as to be lost in the actual repetition of the sacrifice of which it was designed to be a sacred and impressive memorial.

It would have been thought impossible that any mysterious, and especially any sacrificial meaning, could have been discovered in the very first words of the command, "Do this in remembrance of me;"

but the late Bishop Hamilton, in a charge to the clergy of the diocese of Salisbury, finds in every word of the sentence a striking support of the sacrificial character of the Eucharist. "The original words," he says, "of which 'do this' is the translation, mean, in Alexandrian Greek, 'sacrifice this;' and the other word, ἀνάμνησις, is also a sacrificial word, and signifies the offering of a μνημόσυνον."[1]

If such were the case, it would be surprising that an argument so conclusive was never, so far as I know, advanced even by those to whom the Greek, and even the Alexandrian Greek, was their native tongue, and who must have been aware of the technical meaning of the verb ποιεῖν. This consideration in itself would impair the credit of the bishop's assumption; but I hazard the opinion that the worthy prelate could not find a single passage in which τοῦτο ποιεῖτε ever signified "sacrifice this," except when the idea of sacrifice is already distinctly mentioned in terms which define the nature of the transaction; and in such cases τοῦτο ποιεῖτε may denote anything or everything which has been thus defined. For example: when the young man answered our Lord's question—"What is written in the law, how readest thou?"—"Thou shalt love the Lord thy God with all thy heart, and with all thy soul, and with all thy strength, and with all thy mind, and thy neighbour as thyself," the Saviour said, "τοῦτο ποιεῖ (this do), and thou shalt live." But what would be thought of

[1] "Charge of the Lord Bishop of Salisbury," 1867, p. 37.

a principle of interpretation which should affirm that sometimes τοῦτο ποιεῖτε means in Alexandrian or Hellenistic Greek "fulfil the commandments"? A lexicon which should range under the verb ποιεῖν, "To love God and man perfectly," would be deemed a curiosity, and in order to complete a list of meanings thus capriciously invented, would require to exhaust all the possible forms of human activity.[1] This ποιεῖν, which has been so whimsically endowed with the function of performing sacrifice, occurs in the New Testament alone upwards of five hundred times, and never sacrifices in any one of them. It "brings forth," it "tarries," it "gains," it "traffics," it "puts forth" branches, it "calls together" a council, it "commits murder," but always with the help of another word, on which condition it will render any service imaginable. In the Old Testament it occurs nearly two thousand five hundred times, and though its shades of meaning differ, there is but one instance out of the whole, in which Trommius, whose examination of the word has been exhaustive, finds a sacrificial signification, and even there the usual rendering of the verb would fully satisfy the case. The bishop supposes that he has found, out of nearly two thousand five hundred instances in which the verb ποιεῖν is used, sixty-five in which it has a sacrificial import; but not only has he overlooked the fact that this signification is derived reflectively from the special sacrificial

---

[1] For a discussion of the import of the terms ποιεῖν and ἀνάμνησις, see a volume by the Rev. S. C. Malan, entitled, "The Sacrament of the Lord's Supper," a work which deserves to be better known.

circumstances which expressly define its action, but these sacrificial circumstances in the alleged cases were in connection with bloody sacrifices:[1] so that, on the one hand, ποιεῖ does not of its own accord, and in virtue of its own powers, sacrifice at all, and on the other, if it do, it offers a bloody sacrifice, *which the Eucharist is declared not to be*.

But the bishop thinks he has discovered the word in the act of offering " unbloody sacrifices," and gives a series of eleven examples, of which the following may be regarded as specimens.

(1) The first is found in Exodus xxix. 41—ποιήσεις κάρπωμα. Now, doubtless, ποιήσεις κάρπωμα signifies "Thou shalt make an offering;" but not only has the bishop here confounded an unbloody offering with a bloody one, but he has overlooked the fact that κάρπωμα is the word which expresses for itself the offering, and all the function which ποιεῖν has to discharge is "to make." The bishop introduced the word for the purpose of making it perform the whole of the sacrificial work, but this it modestly leaves to κάρπωμα, which is quite equal to the emergency.

(2) The second text is Leviticus ii. 7, where the Septuagint has σεμίλαδις ποιηθήσεται—literally, "The finest flour shall be made." But why did the bishop omit the words immediately connected with them, ἐν ἐλαίῳ (in oil), and which show that Moses was giving

[1] See, on this question, an admirable work by Dr. Harrison, Vicar of Fenwick, entitled, "Dr. Pusey's Challenge Answered;" which is one of the most exhaustive treatises on the real presence in our language.

directions as to the process of preparation? The English version puts it clearly enough—"And if thy oblation be a meat offering (baken) in the frying-pan, it shall be made of fine flour with oil." Neither the Hebrew nor the Septuagint refers in the latter part of the verse to the sacrifice, but to the manner in which the substance to be offered shall be made: and the word ποιηθήσεται retains its ordinary and general signification, "shall be made."

(3) Another instance is from Leviticus ii. 11—οὐ ποιήσετε ζυμωτόν—literally, "Ye shall not make leavened, or of leaven," and the whole passage is sufficiently unambiguous. "Every sacrifice which ye shall offer to the Lord ye shall not make of leaven."

(4) A further instance cited by the bishop is from Leviticus vi. 22, which, literally rendered, is as follows: "The priest anointed instead of him, from his sons, shall make it or do it"—ποιήσει αὐτήν (shall make it); but what is the αὐτήν? If the bishop had looked at the verse immediately preceding he would have found θυσίαν (sacrifice); so that instead of ποιεῖν containing within itself the sacrificial idea, the substantive expressing it is distinctly specified, and the word ποιεῖν is left to do its own proper work of performing. And the remaining instances are of precisely the same character; the verb ποιεῖν in not one of them appearing before us as a sacrificing agent, except as the sacrifice is distinctly mentioned.

An interpretation therefore which was unknown to the Greek Fathers, and to such of the Latin Fathers as understood Greek, which escaped the detection of Paschasius, and Aquinas, and Bellarmine, and, in general, the whole race of Romish controversialists, whose zeal in the defence of the doctrine of Transubstantiation inspired them with an almost superhuman subtlety, and rendered them little scrupulous as to their methods of defence, is one which no single episcopal authority in these latter days can avail to sustain. The verb ποιεῖν, as I have said, possesses an extraordinary amount of versatility and power, but what it does or makes must be expressed by another term, as, of itself, without such assistance, it can no more sacrifice than it can make a world.

So much as to the alleged meaning of this word in Alexandrian Greek, or rather in the upwards of seventy instances out of two thousand five hundred in which the bishop thought he found it supporting his view of the Eucharist; though even in this case he was contenting himself with a narrow basis of generalization for the maintenance of so stupendous a doctrine.

But we have now to see what is the nature of the service which it renders to his cause as viewed in the connection in which it occurs. In the records of the Last Supper, as given by Matthew and Mark, *it does not appear at all*, and therefore nothing sacrificial is commanded there. It occurs only in St. Luke, and in 1 Cor. xi. We take the account given in the latter, because it shows to us the Supper according to the exposition given of it by an inspired apostle.

" For I received from the Lord that which also I

delivered unto you, that the Lord Jesus, in the night in which he was betrayed, took bread, and having given thanks, he brake it, and said, This is my body which is for you: this do in remembrance of me. After the same manner the cup also, when he had supped, saying, This cup is the new covenant in my blood: this do as oft as ye drink it in remembrance of me; for as often as ye eat this bread and drink the cup, ye do declare the Lord's death till he come."[1]

Now the very expression with which the apostle concludes shows unmistakably that the idea of sacrifice is wholly foreign to his mind. The word *for* introduces the key to the whole passage, and in the most marked manner opens up the meaning of τοῦτο ποιεῖτε. Do what? we ask. And the apostle answers, "For as often as ye eat this bread, and drink this cup, ye do declare the Lord's death till he come." But on the bishop's interpretation it introduces an inconsequential inference. It would be imputing to the apostle a most halting logic, to represent him as saying, "Sacrifice this in remembrance of me—*for* as often as ye eat this bread and drink this cup, ye do declare the Lord's death till he come." The showing of the death consisted in the eating of the bread (for bread it is when eaten) and in the drinking of the cup.

In his treatise on the priesthood, Mr. Carter, with a surprising confidence, affirms that "two distinct uses are commanded by holy Scripture to be made of the consecrated elements. By them we are to 'show forth

[1] Alford's translation of Tischendorf's text.

the Lord's death till he come,' and afterwards to receive them in Holy Communion. We make of them a sacrifice, and then they become our food."[1] A more extraordinary interpretation than this is not to be found even in his work, which abounds in curiosities of criticism. Of the "two distinct uses which are commanded by holy Scripture," we find no trace, for nowhere does the New Testament speak of the consecrated elements being made a sacrifice. And as to the "afterwards" of which Mr. Carter speaks, it does not expound, but contradicts the text. The teaching of the apostle is not that when we "have shown forth the Lord's death," we then partake of the consecrated elements; but that when, and as often as we partake of the bread and cup, we do show forth the Lord's death, the two things not being "distinct," as Mr. Carter unwarrantably affirms, but combined in one indivisible act. The "showing forth" is not in order to the participation, but the participation is in order to the "showing forth," and, in fact, absolutely constitutes it. The showing forth is not accomplished except in the act and process of "eating this bread and drinking this cup." A true theory does not require such violent handling of the Divine word, and a theory which can sanction it cannot be true.

A corresponding experiment, moreover, has been made upon the word ἀνάμνησις, with the view of extorting from it some testimony to the sacrificial

[1] "Doctrine of the Priesthood in the Church of England," by T. T. Carter, M.A. Second edition, p. 39.

idea, for the late prelate in question considers it to signify the offering of a μνημόσυνον—a memorial or record. Of such an import of the term, either in its substantive or in its verbal form, there is not one shadow of evidence in the New Testament. In the verbal form it remembers, or recollects, or calls to mind; and in its substantive form it is a remembrance or recollection and nothing more, and in this respect the Hellenistic Greek follows faithfully the steps of the Attic.

The ἀναμνήσις of Plato is a subjective recollection of things known in the past. Hence he speaks of it as a "seizing in thought of the form of a deceased friend;"[1] and Aristotle distinguishes memory (μνήμη) from remembrance (ἀναμνήσις), defining the former as the holding of images in the mind, and the latter as the returning of them when once forgotten. And with respect to the Alexandrian Greek as found in the Septuagint, there is not one unambiguous instance of the use of the term in the sense for which the late Bishop of Salisbury pleaded. That the word, whether in Attic or Alexandrian Greek, signifies, in general, a subjective remembrance or act of memory, and not any outward and objective fact or deed apart from the mind that remembers, is a truth which cannot be lightly questioned by any one who has taken the needful pains to trace the usage of the term. The ἀναμνήσις is not a something which is designed to put another in mind, but an actual putting of oneself in mind, or

[1] Plato. Phædon, p. 213.

an observance which has this purpose in view. The ἀναμνήσις (remembrance) of sins every year was not an awakening of the memory of God, but an expression of the memory of the Jews. The sins were ever in the eye of God, but they were to be remembered and acknowledged by His people, and the yearly sacrifices were meant to express the yearly recognition. And in like manner the ἀναμνήσις enjoined by our Saviour upon His disciples at the Last Supper was not designed to remind Him, as if it were possible that He might forget those for whom He had come to die, and whose names were graven, not alone on the palms of His hands, but on His very heart; but it was designed to be on their part a devout, grateful, and exulting remembrance of Him, and of that great sacrifice which was their hope and their life.

But, in fact, the whole narrative contains not one word which can be construed as having the remotest connection with sacrificial ideas. Every verse in this apostolic exposition precludes as by a strict and purposed selection of terms the notion of a sacrificial oblation. The ruling conception is that of participation, and that alone. The sole command is to eat and drink in remembrance of Christ. And when the apostle passes on from the words of institution to certain inferential considerations, which are meant to rebuke and correct the monstrous abuses which had crept into the Corinthian Church, he confines himself to the same ideas and words. "Wherefore whosoever shall eat this bread, and drink this cup of the Lord, unworthily, shall be guilty of the body and blood of the Lord. But let a man examine himself, and so let him eat of that bread and drink of that cup. For he that eateth and drinketh unworthily, eateth and drinketh judgment to himself, not discerning the Lord's body."[1]

What the apostle means by unworthy participation can occasion no perplexity to those who remember the circumstances which drew forth his allusions to the Lord's Supper. He had heard of the greediness, the gluttony, and the drunkenness which were exhibited by some of the Corinthian Church at that meal, and of the disregard with which others were treated. These were the sins which constituted the unworthy partaking which he so strongly condemned.

And in what manner does he meet this unseemly conduct on the part of the offending Corinthians? The loftiest ground which he could have occupied in administering his stern remonstrance is the one which, according to the theory of Bishop Hamilton, he seems to have overlooked. If indeed it had been true that with the consecrating words of the presiding elder an actual sacrifice was consummated, and that there lay the very body and blood of the Lord Jesus, is it possible on the one hand to conceive that the Corinthians, holding such a view of the awful elements before them, could have prostituted them to such an infamous use; or, on the other hand, is it conceivable that the apostle would have brought into such prominent view, by repetition and emphasis, "this bread

[1] 1 Cor. xi. 27–29.

and this cup"? Then, if at any time supposing that the Corinthians had misunderstood the nature of those elements, the apostle would have rebuked them by reminding them that the person who presided at that sacred ceremony was not a common man, but a priest of the most high God; that the bread and wine which he held successively in his hand, though taken from the general stock supplied for the feast of the Agapæ, vanished at the words of consecration, and became the very body and blood of the Lord, or, at least, their veils and vehicles; and he would have eschewed the terms bread and the cup, inasmuch as they *were* no longer, and could no longer competently *denote*, the sacred substances with which they had become associated, or by which they had been wholly displaced. If such were, indeed, the nature of the Supper, then nothing could have more abashed the Corinthians, or convicted them of the sacrilegious outrage they had been perpetrating, than such an exposition.

But if the sacrificial view of the Lord's Supper is supported neither by the words τοῦτο ποιεῖτε nor by the word ἀναμνήσις, so neither does it derive any warrant from the word καταγγέλλετε, rendered in our version "ye do show," still more unambiguously by Alford, "declare," but which is by some writers so paraphrased as to give it the force of "represent" or "enact," as if the Lord's Supper were a dramatic repetition in some sort of the death of our blessed Lord upon the cross. But this again is an attempt to force upon a word a function which it is incapable of discharging. The word καταγγελλεῖν refuses to lend itself to any histrionic procedure. It will announce, publish, declare, but it will not enact or represent as in a scene. This it never does in any one of the instances in which it occurs in the Scriptures, and no exceptional import can be conceded to it in the case before us.[1]

From this consideration of the terms employed by the apostle in his description of the nature of the Lord's Supper as he had received it from the Lord Himself, it results that not only is the sacrificial conception of that ordinance not sustained by the apostle, but absolutely precluded by him. There is no mention of victim, sacrifice, propitiation, or priest; and all these terms as applied to the Lord's Supper are ecclesiastical inventions.

When Mr. Wilberforce, in his very able work on the Holy Eucharist, asks why the eucharistic service is called "the Christian sacrifice," and adds, that if the term is applied only in a general and metaphorical manner, every act of worship may be styled a sacrifice; I answer that nowhere in the Scriptures is such a denomination applied to the feast of communion, and that to any post-apostolic innovations, either in doctrine or language, which pervert or overlay the original nature of the ordinance, I can attach no importance. Moreover, it is unaccountable, were it

---

[1] Waterland admits that καταγγέλλειν has not the meaning elsewhere of "showing to God," but curiously enough seeks to invest it with the force of ἀναγγέλλειν—a style of criticism which is not worthy of so great a man. See p. 106, "Doctrine of the Eucharist." Second edition, 1737.

not "in a general and metaphorical manner," but in a real and unfigurative sense a Christian sacrifice, that it should not have been marked off by the apostles themselves from all other acts of Christian obedience by this designation. And it is as extraordinary that when apostles have occasion to speak of Christian sacrifices this ordinance never takes its place in the enumeration. Paul receives from Epaphroditus the things sent by the Philippians, which "are an odour of a sweet smell, a sacrifice acceptable, well-pleasing to God;" and the Hebrews are exhorted to offer the "sacrifice of praise to God continually, that is, the fruit of the lips giving thanks to his name;" and are also besought not "to forget to do good and to communicate, for with such sacrifices God is well pleased;" and Peter, writing to the strangers scattered abroad, whom he designates a holy priesthood, reminds them that they are to "offer up spiritual sacrifices acceptable to God by Jesus Christ." But while these sacrificial terms are applied with so little scruple to other Christian acts and services, they seem to be purposely eschewed whenever reference is made (and this is remarkably rare) to that ordinance which Mr. Wilberforce describes as the "crown of public worship, the bond whereby men are attached to Christ, the focus in which all Church ordinances culminate." It is not a little remarkable, and I must add significant, that a term so familiar as sacrifice, and one, moreover, which in subsequent ages became a prominent designation of the Lord's

Supper, should have been avoided by the apostles if they had deemed that Supper a real sacrifice. The absence of the name is explained by the absence of the conception.

It was not at once, indeed, after the death of the apostles, that the sacrificial view of the Lord's Supper obtained universal recognition. For Justin Martyr expressly says: "The most Divine Word, to whom also we perpetually sacrifice the sacrifice of praise, and pour out, as to God, sincere prayers, and sacrifice the sweet smell of our works, making Him a part of ourselves, breathing Him, thanking Him, yearning after Him, praising Him in all things, our blessed Hope, and the Giver of the kingdom of heaven;" and in his dialogue with Trypho he is still more emphatic, and says: "Therefore I also admit that the prayers and thanksgivings offered by worthy people are the only sacrifices that are perfect and well-pleasing to God, for these alone have Christians undertaken to offer; and in the remembrance effected by their solid and liquid food, whereby the suffering of the Son of God, which He endured, is brought to mind."

This latter citation is specially noteworthy, both as showing the distance at which Justin Martyr stood alike from the advocates of Transubstantiation and Consubstantiation, and that the sacrifice of the Eucharist is not one of propitiation, but of thanksgiving; and this, let me add, is in strict keeping with the whole of his teaching, for not even in his most rhetorical passages does he afford the slightest support for the doctrine that the Lord's Supper was a sacrifice in the usual acceptation of that term, but he interprets the prophecy of Malachi—"For from the rising of the sun to the going down of the same my name shall be great among the Gentiles; and in every place incense shall be offered in my name, and a pure offering"—as having its fulfilment in the prayers and giving of thanks which are offered through the name of the crucified Jesus.

Before closing the examination of the evidence of the New Testament upon the point in question, it may be considered necessary to glance at the two passages which have been suborned with no little confidence as witnesses to the sacrificial nature of the Lord's Supper.

The first is that which occurs in 1 Cor. x. 16-21: "The cup of blessing which we bless, is it not the communion of the blood of Christ? The bread which we break, is it not the communion of the body of Christ? For we being many are one bread, and one body: for we are all partakers of that one bread. Behold Israel after the flesh: are not they which eat of the sacrifices partakers of the altar? What say I then? that the idol is anything, or that which is offered to idols is anything? But I say, that the things which the Gentiles sacrifice, they sacrifice to devils, and not to God: and I would not that ye should have fellowship with devils. Ye cannot drink the cup of the Lord, and the cup of devils: ye cannot be partakers of the Lord's table, and of the table of devils."

Now the key to the whole of this expostulation is found in the fourteenth verse, "Wherefore, my dearly beloved brethren, flee from idolatry," and the purpose of the apostle is to warn the Corinthian disciples from any complicity with this heathenism, which, by the very nature of their Christian profession, they had openly abandoned. They were not therefore to mingle in the feasts of that idolatrous system which they had renounced in favour of the Christian faith. The two were incapable of conciliation. Christ and demonism were opposed to each other, and so too were the festive celebrations which represented them; and the participation of both by the same man would be regarded as a practical acknowledgment that sympathy with idol worship was not yet extinguished, and as a dishonour done to the name of Jesus. The apostle speaks of the things which the Gentiles sacrifice, but he does not speak of the things which the Christians sacrifice, and thus complete an antithesis which would have given all the greater force to his reasoning if such material and propitiatory oblations had been offered by them. He speaks of the Lord's table, but not of the altar, though he had just before used the word altar in reference to the Jewish sacrifices. But as if conscious of its incongruity with the whole genius of the Christian dispensation, and the whole purpose of the Lord's Supper, he avoids the term in favour of table. And it is the more extraordinary that he should have done this, for on the supposition that the emblems became by consecration the sacrifice of the real body and blood of the Lord, the very table at which the early disciples sat, or reclined, must have been the altar likewise, for the same table sufficed for the president and the other communicants. But if the table were also an altar, why was this designation passed by when it would have given such impressive emphasis to the sacrificial conception?[1]

[1] I am glad to be able to fortify the reasoning contained in the text with the authority of Canon Lightfoot, who says:—"Some interpreters again, from a comparison of 1 Cor. ix. 13 with 1 Cor. x. 18, have inferred that St. Paul recognises the designation of the Lord's table as an altar. On the contrary, it is a speaking fact that in both passages he *avoids* using the term of the Lord's table, though the language of the context might readily have suggested it to him if he had considered it appropriate. Nor does the argument in either case require or encourage such an inference. In 1 Cor. ix. 13, 14, the apostle writes, 'Know ye not that they which wait at the altar are partakers with the altar? Even so hath the Lord ordained that they which preach the gospel should live of the gospel.' The point of resemblance in the two cases is the holding a sacred office, but the ministering on the altar is predicated only of the former. So also in 1 Cor. x. 18, *et seq.*, the *altar* is named as common to Jews and heathens, but the *table* only as common to Christians and heathens; *i.e.*, the holy Eucharist is a banquet, but it is not a sacrifice (in the Jewish or heathen sense of sacrifice)." —P. 264.

"I am aware," says Bishop Kaye, in his sermon on the Eucharist, "only of one passage in the New Testament which can, with any plausibility, be alleged in support of the opinion that the apostles contemplated the continuance of propitiatory sacrifices in the Church of Christ. It is that in which the apostle says, 'We have an altar whereof they have no right to eat who serve the tabernacle.' An altar, it is contended, implies a sacrifice to be offered and a priest to offer it; and hence it is inferred that in the Eucharist,

The other passage which has been regarded as contributing not a little strength to the Catholic view of the Eucharist is Heb. xiii. 10: "We have an altar, of which those serving at the tabernacle have no right to eat." Nothing but a theory in sore distress could repair to such a passage for succour, for the context both before and after forbids its perverted application to the sacrificial theory of the Lord's Supper. The writer, be it remembered, throughout the main portion of this epistle, has been comparing and contrasting two dispensations, one of which, as he says in the previous verse, has been distinguished by "meats," and the other is distinguished by "grace;" and he says it is good that the heart be established with grace, and not "with meats, which have not profited those that have been occupied therein." These "meats" have pertained to carnal ordinances and a worldly sanctuary. They have had relation to a dispensation in which there was an altar. We also "have an altar" in this dispensation of grace. One altar, let it be observed, and not many. One altar in and for the dispensation, and not an altar in every church. And of this altar those who serve in the tabernacle have no right to eat. "For as the bodies

---

Christ is offered as a sacrifice in the proper sense of the word. It is true that some commentators have understood this passage of the Eucharist; though, if we compare it with the context, we shall find good reason to think that the altar which the apostle had in his mind was the altar of Christ's cross. Let it be granted, however, that there is an allusion to the Eucharist; still the sacrifices to be offered are not material, but spiritual; not propitiatory, but of thanksgiving; the sacrifices (as we have just seen) of praise and good deeds."—"Bishop Kaye's Charges," p. 426.

of those beasts whose blood is brought into the sanctuary by the high priest for sin, are burned without the camp; so Jesus also, that he might sanctify the people with his own blood, suffered without the gate."

The sin-offerings of the ancient dispensation are here unquestionably contrasted with the sacrifice of Christ, and consequently the altar must be the cross upon which He died, for it is to the death of Christ, and to the place where He was crucified, that the writer alludes. And the eating of which he speaks denotes the participation of those benefits which Christ procured for man, but of which they cannot partake who continue to reject Him, and serve at the tabernacle; for in persisting in such service they are practically denying that another priest, another altar, and another victim have abolished for ever the typical ordinances by which they were foreshadowed. The contrast of the "grace" of the new dispensation with the "unprofitable meats" of the old, conveys a very significant intimation that when he speaks of an altar of which the adherents of Judaism have no right to eat, he contemplates those transcendent blessings which have made the feasts of the gospel emphatically a feast not "of meats" that profit not, but a feast of grace; and therefore a feast of "fat things, of things full of marrow, of wine upon the lees well refined."

Thus far I have endeavoured to show, from an exposition of the teaching of the New Testament—the only final authority on this question—that the Lord's Supper was meant to be a commemoration of the death of our Lord, and not a commemorative sacrifice; a simple feast at a table whereon lay the emblems of a love which poured itself out in death, and not, in the first place, an altar upon which a priest immolates the one sacrifice afresh, and then a table at which the communicants consume the broken body and the shed blood. Nowhere do the Scriptures speak of the emblems as a sacrifice, of the table as an altar, or of the minister as a priest; and yet, as we have seen, no terms could have been so appropriate as these if the Catholic conceptions of the sacrament had been those which apostles held and sought to perpetuate in the Church. That the apostles have not availed themselves of such language is not due to the fact that they were unfamiliar with it, for it formed part of their earliest and most inveterate associations; but because they were the authoritative expounders of a dispensation with which such terminology had no consonance, except in a sense wholly figurative, or in its application to Him who had made the one sufficient oblation. It is true that, with the characteristic precocity of error, no long period elapsed before all these words were seen rising up in the literature of the Church, at first somewhat scantily, and then in rank luxuriance; at first, too, with meanings wholly different from those they had in Judaism and heathenism, but at length with a dangerous similarity. For some time the word "sacrifice" in the writings of the subapostolic Fathers had a meaning innocent enough. It denoted the bread and wine which were offered in the Lord's Supper as a thank-offering to God, and this without any idea of propitiation whatever.

And here I might have concluded the evidence of Scripture against the sacrificial view of the Lord's Supper, and in favour of its being a commemoration of a sacrifice; but the doctrine of the real presence held by the Roman Church, and revived almost, if not entirely, in the same sense, by a certain section of the Anglican Church, renders it necessary to examine in the light of the same inspired teaching the arguments by which it has been maintained. In speaking of the revival in the same sense, I mean as to the *essence* of the doctrine, for the distinction between the mode of the presence of Christ, as to whether it be by Transubstantiation or Consubstantiation, is a matter of indifference when the tenet of the real bodily presence is held in common. If the body of our Lord be assumed to be in the elements as a body sacrificed for man by the words of the priest, it is a refinement which deserves no discussion, whether that body be transformed from the original substances of bread and wine, or coexists with them. The two doctrines easily pass into each other, the latter being, however, the less consistent of the two with the language of Scripture. The question is not so much in connection with what substances or properties is the real body of our Saviour present, as whether the real body be in connection with any substances or properties. Nor is the question whether our blessed Lord be present at the sacrament with His disciples, confirming to them the spiritual blessings which are symbolized and pledged to all faithful communicants; but whether He be bodily, and as a sacrifice, in the visible elements of the sacrament. The latter is held by Romanists and many of the Neo-Catholics alike: the former we believe to be the teaching of the Divine Word.

The Council of Trent heads its second chapter on the Sacrifice of the Mass as follows:—"The visible sacrifice on the altar is propitiatory, not only for the living, but also for the dead in Christ who are not yet fully cleansed."

The Neo-Catholic definition of the eucharistic sacrifice follows closely in the steps of the Tridentine symbol. "By the eucharistic sacrifice," writes one, "is not meant merely a sacrifice of prayer and praise; nor does the eucharistic sacrifice merely mean the offerings of ourselves, our souls, and bodies to be a reasonable, holy, and lively sacrifice unto God; still less does it mean the offering of bread and wine for use in the sacrament, which, nevertheless, because they are thus offered, are called oblations; but the eucharistic sacrifice is Christ Himself supernaturally present in the sacrament, the Victim slain once for all upon the cross, but continuously offered before God in memory of that death by His own natural presence in heaven, and by His supernatural presence in the sacrament here on earth." [1]

A still more undisguised endorsement of the Romish

[1] "Some Thoughts on Low Masses," by the Rev. E. Stuart, p. 31.

definition, by one of the Catholic revivalists, is the following:—" The Church of England holds precisely the same view of the sacrament of the Lord's Supper as the Church of Rome."[1]

And Dr. Pusey so little resents the Romish doctrine, that with a quiet and undeserved slur upon the learning or honesty of those who compiled the Articles of the Church of England, he says: " My own conviction is that our Articles deny Transubstantiation in one sense, and that the Roman Church, according to the explanation of the Council of Trent, affirms it in another;" thus suggesting that a little intelligent explanation might bring the two into the most perfect accord.[2]

In the citations just given there are two assumptions, both of which are constantly made alike by the Romish and Neo-Catholic theologians of the more advanced school. The first is that the body of our Lord is really present on the altar, and the second, that it is there to be sacrificed. Without retraversing the ground already trodden in the previous lecture as well as in this, we shall submit these positions to the test of Scripture and reason. In doing this it will be needful to direct attention to a series of theological distinctions and refinements which have been set up for the purpose of evading otherwise insuperable difficulties, and which have exposed the whole of theological science to the imputation of being an arena for the display of juggling with words.

[1] "The Kiss of Peace," by the Rev. Gerald Cobb, p. 105.
[2] See Appendix D.

That the body of our Saviour is in heaven, and not on earth, is a matter which, if language has any unambiguous meaning, is set at rest by a superfluous amount of evidence. It is seen in the assurance of our Lord that it was "expedient for his disciples that he should go away, in order that the Comforter might come;" it is seen in the historic record that "when he had spoken these things, while they beheld, he was taken up, and a cloud received him out of their sight;" and in the words of the angels who stood by the disciples as they sorrowfully witnessed His vanishing form, and said, "Ye men of Galilee, why stand ye gazing up into heaven? This same Jesus, which is taken up from you into heaven, shall so come in like manner as ye have seen him go into heaven." It is seen in the apostolic declaration that "the heaven must receive him until the time of the restitution of all things." Exhortations are grounded upon the fact of his bodily presence being in heaven, and not on earth. "Seek those things which are above, where Christ sitteth at the right hand of God." When He appears again it "is to be the *second* time without sin unto salvation." Meanwhile He is in heaven, and from henceforth "expecting until his enemies become his footstool." To be at home in the body was (even though the apostle partook of the Lord's Supper) to be absent from the Lord; and to be "absent from the body" was to be "present with the Lord."

These inspired testimonies should be sufficient to place beyond the range of controversy the fact of our

Saviour's bodily presence in heaven, and of His presence there in such sense as to preclude the presence of the same body on earth. Otherwise, why is His body expressly localized in heaven at all, or why was it said to have ascended thither, if it be indifferently and equally in heaven and on every altar in the world where the priest has breathed the consecrating words, "This is my body"? According to the Romish theory our Saviour has not, in fact, gone away wholly except in the *form* of His body, inasmuch as He is in the *substance* of that body more present than ever, because simultaneously present in more places than ever. And it is the critical difficulties created by this enormous assumption which have whetted the theological dialectic to such an edge of subtlety, that hair-splitting has become comparatively a coarse operation. There is not one word that figures in this controversy which can be said to have a definite and uniform significance; not "substance," not "body," not "flesh," not "blood," not "presence," not "real," not "true," not "identical," not "here," not "there." These terms cross the stage, and as they cross, change their forms and features in the most perplexing and baffling manner. As if to exclude all possibility of mistake as to what is the nature of the body which is in the Eucharist, the Church of Rome multiplies terms of definition. It is *vere* (truly), *realiter* (really), and *substantialiter* (substantially) there, and these words are still further defined. By truly (*vere*) it means not figuratively; by really (*realiter*) it means not simply efficaciously by faith; and by *substantialiter* (substantially) it means not simply objectively through the operation or virtue diffused by Christ."[1] And as we have seen already, in this body thus elaborately defined, the Church of Rome includes the flesh, bones, and nerves of the Saviour, together with His soul and divinity.

But an arrest is suddenly laid upon the understanding when about to affirm that the same body cannot possibly exist in two places at one and the same time, still less in a thousand places; for it is reminded that the body is present on the altar, but not as in a place; within the species which are in a place, but not as in a place; in the hands of the priest, which are in a place, but still not as in a place; on the tongue of the communicant, which is in a place, but still not as in a place, because the presence has no " relation to quantity more or less." Assuredly the definitions and their expositions seem to confront each other with such startling antagonism, that if the former had been "*not* truly," "*not* really," "*not* substantially," the latter would have been in most admirable harmony with them. The introduction of the negative would on this point be a true eirenicon between the teaching of Rome and that of the apostles.

The fortune of these words has been singular in the conflicts between the Papal and Protestant Churches. They have been treated both as enemies and as friends, alternately anathematized and blessed. To know that *realiter* means " really," is to know but little. For what

[1] "Dens' Theology," vol. v. p. 279.

does "really" mean? In the mouths of the scholastic theologians it has an astonishing variety of significations. It is "really" as opposed to "nominally"—"really" as opposed to "figuratively"—"really" as opposed to "ideally"—"really" as opposed to "spiritually"—"really" as opposed to "sacramentally"—"really" as opposed to "virtually"—"really" as opposed to "formally." And the same fortune has been shared by the phrase "real presence," an expression which has covered the most contradictory doctrines. The unsophisticated masses of mankind would conclude that "the real presence of a body" meant the "presence of a real body," but the monstrous dogma for which the Church of Rome is primarily responsible has created the necessity for a whole world of refinements which have been the curse of theology to this day. Even Reformers have both accepted and rejected all these technical distinctions, sometimes in the same sense, but more frequently in different senses, and have thus produced endless confusion in the minds of subsequent writers, who have taken but little pains to understand in what senses the terms were approved, and in what condemned.

Cranmer in his later years spoke as strongly against the real presence as against the Popish doctrine of Transubstantiation; and in his answer to Smith's Preface in his "Treatise on the Lord's Supper," he says, "But this I confess of myself, that not long before I wrote the said catechism, I was in that error of the real presence."[1]

[1] Cranmer's Works. Park. Soc. part i. p. 374.

Bishop Jewel argues at considerable length against the real presence, and speaks of those "new-fangled words, '*really*,' 'corporally,' 'carnally,' &c.; which words Mr. Harding is not able to show that in this case of being *really* in the sacrament any one of all the old Fathers ever used."[1]

Foxe, speaking of the difference between the Lutherans and Zwinglians, says: "They both do confess the presence of Christ, and disagree only upon the manner of the presence, which the one part do affirm to be *real*, and the other *spiritual*."

Ridley says: "The blood is in the chalice indeed, but not in the *real presence*." If he may use the terms "truly and really" with his own interpretation, he will use them, but not otherwise. He says: "If you take *really* for *vere*, for 'spiritually,' by grace and efficacy, then it is true that the natural body and blood of Christ is in the sacrament *vere et realiter* (indeed and really); but if you take these terms so grossly that you would conclude thereby a natural body having motion to be contained under the forms of bread and wine (*vere et realiter*), then really is not the body and blood of Christ in the sacrament, no more than the Holy Ghost is in the element of water in our baptism."[2]

Bishop Bilson says: "By these things we have Him in this world not *really*, 'locally,' or 'corporally,' but truly, comfortably, and effectually, so as

---

[1] Jewel's Works. Park. Soc. vol. i. p. 449.
[2] Last Examination before the Commissioners, p. 273. Park. Soc.

our bodies, souls, and spirits be sanctified and preserved by Him against the day of redemption."[1]

Bishop Beveridge says: "If the bread be not *really* changed into the body of Christ, then the body of Christ is not *really* there present; and if it be not *really* there present, it is impossible it should be *really* eaten and received into our bodies as bread is."[2]

Richard Hooker says: "The *real presence* of Christ's most blessed body and blood is not therefore to be sought for in the sacrament, but in the worthy receiver of the sacrament. . . . As for the sacraments, they *really* exhibit, but, for aught we can gather out of that which is written of them, they are not *really*, nor do *really* contain in themselves that grace which with them, or by them, it pleaseth God to bestow."[3]

Thus these terms have all an equivocal meaning, and the same writer may be considered as holding or rejecting the real presence, the true presence, the substantial presence, according as they denote severally the corporal or the non-corporal presence of Christ in the elements themselves. The real presence of Christ, by His Spirit and grace, has been denied by no Evangelical Church, but the real presence of the natural body of Christ, in a sense so absolute that it was *in*, or *with*, the elements, and partaken by all who received them, irrespective of their character, was repudiated by the great body of the English Reformers. But some of them were

[1] Last Examination before the Commissioners, p. 722. Edit. 1585.
[2] Ibid., pp. 482, 3. Oxf. Ed. 1846.
[3] "Eccles. Pol." vol. ii. pp. 352, 353.

addicted to language which bordered dangerously on the Romish views, and this was even more conspicuous in several of the Caroline divines. From this charge, however, must be excepted, among others, Jeremy Taylor, whose work on the real presence marked an epoch in the history and literature of this question, and who has shown himself in this treatise to be a consummate logician as he is elsewhere seen to be the prince of rhetoricians.

Nothing, for example, can be clearer than the following:—" We, by the real spiritual presence of Christ, do understand Christ to be present as the Spirit of God is present in the hearts of the faithful, by blessing and grace, and this is all we mean besides the tropical and figurative presence.

" So that now the question is not whether the symbols be changed into Christ's body or no, for it is granted on all sides, but whether this conversion be sacramental or figurative? or whether it be natural and bodily? Nor is it whether Christ is really taken, but whether He be taken in a spiritual or in a natural manner? *We* say the conversion is figurative, mysterious, and sacramental; *they* say it is proper, natural, and corporal; *we* affirm that Christ is *really* taken by faith, by the spirit, to all real effects of His Passion; *they* say He is taken by the mouth, and that the spiritual and the virtual taking of Him in virtue or effect is not sufficient, though done also in the sacrament. *Hic Rhodus, hic saltus.*"

These statements, however, of Taylor, would by no means satisfy the modern reactionists, some of whom have only relinquished the term "corporal," from prudential considerations, in favour of the word "objective," which they understand in the same sense, though it enjoys the privilege of not having been as yet banned by any judicial decree.[1]

The expedients which have been devised for the purpose of reconciling the "objective presence" of our Saviour's body with the Scripture doctrine that "he sitteth at the right hand of God," are the most extraordinary to be found in the whole history of human speculation. The liberties which have

---

[1] Speaking of the word "objective," Canon Trevor, in his essay on the holy Eucharist, says: "The term is a metaphysical one, imported into English theology within our recollection. It was coined by the German philosophers to indicate an object existing independently of the observer in opposition to an idea within his own mind, which they call a subjective impression."

The worthy Canon is certainly astray in the history of the word. So far from its having been "imported into English theology within our recollection," it is a familiar friend well known to the theologians of the seventeenth century. It is true that for some reason or other it became for a time an exile, greatly to the loss of our language, both in its theological and philosophical aspects. There is no fear, however, of its falling again even into temporary desuetude. It was a scholastic term long before the birth of the German philosophers by whom it was not *coined*, but simply *adopted*.

In his invaluable work on the "Blessedness of the Righteous," John Howe speaks of the "*objective* glory which the saints are to behold" (chap. iii.); and again he says: "Supposing that likeness here do (as it hath been granted it may) signify *objective* glory also as well as *subjective*" (chap. v.).

And John Owen says: "Nothing that Christ undertook or underwent did or could constitute Him *subjectively*, inherently, and thereon personally a sinner, or guilty of any sin of His own" (vol. v. p. 201, Gould's edition); and again: "The righteousness of Christ is not transfused into us so as to be made inherently and *subjectively* ours, as it was in Him" (vol. v. 218); and again: "As to the extent of Divine revelations *objectively*" (vol v. p. 59).

been taken with the words "really," "truly," "substantially," have been already indicated; but these are trifling compared with the manipulation to which the word "body" has been subjected, under which its meanings have varied from finite to infinite, and from material to spiritual, until the very nature of body has disappeared in its contradictory definitions.

Mr. Wilberforce, whose work on the holy Eucharist has been the armoury from which most recent neo-catholic writers have drawn their chief weapons, both with and without acknowledgment, devoted considerable strength to the endeavour to reconcile the *real bodily presence of Christ* in heaven with His *real bodily presence on earth*. He appeals to our modesty, to our ignorance of the nature of substance, with the view of checking that very speculation for which he allows himself an unlimited license. In reply to the statement that it was impossible that our Lord could impart to His disciples "that body and blood which pertained to Himself," he says: "But how can the possibility of such a thing be denied, considering the imperfect state of our knowledge of physical substance?" It were sufficient to reply to such an observation, "And how can the possibility of such a thing be *affirmed*, considering the imperfect state of our knowledge of physical substance?" For where there is no express revelation on the matter, to affirm is as hazardous as to deny; and we have no express revelation that the real body of our blessed Lord can be both in heaven and on earth at the same time, while we have the most indubitable assurance that the heavens have received Him "until the times of the restitution of all things." But though we regard this as a sufficient reply to the *caveat* of Mr. Wilberforce, as grounded on our ignorance of the nature of physical substance, other considerations must not be disregarded. Is anything known of "physical substance"? Are these terms terms only, or do they originate corresponding conceptions, and do the conceptions correspond with any objective truth? If not, then the whole question is quashed, alike for those who hold Mr. Wilberforce's views and those who differ from them.

The question of the real presence of the body of Christ cannot in such case be discussed, for it would be the discussion of that of which confessedly nothing is known. But, indeed, the question is not one concerning substance in general at all, nor is it concerning body as body. It is concerning the Lord's body, that which He took of the Virgin; and to elude the consideration of this by hiding in certain philosophic and shallow common-places touching the mystery of substance, is to beat the air. Are any of the maintainers of the real presence of the body of our Lord, objectively viewed, prepared to affirm that of *this* substance in particular nothing is known? Is it not known that it had form, size, colour, separateness from other substances whether personal or impersonal, power of movement from place to place; and that therefore as such it did not occupy all places at one and the same moment? Are these things not known? If not, nothing is known touching our Lord's body, nor touching any other body; for the cloud of mystery will settle with equal darkness over all substances whatsoever, if indeed in such case we should be prepared to believe that there is any substance at all. If, on the other hand, these things are known, all reasoning entitled to the name must proceed on the basis of these things, and not abjectly close its eyes in the presence of the "mystery of substance." That our Saviour's body was never, while on earth, when its reality was meant to be established and its qualities to be revealed, in two places in the same indivisible instant, is clear from the Scriptures themselves. If it were in the manger, it was not in the temple; if it were on the sea, it was not on the land; if it were on the mountain, it was not in the valley; if it were in Jerusalem, it was not at Bethany; and when the resurrection was accomplished the angel uttered the truth without mysticism or mystery, when he said, "He is *not here*, he is risen."

Nor can this reasoning be impugned by any considerations such as those which Mr. Wilberforce, Dr. Pusey, and their followers adduce touching the mysterious powers attributed to the body of Christ. We are reminded that it could walk on the water, that it could fast forty days, that it passed through the doors within which the disciples were assembled (which is a questionable interpretation), and that it arose from the sepulchre while the stone was not rolled away, which is false. But in what manner do such considerations as these touch the question at issue, which is one of *presence*, and *that alone*. If it had been shown that when our Lord was walking on the sea He was also walking on the land, working miracles at Nain, addressing the multitude at Capernaum, sitting on the Mount of Olives, and sleeping at Bethany; that when He was fasting for forty days He was also, in virtue of the "mystery of physical substance," partaking of His daily repast with His friends; that when He had passed through the closed doors He was also without the doors; at one and the same moment saying to His disciples in the upper room, "Peace be unto you," and walking in the suburbs of Jerusalem, enjoying the fresh coolness of the evening air; no further demonstration would have been needed of the capacity which His body possessed of being at more than one place at the same moment of time. But the illustrations cited by the advocates of the real presence are not only wide of the mark, but they have no relation to it except that of investing it in a cloud. That a human body can walk on the waves, and fast forty days, and perform a thousand miracles, under the direction and energy of Almighty power, is not controverted by any one; but that an organized body, whose very definition demands that it be circumscribed in space, should be here and not here, or here and elsewhere, is a proposition to which nothing but the anguish of a theological dilemma could have reconciled any thoughtful man. In no school of philosophical opinion, either ancient or modern, has any definition ever been given or conceived of a body organized and yet unlimited, and therefore unlocalized. And the Fathers were as clear and unambiguous on this matter as the philosophers.

"That," says Gregory Nyssen, "is not a body which wants colour, figure, solidness, space, weight, and the rest of its attributes."[1]

"There can be no body," says Augustine, "either celestial or terrestrial, aerial or aqueous, that is not less in a part than in the whole; nor can it in any wise have another part in the place of this part, but must have one here, another elsewhere, throughout the several distant and divided spaces of place."[2] And again, in his book against Faustus, he says "that Christ, according to His corporal presence, cannot be at the same time in the sun, and in the moon, and on the cross."[3] And again: "Our Lord is above, yet also in *truth* the Lord is here; for the body of our Lord in which He arose *must be in one place*; but His truth is diffused everywhere."[4] And yet again: "In regard to the presence of His majesty, we have Christ always; in regard to the presence of His flesh, it was rightly said to the disciples, 'Me ye have not always;' for in regard to the presence of His flesh, the Church had Him a few days, now she has Him by faith, and does not see Him with her eyes."

[1] "De Opific. Hom." c. 24.   [2] "Contra epis. Manich."
[3] Lib. xx. c. 11.   [4] Tract 80 in Ioan.

Theodoret, when speaking of the Divine substance, says: "Only the Divinity as being undetermined is not confined to place;"[1] but speaking of the Saviour's body after His resurrection, he says: "Still it is a body, having its former circumscription."[2]

Fulgentius also observes: "If the body of Christ be a true one, it must be *contained in a place*."[3] And again he says: "Everything so remains as it has received of God that it should be, one on this manner, and another on that. *For it is not given to bodies to exist after such a manner as is granted to spirits.*"[4]

But indeed the testimony neither of philosophers nor Fathers can impart additional certainty to the conviction inspired by the unsophisticated common sense of mankind, that body, *as* body, and *because* body, must be locally restricted, and can only be in one place, as it is not at the same time in any other; and I repeat the assertion, that nowhere in the holy Scriptures, which are our ultimate authority on this and every other matter of faith, is the *body* of Christ, in the natural sense of these words, ever said to be simultaneously in more places than one, whether before the resurrection, or after the resurrection, or since the ascension; whether as a physical body, or as a glorified body. If such passage had existed it would have been triumphantly produced, but to this day it has eluded the keenest vision of the subtlest defenders of the real presence.

An attempt has been made by many writers of the

[1] In Gen. qu. 3.
[2] Dial. 2.
[3] "Ad Thras." lib. ii. c. 18.
[4] "De fide ad Petr." c. 3.

school now under review to neutralize such considerations as have just been presented by the creation of certain distinctions which are wholly verbal, and embody no corresponding conceptions. The word *superlocal* is one of these inventions, under which it is sought to convey the idea of the real presence as a body which is not locally present. But even the genius of Dr. Newman cannot entitle such expressions to respect. The superlocal presence of a body is a phrase which involves a self-contradiction, inasmuch as it excludes an essential property in the definition of body. There are but three conceptions which can be formed of the presence of body, and but three affirmations that can be made concerning that presence. It may be said to be present in its form and substance ; it may be said to be present in its influence ; and it may be said to be present both in its form and substance and in its influence. The sun is present in its form and substance in that place which it occupies in the heavens—it is present in its influence wherever its light and heat and attraction extend — it is present in its form and substance and influence together, only in the spot which is assigned to it among the other celestial bodies. Now with respect to the presence of the body of Christ exclusively as an *influence*, this is repudiated alike by Romanists and Ritualists as an insufficient explanation, but any other presence on earth is inconceivable and unrevealed.

As Bishop Bilson has said, with a rugged plainness which is characteristic of his writings : " That which entereth the body must be local and corporal. That which feedeth the soul must be spiritual and intellectual. The soul hath no local receipts, nor corporal instruments for her kind of eating, but only faith and understanding. So that if the flesh of Christ in this mystery be material and local, how can it feed the soul? If it be spiritual and intellectual, how can it be chammed with teeth, or closed in the straits of the stomach? Local, not local; corporal, not corporal, be plain contradictions, and by no means incident to the natural flesh of Christ. One it must needs be, both it cannot be, though you would sweat out your hearts with wrangling."

In order still further to facilitate the reception of the doctrine of the real presence as held by these writers, we are reminded that the body of our blessed Lord acquired new properties by its glorification, in virtue of which that is possible which otherwise would be impossible. The accession of new attributes to that body in virtue of its glorification is not denied, while at the same time it is reverently demanded whether the sacred writers afford us any hint that among these new attributes is that of being in any other place than heaven at any one indivisible instant of time. To expatiate in general terms upon the wonderful exaltation and increase of functions and powers which the Redeemer's body may have obtained through its glorification, is a dangerous procedure apart from explicit revelation, and such revelation as certifying such a presence we have not, but, as we have seen, the exact reverse.

Moreover, in what portion of the New Testament writings is the warrant found for the doctrine that it was the glorified body of our Saviour of which the bread and wine were either emblems or veils, significant symbols or communicating channels? Is it, or was it ever maintained by any Church, that our Lord's body was glorified on the night when He instituted the Supper? that it was glorified before the crucifixion and the resurrection? If the apostles partook of the true sacrament, it is manifest that it could not then be the sacrament of the *glorified* body, and if no sacrament is true but that which is a repetition of theirs, it cannot now be the sacrament of a *glorified* body. The sacrament was that of a body as broken, and of blood as shed, and therefore of a body sacrificed and dead; for with what reason can any one speak of a body literally broken, and blood literally shed, as the body and blood of one that is corporeally living, much less *glorified*? The imagination may wanton at will in the region of speculation as to the new and wonderful capacities which may be conceived as attaching to a body in its glorified state, but inasmuch as the original and typical sacrament instituted by our Saviour Himself was not and could not be the sacrament of His glorified body, all this theological refinement is but labour in vain.

More than one half of Mr. Wilberforce's volume on the holy Eucharist, and still more of Dr. Pusey's work on the real presence, would not have been written at all if due attention had been paid to the fact that no language can be found, either in the teaching of our Lord or of His apostles, which either affirms or justifies the inference that the body commemorated is the glorified body, or that the glorification of the body renders its objective presence possible on every altar throughout the world. The exposition which the apostle gives of the Supper is not, "For as often as ye eat this bread or drink this cup ye do show the glorified body of our Lord;" but, "Ye do show the Lord's *death* till he come." If therefore the body which is alleged to be on the altar be not the *dead* body of our Lord, it is not the body which is broken; and if it be the dead body, it cannot be the glorified body, which "dieth no more, and over which death hath no more dominion."

The theory of the presence of the glorified body was invented for the purpose of supporting the doctrine of the multipresence (to use a barbarous term) of the natural body of our Lord. Reason was affronted and outraged by the infinite contradictions which grew out of such an assumption as that of the multipresence, and hence recourse was had to the supernatural energies and powers supposed, and without proof, to be inherent in the glorified body. But the expedient has proved fatal to itself. It has destroyed the identity of the body now alleged to be offered by the priest with that body given by our Lord to His disciples, and has become a sacrificial commemoration of a body which cannot be sacrificed. By no subtlety of reasoning can this contradiction be either evaded or solved. If it be the dead body it cannot be at the same time the glorified body, and if it be the glorified body it cannot at the same time be the dead body. To cite the passages in which the Saviour announced His presence with His disciples,—" Where two or three are gathered together in his name," and "wherever his gospel should be preached, even unto the end of the world," is but to complete the perplexity; for it is to acknowledge that that presence is not restricted to the sacrament, but is pledged to those who unite in prayer, and who declare His truth. No writer with whom we are acquainted has refuted the doctrine of the glorified presence in the sacramental symbols with more directness and force than Bishop Andrewes, who says: "A live lamb is not it, it is a Lamb slain must be our Passover, Christ's body that now is. True—but *not* Christ's body *as* it now is, but as it then was when it was offered, rent and slain, and sacrificed for us. *Not as* now He is, glorified, for so He is not, so He cannot be *immolatus*, for He is immortal and impassible. But as He then was when He suffered death, that is, passible and mortal. We are carried back to Christ as He was at the very instant and in the very act of His suffering. By the incomprehensible power of His eternal spirit, not He alone, but He as at the very act of His offering is made present to us, and we incorporate into His death, and invested in the benefits of it. If an host could be turned into Him now, glorified as He is, it would not serve; Christ offered is it, thither must we look."[1]

[1] Sermon on the Resurrection.

LECTURE VI.

THE PRIEST AT THE ALTAR (CONTINUED): THE LORD'S SUPPER.

LECTURE VI.

THE PRIEST AT THE ALTAR (CONTINUED): THE LORD'S SUPPER.

THE two preceding lectures have been occupied in the consideration of those representations of the Lord's Supper which are taught by the Romish Church, and by such members of the Anglican Church as have practically adopted on this matter the canons and decrees of the Tridentine Council. The claims of the interpretation, which is vaunted as literal, have been subjected to a careful and patient examination, and have been evinced to be not only incapable of support, but in egregious disconsonance with the letter of Scripture. We have shown that the words of our Lord have been violently wrested from their natural signification; that an unauthorised meaning has been assigned to the word *body*, which, instead of expressing a conception understood by all, has been made to denote a metaphysical abstraction, a phantom of the imagination, having presence but no locality; nerves, bones, and sinews, but no magnitude; and substance divested of its ordinary and universally acknowledged accidents. It has been shown that no sense can be literal which first evacuates language of the import which it uniformly bears among the people to whom it is addressed, and that such has been the operation performed by the Romish Church upon the words of institution. In no language, ancient or modern; among no people, civilized or savage; in no form of literature, except such as has been created by the exigencies of the theory of Transubstantiation, did the word "body" as a designation of the human frame, whether that of Christ or of any other man, denote a substance apart from species or accidents, and of which it could be predicated that it had no relations to space. The dogma in question therefore holds warfare alike with Scripture, philosophy, and the common sense of mankind. We have shown that the words of institution not only afford no countenance to the sacrificial conception of the Lord's Supper, but absolutely preclude it; and also that with respect to the alleged real presence of the body of our Lord in the elements of the sacrament, it cannot be the presence of that very body in which He instituted the Supper, and of which He spoke as being broken, for that is subject to the restrictions of space; neither can it be the presence of His glorified body, for His body could not be glorified before as yet it had been sacrificed on the cross.

In concluding, with this lecture, the consideration of the sacerdotal view of the Lord's Supper, and the vindication of the definition which I have already given of the nature of the ordinance, it will be necessary to consider the element of propitiation, which both Romanists and certain Anglicans have imported into it; for, as we have seen, it has been defined, not only as a sacrifice, but as a propitiatory sacrifice, both for the living and the dead.

The history of the origin and growth of the sacrificial idea in connection with the Eucharist, is by no means difficult to trace. The circumstance out of which it was developed was simple and innocent. As early as Justin Martyr the words "sacrifice" and "offering" were applied to the feast, but then and for a considerable period afterwards without any conception of propitiation. They were applied to the contributions of bread and wine which the people brought, and out of which materials were taken for the sacred meal. These contributions were termed not only offerings ($\pi\rho o\sigma\phi o\rho\alpha\iota$), but also sacrifices ($\theta v\sigma\iota\alpha\iota$); but so far from such terms being designed to embody and inculcate a propitiatory conception, the very same terms (the latter most emphatically) were applied to the prayers and thanksgivings which were presented to God at the feast of communion. And as if to debar the gross and material interpretation which has been put on Justin's words, he declares, as we have seen, that "prayer and thanksgiving offered by the worthy are the only perfect and acceptable sacrifices ($\theta v\sigma\iota\alpha\iota$); and that these only have Christians received commandment to offer at the commemoration of their dry and wet food, in which they commemorate the sufferings that the Son of God endured for them."

Little by little, however, as priestly power and arrogance developed in the Church, these offerings of the people acquired a greater sanctity, until, at length, they were regarded as sacrifices in a more material sense, and finally became clothed with propitiatory efficacy, which converted the Eucharist into a service of expiation. And now it is common for the defenders of sacerdotalism to appeal to the sacrificial terms employed by Justin Martyr and Irenæus, for the purpose of establishing the antiquity of their view, overlooking the enormous change of meaning which these terms have meanwhile undergone; and not the terms alone, but the whole form and ritual of the eucharistic service, which, as celebrated in the Greek, Roman, and certain portions of the Anglican Churches, would not be recognised by those early Fathers as having aught but the faintest resemblance to the feast of commemoration as known by them.

But not even Justin Martyr and Irenæus are our ultimate appeal on this matter. They have a chronological value, in so far as they depose to the nature of the Eucharist as observed in their days, and to the views which they themselves held in common with their Christian brethren. Beyond this we owe them, and we pay them, no deference, on account of the rapidity with which corruption, both in doctrine and practice, crept into the Church, and that too mainly through the influence of those who were set for the defence of the apostolic faith.

It is but little to say that the propitiatory aspect of the Eucharist is destitute of all scriptural authority: it commits violence against both its letter and spirit, assailing, as will be seen, the transcendent value and sufficiency of that one offering whereby Christ hath perfected for ever them that are sanctified.

Strange indeed, and yet true as strange, that the most solemn Christian service, in which the faith, the reverence, the awe, the love, and even the ecstasy of the believer, is supposed to find its highest expression, should, if without intention, yet not the less really, dishonour the sacrifice of the cross. We have seen already that nowhere is the Lord's Supper termed in Scripture a "sacrifice"—it is almost needless to add that nowhere is it termed a "propitiation;" and this is the more extraordinary on the supposition that the conception itself were true, inasmuch as both the conception and the term were familiar enough to the minds of the apostles. Can the hypothesis be entertained for an instant that those inspired men, who were charged with the sacred function of expounding the mysteries of the kingdom of God, concealed that very aspect of the Eucharist which, if true, casts every other into the shade? For who would speak of "commemoration" if a "propitiation" were being offered? or how, in fact, could the same service be both in one?

The writer of the Epistle to the Hebrews, though concerned primarily with the exposition of the gospel in its relation to Judaism, which it abrogates not so much by statute as by fulfilment, supplying the antitype and substance of its types and shadows, precludes by anticipation the whole Romish doctrine of the Mass as a propitiatory sacrifice. It avails nothing for the Romanists to allege, as they do, that the epistle had a retrospective reference, and was meant merely to show that the functions and services of Judaism were practically abolished by the redemptive work of Christ. The doctrine of the epistle is absolute. It looks before as well as after. It fills in the whole sphere of vision with one propitiation, and that one propitiation once offered, and this shuts out alike the inventions of Rome and the provisional and temporary sacrifices of the ancient economy. By an elaboration amounting to repetition of this one idea, and by the emphasis which it lays upon the solitary but sublime fact of the Saviour's expiatory death, it leaves no room for any other propitiation, whether by Himself or any other person.

Prominence is given to the oneness of the Priest and the oneness of the propitiation. This Priest has an intransmissible priesthood. This Priest doth not offer oftentimes the same sacrifices. This Priest has entered heaven itself, now to be made manifest before the face of God for us. This Priest does not offer Himself often, as the high priest entereth into the holy place every year with the blood of others, for then it were necessary that He should oftentimes have suffered since the foundation of the world. This Priest now, once at the end of the world, hath been manifested for the putting away of sin by the sacrifice of Himself. The death of man is appointed once, and there is one judgment after death, and so this Priest, Christ our Lord, having been offered *once* to bear the sins of many, shall appear the second time without sin unto salvation to them that wait for Him. This Priest, "after he had offered one sacrifice for sins for ever, sat down at the right hand of God; from henceforth expecting till his enemies be made his footstool. For by one offering he hath perfected for ever them that are sanctified." And, finally, it is written of this Priest and of the all-sufficiency of His one propitiation, "Now where remission of these is, there is no more offering *for sin*."

It is impossible to conceive of any language being framed which should express with greater precision and force the one great truth, that a propitiation has been offered by the great High Priest of our profession, whose efficacy sums up and satisfies all the sacrifices of the ancient dispensation, and renders any future sacrifice an impertinence and a mockery. The same oblation which ended the types was also to debar repetitions of itself; for it would be indeed a marvellous thing if a new series of sacrifices were to take the place of those whose inefficiency as saving ordinances the writer had so strenuously asserted and so triumphantly proved. The glorious completeness of our Saviour's death would be compromised as much by sacrifices which affect to rehearse it, as by the continuance of those which prefigured it, and even more so;

for the typical sacrifices had been stamped with Divine authority, and might be continued through ignorance and misconception, but the offerings which assumed to repeat the propitiatory oblation of our Lord are unwarranted inventions, forbidden alike by the spirit and the letter of the New Testament. The session of Christ at the right hand of God after His one offering, once for all, and for all men, conveys in a manner the most sublime and impressive the truth that the stupendous sacrifice which through ages He had been contemplating, and for which He had been preparing, had at length reached its consummation. Hitherto He had as it were *stood*, the great Priest and Victim, ready to be offered up in the fulness of the times. But now He *sat down*, as one that rested from His toil and unknown agony, as one that contemplated with ineffable joy the completeness of His sacrificial work, which was incapable henceforth equally of supplement and repetition, and as one that was glorified with the glory which He had with the Father before the world was.

It will naturally awaken surprise that in the presence of evidence so abundant, emphatic, and unequivocal, any Church claiming the name of Christian, and acknowledging any deference to the authority of revelation, should make propitiatory sacrifice the chief feature of its ritual; and it may be inquired whether this is done in open defiance of the written Word, or whether some attempt is not made to find in it, at least, a semblance of support? It is not the manner of the Church of Rome to confess that any of its distinctive dogmas and practices have no other foundation than tradition or its own arbitrary decrees. Whatever truth there might be in such acknowledgment (and for the most part it would be absolutely true), there is always some endeavour to connect its teaching with the authority of the Bible, however extraordinary may be the principles of interpretation which it employs. It professes to find at least the seed of its doctrines and precepts in the Scriptures, content that tradition shall accomplish the work of full development. And yet, touching the majority of its distinctive tenets, its appeal to Scripture was made only after the tenets themselves had been adopted, inspiration being not their source, but their falsely alleged confirmation. This statement is strikingly illustrated in reference to the point in hand, the Church of Rome having discovered a support for its doctrine of the propitiatory sacrifice and its correlative officer, the priest, in Acts xiii. 1, 2, where we are informed that "as Barnabas, and Simeon that was called Niger, and Lucius of Cyrene, and Manaen, the foster brother of Herod the tetrarch, and Saul, ministered to the Lord, and fasted, the Holy Spirit said, Separate forthwith Barnabas and Saul for the work whereunto I have called them."

It is in the expression "ministered to the Lord" that the Mass is found, the original word being λειτουργούν-των, which is affirmed, and with truth, to be in the Greek Church a common technical term for the celebration of the Eucharist. We have, therefore, in the first place, five men who are distinctly called "prophets and teachers" transformed into priests, each and all at one time and in one place offering the propitiatory sacrifice of the Mass, and all this on the strength of the word λειτουργεῖν, which means to offer Mass! Was Epaphroditus then a priest offering Mass to Paul, because Paul calls him a λειτουργὸς (servant) to his need? And are the angels priests because they are termed God's ministers (λειτουργοὶ)? and do they perform Mass because they are called ministering spirits (λειτούργικὰ πνεύματα)? Or were the Gentiles supposed to be offering the sacrifice at the altar when they ministered to the Jews by their beneficence in carnal things (ἐν τοῖς σαρκίκοις λειτουργῆσαι)? or had the Philippians been offering Mass to the apostle when he speaks of their "ministration toward" him (πρὸς με λειτουργίας)? Or, finally, are kings or rulers clothed with sacerdotal power, by which they can offer the stupendous oblation, because they are called by the apostle servants of God (λειτουργοὶ γὰρ Θεοῦ εἰσιν)? In what manner the five prophets or teachers were ministering to the Lord the narrative is silent, though it is significant that Chrysostom, himself a Greek, and strongly imbued with sacerdotal sympathies and ambition, asks the question distinctly, What is this ministry? and answers it as distinctly "κηρυττοντων" (preaching the gospel); an exposition which, while I confess its doubtfulness, suffices to show that there is no *consensus patrum* in favour of the Romish interpretation?

It may seem a serious accusation against the doctrine of the Church of Rome, but I make it with due deliberation, that it practically denies all immediate efficacy, upon the condition and prospects of man, of the death of our Lord. It establishes a possibility, and nothing more. It is the first in a series of propitiations which all depend upon it, but without the offering of which it is destitute of all value. The one oblation upon the cross does not secure for man blessings which are to be appropriated through faith, and that alone; but it demands fresh oblations, through which its virtue is communicated and sealed. "It must be taught," says the Catechism of the Council of Trent, "that the sacred and holy sacrifice of the Mass is not a sacrifice of praise and thanksgiving only, or a mere commemoration of the sacrifice performed on the cross, but also a true propitiatory sacrifice, by which God is appeased and rendered propitious to us. If, therefore, with a pure heart, a living faith, and affected with an inward sorrow for our transgressions, we immolate and offer this most holy Victim, we shall, without doubt, obtain mercy of the Lord, and grace in the time of need; for so delighted is the Lord with the odour of this Victim, that, bestowing on us the gift of grace and repentance, He pardons our sins. Hence this usual prayer of the Church: 'As often as the commemoration of this Victim is celebrated, so often is the work of our salvation being done;' that is to say, through this unbloody Victim flow to us the most plenteous fruits of that bloody Victim." No language could more strikingly prove that, in the opinion of the Romish Church, the death of Christ upon the cross was not the one sufficient oblation accomplishing the atonement for the sins of the whole world; and nothing more is required to evince the unscriptural and paradoxical character of the theory in question than the following language from the same catechism: "We therefore confess that the sacrifice of the Mass is and ought to be considered one and the same sacrifice with that of the cross, for the Victim is one and the same, namely, Christ our Lord, who offered Himself once only a bloody sacrifice on the altar of the cross. The bloody and unbloody Victim are not two, but one Victim only, whose sacrifice is daily renewed in the Eucharist, in obedience to the command of our Lord: 'Do this in remembrance of me.' The priest is also one and the same Christ the Lord."

We are required, therefore, to believe in the perfect harmony of the following propositions, both with each other and the doctrine of Scripture. That our Saviour offered Himself once only a bloody sacrifice on the cross; that He offers Himself on every altar an unbloody sacrifice; that the unbloody sacrifice is the same as the bloody sacrifice; that while without shedding of blood there is no remission of sins, yet without shedding of blood there is remission of sins; that by His one offering He hath perfected for ever them that are sanctified, and that by His one offering alone none are perfected; that one and the same

Victim offered in sacrifice is not only once offered but oftentimes, and is immolated, though as unbloody it is incapable of immolation. The faith which can prove itself equal to the task of accommodating all the paradoxes involved in the dogma of Transubstantiation, will find no difficulty in the propositions just enumerated, but to a less capacious credulity they are absolutely incredible. The considerations already presented render unnecessary the further discussion of statements which are as revolting to the first principles of reason as they are at open issue with the repeated and unequivocal declarations of the Divine Word.

Rome, however, has no monopoly of these innovations upon Scripture. Phraseology is in vogue in the bosom of the Protestant establishment of our country, which embodies errors scarcely less grave than those which have been just exposed. For when the propitiatory nature of the Lord's Supper is not distinctly avowed, other language is employed which involves the same idea, while the ritual which has grown up in certain Churches is clearly intended to give it the most impressive scenic representation. Whence have come the phrases, "continuous sacrifice," "perpetual offering," "the continuation of the one sacrifice by the one priest"? They are not found in Scripture, nor is there any expression from which they can plead an adequate justification. "Offering," as applied to our Saviour's death, has in Scripture one definite meaning, and never any other; and to seek to expand it so as to include the nature of His present work in heaven, is a wanton tampering with the Divine Word. His offering of Himself was, according to apostolic teaching, confined to the act and fact of His death, and to that alone. Whatever relation His life might bear to His atonement and propitiation, it is never included in the term "offered." It contemplates neither what preceded His death, nor what followed it, whether on earth or in heaven. "He was once offered;" "he offered one sacrifice for sins;" "there is no more offering for sin." The offering of Christ was synonymous with the suffering of Christ. He could not offer Himself again without suffering again. He could not offer Himself perpetually without suffering perpetually. This fact the writer to the Hebrews sets at rest by one impressive declaration, viz., that Christ was "not to offer himself often, as the high priest entereth into the holy place every year with blood of others, for then it were *necessary* that he should oftentimes *suffer* since the foundation of the world." With what consistency, therefore, can writers who shrink from the assertion that Christ is suffering in heaven, dissolve the identity between the suffering and the offering of Christ, and thus set at naught the authority of inspiration.

Nothing can be more reprehensible than such language as the following: "St. John saw our Lord thus offering Himself, His death wounds still visible on His body." Now John saw no such "offering,"[1] and his

[1] Carter's "Doctrine of the Holy Eucharist," p. 14.

language expressly repels the interpretation. He saw a "lamb as it had been slain," that is, as it had been offered; and the very term ἐσφαγμένον prohibits the conception of its being a proceeding or continuous act of offering. This is indeed admitted by the same writer in another place, but he maintains still, in defiance of scripture language, "that He (Christ) is being gazed upon in heaven as a Person still offering Himself as a sacrifice." We must prefer the text to the gloss which is in contradiction of it. Christ is being gazed upon in heaven as a Person that *has been slain* or *offered*, and not as a Person still offering Himself as a sacrifice. Moreover, there is one significant expression in the Apocalypse which this writer has unaccountably overlooked, and the obvious interpretation of which would have protected him from the serious mistake into which he has fallen. The Lamb which John in vision saw was neither on an altar as a victim, nor before one as a priest, but was in "the midst of the throne," a position quite consistent with an offering of Himself once made, and possessing an infinite and eternal efficacy, but wholly incompatible with the conception of a continuous offering, that is, of a continuous suffering and death.

This employment of the language of Scripture in a sense of which Scripture knows nothing, is characteristic of all the writers of this Neo-Catholic school, and is partly the cause and partly the effect of that confusion of thought which is one of the most prominent features in all their productions. In his preface to the

"*Directorium Anglicanum*," the writer says: "To these considerations it may be added that there is one book of Holy Scripture—the Apocalypse—which reveals to us the ritual of heaven. That ritual is the normal form of the worship of the Christian Church. The full scope and burden of the Epistle to the Hebrews is this: that the law was a shadow of good things to come, and not the very image of the things; that in the law we have but a copy ($\dot{v}\pi o\delta\epsilon\iota\gamma\mu a$), but that in the gospel we have the object itself as in a mirror, the very image ($a\dot{v}\tau\dot{\eta}$ $\dot{\eta}$ $\epsilon\iota\kappa\dot{\omega}\nu$), the express image or stamp. The Jewish ritual was therefore a type or shadow of the ritual of heaven which would be hereafter, not as then existing, at least in the form it was to assume in the fulness of time. If the Jewish ritual had been a copy or pattern of things existing in heaven at that time, it would have been an image thereof, not a shadow or type. But 'coming events cast their shadow before,' and (it is written with reverence) the worship of heaven, always objective, became amplified, and, so to speak, ocularly objective (as God could be seen of man), when the hypostatic union took place; when bone of our bone, flesh of our flesh, was worshipped by the angelic host in the person of the Incarnate Word in His glorified humanity, at the right hand of God the Father Almighty. Moses was admonished when he was about to make the tabernacle. 'For see,' saith He, 'that thou make all things according to the pattern showed thee in the mount.' The Jewish ritual was the shadow cast upon earth from the throne of God of the worship which was to be in heaven after the incarnation and ascension of the God-Man, our Lord Jesus Christ, who pleads before the throne His sacrifice, at once the Victim, the 'Lamb as it had been slain,' and High Priest. The ritual of heaven is objective, and the principal worship of the Church on earth is equally so by reason of its being identical with the normal and apocalyptic ritual, and thus containing a great action, even the perpetuation of the sacrifice made on the cross, in an unbloody manner on the altar." [1]

The several statements contained in the above citation might justify a treatise, affording as they do a series of the most remarkable misapprehensions both of the function of the Apocalypse as a didactic book on Christian worship, and of the reasoning of the writer to the Hebrews. Are the expositions either of Christian doctrine or of worship which are found in the calm prose of the apostolic letters so obscure that they need to be interpreted by a book which by the consent of all divines in all ages is the most perplexing and incomprehensible? The subornment of the symbolism of the Apocalypse, in order to establish any ritual observance, ought at least to be made on some definite and consistent principle, and should not reveal an arbitrary eclecticism, which leaves us wondering quite as much at what is left as at what is taken. If the priest of modern times burns incense because the apocalyptic angel is said to have done the same, why does he not imitate the same angel when he fills his "censer with

[1] Pp. xi. xii. Preface.

fire of the altar, and casts it upon the earth," evoking "voices, and thunderings, and lightnings, and an earthquake"? Does the writer believe that the vision which John saw had a real, objective, historic existence in heaven, and that there was a material altar, a material censer, material incense, and that material fire was flung from heaven upon earth? Does he believe that beyond the vision itself there actually "stood in the midst of the throne, and of the four living creatures, and in the midst of the elders, a Lamb as it had been slain, having seven horns and seven eyes"? Does he believe that there were objective vials full of odours, and objective vials full of the "wrath of God"? He speaks of the ritual of heaven. Where is that ritual found as an unsymbolic order of worship, demanding that we interpret it after a literal fashion, and regard it as a heavenly scheme for earthly imitation? He speaks of the "normal and apocalyptic ritual," but do we not read in the same book that John saw no temple in heaven, and that its inhabitants "need no candle, neither light of the sun, for the Lord God giveth them light"? If the book of the Revelation is to be treated as a directory of the order of worship in the Church on earth, let its regulations be impartially cited, and it will be seen how impossible it is to translate them into a modern ritual.

When this same writer says that "the Jewish ritual was therefore a type or shadow of the ritual of heaven which would be hereafter," he is assuming as a fact that which rests on no evidence whatsoever, and he is overlooking the important truth that the writer to the Hebrews does not regard the Jewish economy and worship as a shadow of the Christian economy and worship, but as a shadow of the work of Christ. It is the many priests which are the shadow of the one Priest; the many sacrifices which are the shadow of the one Sacrifice; and the ritual or formal worship of the Christian Church is not once adverted to in the whole of his elaborate argument!

The view just presented by the writer in question serves, however, a special purpose in connection with the spectacular aspect of the Eucharist, which it is the determination of the Ritualists to assimilate more and more to that of the Romish Mass. It is their delight to represent the transactions of heaven and earth as corresponding with each other. Within the veil there is a continuous sacrifice offered by Christ, and without the veil there is a continuous sacrifice offered by Christ through His duly appointed priests. There is an unceasing propitiation in heaven, and there is an unceasing propitiation on earth, by which the celestial sacrifice is supposed to be commemorated, symbolized, represented, and applied. Not that the earthly is once more the type of the heavenly. It is this, and more. It is complementary and co-essential. As we have shown, the heavenly possesses, in their view, no practical efficacy, either on the soul of man or its destiny apart from the earthly. The priest therefore is as necessary as the Saviour, the Mass as the cross upon which our blessed Lord accomplished the one sufficient atonement for sin; and it is the assumed prerogative of the priest to determine, without right of protest on the part of the layman, whether he shall be permitted to partake of the sacrament which avowedly contains and communicates the body and blood of Christ. This is the doctrine of the Church of Rome, and it is rapidly becoming the doctrine of many of the priests in the Church of England.

I shall not indulge in the uncharitableness which would charge its advocates with a conscious travesty of the Divine Word, and with building up a system of sacerdotal assumptions and claims for the purpose of exercising a ghostly influence over their fellow-men. I shall not deny that, tremendous as these assumptions and claims may be, and disastrous as their influence has been upon the welfare of mankind, they have nevertheless been put forth by men of transcendent genius, and whose lives, for their self-denial and exhausting toil and devotion, have never been surpassed; but if charity imposes its obligations, so does the homage which I owe to truth. And this constrains me, in the light of the argument which has been just pursued, to declare with the utmost plainness of speech that the sacrificial and propitiatory view of the Lord's Supper is a gross perversion of the Divine Word; that the attempt to discover it in the Scriptures was an afterthought; that it derogates from the infinite sufficiency of the Saviour's death; that it practically assigns to the priest an authority which casts into distance and shadow the great High Priest, into whose presence and light it is the privilege of every child of God to enter, and thus renders the salvation of men contingent upon the *opus operatum* of one, the efficacy of whose sacerdotal acts depends upon the concurrence of a multitude of conditions, of the presence of all of which no communicant can be assured, and yet the absence of which would vitiate and nullify the whole sacrament.

It is true that out of this conception of the Divine Word has grown up a service which, if its fundamental error could be overlooked, is one of the most impressive spectacles in the world. Whatever human taste could suggest, or human art accomplish, has been combined for the purpose of investing with impressiveness and glory the celebration of this " tremendous sacrifice." Architecture has reared her noblest fanes; music has sung her choicest strains to subdue the soul with her sobbing *misereres* and to ravish it with her triumphant and ecstatic *glorias;* painting has filled her canvas with glowing Madonnas and with her crucifixions and entombments, her ascensions and her assumptions, and her heavenly coronations. Fabrics rich in colour as the rainbow, and symbolic of the succession of fasts and feasts, have formed the vestments of the priests; altars and crosses have blazed with gold and gleamed with precious stones, and every avenue of sense has been plied with its appropriate appeal and gratification; but as we behold the prostrate crowd before the elevated host, we cannot forget that Christ sitteth at the right hand of God, and that by His one oblation He hath "perfected for ever them that are sanctified."

Enough has been said with the view of exposing the unscriptural nature of the doctrine which invests the sacrament of the Lord's Supper with propitiatory efficacy, and I now proceed with as much of condensation as possible to complete the exposition of that definition of the ordinance which was given in the previous lecture. It was described "as a simple meal appointed by our Lord Himself, and enjoined upon His disciples as a monumental assurance and seal on His part of His infinite love as shown in His sacrificial death, and as a commemoration on their part of that same death, through the participation of its emblems of bread and wine."

This definition recognizes what has been too much obscured in some Churches, the Divine aspect of the sacrament. It is appointed by our Lord. It is not an observance originating in the gratitude and love of the followers of Christ, a merely apostolic custom handed down from generation to generation. Whatever institutions may exist in the Church, which owe their sole authority to the faith and affection of the Church, this is not one of them. Like the Passover, which, as we have seen, suggested some of its forms, it bears the mark and seal of Divine appointment, and its significance can never be fully apprehended so long as it is regarded purely from the subjective side—as if it were instituted by the Church itself, as a medium for the expression of its adoring love, and not instituted by Christ for the expression of His love, and for its commemoration by all His followers till He come.

It is easy to conceive that the disciples of our Lord, if left to themselves, might have devised some act of remembrance, festive, or in some other form. It would not have been strange, indeed, if they had observed from year to year the very night in which He was betrayed, while it would have been strange if with, or without, some memorial observance, they had forgotten it. They were in no danger of such oblivion, nor was the Supper appointed in the view of any such peril. Even apart from its existence altogether, it is inconceivable that they should forget Him in whose fellowship they had found their highest joy, from whose lips they had learned the noblest wisdom, and from whose death they were to obtain the hope of eternal life. Though there had been no feast of commemoration, they would still have been His apostles—would have preached the gospel—would have wrought miracles—would have confronted their adversaries with unblenching fortitude and faith, and would have welcomed the sufferings and the crown of martyrdom. Other things and persons might fade from their memory, but their Saviour never, so long as that faculty retained its power or their hearts their love. They might have felt wounded at the misgiving which such an ordinance insinuated as to their fidelity, if they had regarded it as nothing but a help to a precarious or faithless recollection. And if their love could die, and with it the fond remembrance of their Lord, no sacrament could rekindle its life: the fatal mischief would lie deeper than it is given to any outward ordinance to reach.

But the Supper was not grounded on any such distrust. The Saviour had no fear of being forgotten, but He yearned that He should be rightly remembered as One whose death was the life of apostles and of all who should believe on His name. The Supper becomes thus a historic objective monument, witnessing to all generations the fact of His Divine and unquenchable love for man, a love infinite in its degree and special in its quality, as it was the only love which could shed its blood for the remission of sins. It becomes thus embodied among the unquestionable historic verities of the world. In itself it declares perpetually a fact which is largely independent of the views which men may entertain touching the person of Christ, or the nature of His mission and work. These views may be conflicting and changeful, but so long as the sacrament of the Lord's Supper is observed, and the records which contain the circumstances of its original institution are preserved and accepted, it will be impossible to deny that it had its origin in a Divine command; that that command was the expression of a love which passeth knowledge; and that that love was one which, by death, laid the foundation for the redemption of man. The sacrament is therefore primarily an institutional enshrinement and demonstration of the love of Christ. It is a declaration embodied not in a sentence, but a rite. It stands before the eyes of the Church and the world a sublime column, inscribed with characters of mercy that are ineffaceable, announcing the Lord's death till He come. No language can be too strong which gives adequate and impressive emphasis to the truth that the sacrament of the Lord's Supper was not the outburst of the enthusiastic affection of the apostles, but was the appointment of their Saviour, and comes therefore clothed with an authority which pertains to all His commands. His love to them—their love to Him—this is the order of the conceptions which underlie the ordinance, and the former abides unchangeable, embalmed in the testimony of a positive institution, though the latter should lose its fervour or die. The sacrament will remain a witness and a warning, even if its participators should eat and drink unworthily.

This view of the Eucharist, objective and heavenly, is one which, while it has not been ignored, has been largely obscured in some representations of the commemorative theory which have regarded the ordinance too exclusively from its subjective side. It is the extreme antithesis to that other theory which has almost lost the spiritual commemoration in the reiterated propitiatory oblation, while it has furnished too much ground for the objection that any other service of commemoration would have set forth with equal impressiveness the sublime and sacred relationship which Christ sustains toward man. There are other seasons and other services in which the Christian remembers his Lord. He reads of Him in His Word; he presents his prayers in His name; he celebrates His work and glory in his hymns of praise; he makes Him the subject of his hallowed meditation when his heart burns within him, and he feels in his solitude least alone. But all these seasons and forms of commemoration are specifically different from that of the Eucharist, in which not only does man *think* of Christ, but Christ *speaks* to him, and *speaks* through emblems which set forth the fact that the redemption of man is accomplished by the death of Christ, and that the life of man is sustained by a believing communion with Him.

In the definition which I have given of the Eucharist, I have spoken of it as a monumental assurance on the part of Christ of His *sacrificial death*, and it is this characteristic to which the Saviour gives striking prominence in His own exposition, " This is my blood of the new covenant, shed for many for the remission of sins." It is impossible by any fair principles of interpretation to eliminate from these words the fact which places the death of Christ beyond the category of the deaths by which other prophets and reformers have sealed their testimony with their blood. It is to His death, and to that alone, that the Saviour here calls the attention of His disciples. It is this, and this alone, which He expressly requires them to commemorate. His life they could not forget. The years of their fellowship with Him could never fade from their memories. His wondrous miracles, His gracious words, His unselfishness, conspicuous in every act of His life, His unconquerable patience, His matchless tenderness to sinners, combined with His unsparing condemnation of sin, would live within them and become glorified in memory with the flow of years. But it was not to His life—the only perfect life the world has ever known—that He here gives prominence and makes allusion. He was in the penumbra of that darkness which deepened until He died, and it was His death, not His example or His teaching, that now filled His soul.

Nor was it His death alone, but His death as having special relation to the *forgiveness of sins*. In the words in which He expounded the nature and purpose of His death, He seems to sum up the scattered allusions to the same event which had fallen incidentally from His lips during the three years of His public ministry. He had spoken of Himself as the Good Shepherd that layeth down His life for the sheep; whose life no man took from Him, but who laid it down of His own accord, and of His own accord took it again; as one who had come, not to be ministered unto, but to minister, and to give His life a ransom for many; as having a baptism to be baptised with, and being straitened till it was accomplished. Throughout His life the shadow of His death upon the cross was projected to His feet, and invaded even the effulgent glories of the Mount of Transfiguration; and now, when He might well be supposed to give supreme prominence to that aspect of His mission which sustained the most wide, deep, efficacious, and abiding relations to the immortal interests and destinies of man, he isolates and emphasises the fact of His death.

To denominate His death a martyrdom is to rob it of its specific function and meaning, and this, too, in the face of His own exposition and of the teaching of His apostles in after days. All martyrdoms by which fidelity to truth, or to that which may be misapprehended for truth, is sealed, are of equal value. They all proclaim the homage of conscience to an authority regarded as supreme, and nothing more. In this respect the martyrdoms of Socrates, John the Baptist, James, Paul, Polycarp, and Hooper, are on the same level with that of the Lord Jesus Christ; while in respect to their fortitude, their calmness, or even triumph, they stand in striking and favourable contrast with it.

Though it has been said that the blood of the martyrs is the seed of the Church, it is not the death of martyrs that has finally given them their chief moral power over mankind. When martyrs have not only been sincere, but have also been heroes for the truth, whether the truth of science, politics, or religion, the scenes which most enchant succeeding generations are those in which whilst living they have done battle with error and established traditions. True, there is an irresistible pathos connected with their dying hour, but that fills but a small space in the memories of mankind compared with the truths which they held aloft with unflinching determination amid the obloquy, the scorn, and the persecutions of their contemporaries.

Around Paul, as he unveiled the unknown God before the Athenian idolaters on Mars' Hill, and as he confronted Felix, and filled him with terrors, when he reasoned of righteousness, temperance, and a judgment to come — there gathers a deeper interest than is created by his martyrdom in Rome. It is not to his death, as such, that we look as the event which will bring to him any accession of influence over his fellow-men, least of all do we regard it as that supreme moment which will give him his chief claim upon the admiration of the world. His death terminates his active usefulness, and henceforth his writings and labours alone survive as the undecaying powers by which succeeding generations are to be progressively raised to fellowship with God through Jesus Christ. It is to these forces, set in motion while the apostle was living, and not created by his death, that the world owes mainly the influence which the apostle has exerted, his death giving emphasis to his faith and sincerity, and little more.

But these considerations lose their value, if not wholly, yet in great measure, when applied to the death of Christ. That was never regarded by Himself, nor after His resurrection by the apostles, as the termination of His beneficent work. His death was the crown and consummation of the whole. He was to be lifted up, that whosoever believeth in Him should not perish, but have everlasting life; and it was because He was lifted up that He should draw all men unto Him. It is around His death that the chief interest gathers, not in despair, as if it would put a disastrous end to His usefulness, but in grateful and triumphant joy, because He shall make His soul an offering for sin. It is this event as a new power, the power of God unto salvation, which constitutes the great theme of the New Testament, and which transforms what would otherwise be a martyrdom into a sacrifice and a propitiation. In other deaths the active beneficence of martyrs succumbed and expired. In this death it reached its climax, opening for the repentant malefactor and for all believers the door of the kingdom of heaven. In what sense, indeed, consistent with the ordinary laws of thought and language, could any martyr be said to have shed his blood for the remission of sins? None of whom we read, with the exception of our Saviour, ever pretended that his death would sustain such relation. Few of them indeed everanticipated death as a violent termination of their teaching and toil. It came as an abrupt and unexpected outrage, and not, as in the instance of our Lord, as an event minutely predicted in its circumstances, and expounded beforehand in its scope and efficacy. The death of other martyrs revealed and aggravated the sins of men, but the death of Christ not only revealed and aggravated the sins of those who took Him, and with wicked hands crucified and slew Him, but laid the foundation for their forgiveness, and was designed to accomplish this end.

No interpretation which seeks to attenuate the expression, "remission of sins," by regarding it as denoting simply the subjective influence of our Saviour's death upon the heart of man, can be regarded as sufficient. For not only must we ask how it happens that such subjective influence is not claimed for other martyrdoms equally sincere, and in their outward circumstances more heroic and unflinching, but we must urge that the remission of sins is that forgiveness which, in the Lord's Prayer and in the parable of the King and the two Fellow-servants, "forgives debts" —an act of grace which is surely wholly objective.

The first, the most prominent, but not the only aim of the death of Christ, was accordingly the "forgiveness of sins;" and on this account His death occupied an exceptional and unparalleled position as the one solitary propitiation, whose efficacy, alike in relation to the government of God and the eternal destinies of mankind, entitled it to an institutional and commemorative permanence in the Church until the Lord should come. No other event of His history has He commanded us to celebrate by any special ordinance whatsoever. Neither His wonderful nativity, nor His baptism in Jordan, nor His transfiguration on Hermon, nor His triumphant entry into Jerusalem, nor His ascension into heaven, is commemorated by an institution expressly appointed by Himself. This unique honour is reserved for that death which was symbolized by bread and wine, and by bread and wine which were not displayed on the table as visible emblems, to be simply gazed at as significant tokens of a broken body and of shed blood, but which were to be partaken, because, as elements that nourish the outward man, they set forth the need of that higher spiritual nourishment for the soul which was to be found in the believing participation of Christ. It is not necessary that I should add more touching that portion of the definition already given which asserts the sacrificial character of the Saviour's death, and I must leave wholly out of view such considerations as would demand a place in a treatise on the Atonement. I have restricted myself to such brief and incidental presentation of the subject as the exposition of the words of our Lord seemed to require.

It is therefore as a historic monument of the sacrificial death of Christ that the ordinance was instituted, and it is as such that it is to be commemorated. As the monument is not the death, so neither, as we have already seen, is the commemoration a sacrifice. One of the earliest designations of the Eucharist, and that too a designation which ought by anticipation to have rendered impossible that stupendous sacerdotal development which it has attained both in the East and West, is the breaking of bread. With such a name, a propitiatory sacrifice has no affinity. They in fact reciprocally exclude each other. We are informed in Acts ii. 42, that the converts "continued steadfastly in the apostles' doctrine and fellowship, and in breaking of bread, and in prayers." The application of this passage to the Eucharist has been questioned by some writers, but with insufficient reasons, and those mainly of a controversial and strategic kind, in order to wrest from Rome an argument for communion only in one kind. Nothing, however, but a strained interpretation can fairly deny that in Acts xx. 7 the breaking of bread is the Eucharist. "And upon the first day of the week, when the disciples came together to break bread, Paul preached unto them, ready to depart on the morrow;" and the expression which the apostle employs in the First Epistle to the Corinthians, "the bread which we break," confirms the conclusion that it bore allusion to the sacred meal. The attempt of the Romanists to build on this designation an argument in favour of their mutilated communion is manifestly suicidal; for if it be inferred from the circumstance that no mention is made of wine, that the sacrament was administered without it, it must of necessity have been consecrated without it, a fact which, according to the teaching of that Church, would vitiate the whole service. It would also follow that Paul himself, or whoever on that occasion consecrated the bread, and was therefore in Romish phrase the celebrant, received the communion but in one kind, a position equally in conflict with the doctrine of the integrity of the Mass. It is clear that the phrase, "the breaking of the bread," is an instance of a common figure of speech, which designates the whole by a part, and acquires at length a definite technical force. Another name by which the Eucharist is designated is the Lord's Supper (κυριακὸν δεῖπνον); as when the apostle says (1 Cor. xi. 20), "When ye come together into one place, this is not to eat the Lord's supper." The application of this passage to the Eucharist has been called in question by many Roman Catholic writers, but a dispassionate consideration of the context will show that no other than the sacramental interpretation will harmonize with the drift of the apostle. He is rebuking the Corinthians for their disorder. He tells them that the meal of which they partake is *not* the Lord's Supper; that is, whatever it may pretend to be, it does not correspond in fact with that Supper which the Lord appointed. It was a selfish and unseemly banquet, destitute of all reverence and brotherly consideration. To allege that the meal in question was only the Agape, and did not even assume to be the Lord's Supper, is to destroy the relevancy and force of the apostle's argument; for why should he enter upon an articulate statement of what he had received from the Lord, as to the nature and form of the ordinance, if he did not mean to reprobate the corruptions by which the Corinthians had degraded and defiled it? To give a picture of one thing, in order to correct what does not pretend to be the same thing, is a species of logic to which the apostle was never addicted.

The elements employed in this Supper were bread and wine, and these alone, materials which, in their simplicity and commonness, harmonise with the whole spirit of the Saviour and the genius of that dispensation which He founded. These were set apart by thanksgiving and prayer, but remained in their essential quality the same as before. They acquired a new meaning and nothing more, retaining the names, in the very act of being eaten and drunk, which they held previous to the prayer of the Lord. They possessed the same properties for the nourishment of the body as ever, without addition or modification, nor did they acquire any spiritual attribute by which they could affect either the substance or the moral condition of the soul. From the opinions afterwards propounded by some of the Fathers, that the consecrated elements became charged with the power of imparting immortality, I must express the strongest dissent, as well as from the inflamed and reckless rhetoric in which the great majority of them were in the habit of indulging when speaking of this simple meal. In their calmer moods their language is unexceptionable, but their calmer moods, as evidenced by their writings, would seem to have visited them but seldom; and it has been a sore mischief that subsequent ages have chilled and hardened their tropical rhetoric into the rigid stiffness and precision of logical forms. The same Fathers who have expended their exuberant wealth of imagery upon the wonderful efficacy possessed by the consecrated elements, have also alleged that " baptism, or the baptismal water, is red, when once it is consecrated, by the blood of Christ; that " in baptism we are dipped in blood;" that " the Ethio ian eunuch was baptised in the blood of Christ;" that "the flesh of Christ is eaten and His blood drunk in the laver of regeneration;" that "the water of baptism is the water which flowed out of Christ's side at His Passion;" and in the same tumid fashion they have celebrated the wonders of the sacred oil and the altar of stone. Extravagance like this, even in the fervour of impassioned devotion, is indefensible, and could not have been indulged in if its authors had been more careful to preserve the form and spirit of the original ordinances themselves.

The due recognition of the fact that the elements of the Lord's Supper, after the so-called consecration, are but bread and wine, would have rendered impossible the alleged mystery and the untold abuses of the Mass.

The representation which, in common with many others, I have given of the Lord's Supper, has been regarded and denounced as a fearful depravation and impoverishment of the sacrament, robbing it of that impressiveness and ritual glory with which it has been invested by many of the Churches of Christendom. But this objection I hold as of little moment, so long as the simplicity of the ordinance can be vindicated in the light of apostolic authority. An ordinance as left by our Lord Himself, and as observed by His apostles and the Churches under their care, can lack no impressiveness which is inherent in its essence and avowed purpose. The impressiveness of the Supper cannot be rendered greater than it was at first, except by adjuncts, the influence of which requires to be carefully analysed, lest, from being spiritual, it become wholly sensuous and deceptive. It is easy, with the resources of musical and decorative art, to surround any ceremony, whether religious or civic, with a spectacular splendour which captivates the imagination, and, for the time, subdues or elevates the feelings; but the evanescence of results thus produced is proof enough of their impotence to effect any abiding moral impressions upon the heart and life. The social, moral, and religious condition of Italy and Spain, where scenic grandeur and solemnity in the celebration of the Mass have had uninterrupted sway for centuries, yields but a doubtful verdict in favour of those human accretions which have converted the Lord's Supper into a drama. In the presence of all that splendour, with its help, or in spite of it, these nations have sunk to the lowest condition among the nations of Europe that profess in any form the Christian faith. There are other elements, I know, that cannot be overlooked as having contributed to this result, but the Mass has been found powerless, at least, to arrest this mournful corruption and decay.

But I do not concede the truth of the allegation that the account which I have given of the Lord's Supper is a depravation and impoverishment of the sacrament. In what sense can it be thus designated? Is it a trifling thing to eat bread and drink wine, which, in accordance with the Saviour's request or command, have acquired a special and sacred import? Is it a trifling thing to partake of them in the presence of Him whose eyes are as flames of fire, and to profess, as we eat and drink, that we have been renewed by the Spirit, cleansed by His blood, and have consecrated ourselves to Him? Is it a trifling thing if our profession be insincere, and our lives consciously profane, or worldly and sensual, to take as from His hands, wearing the scars of an infinite agony, the emblems which He has appointed to be at once the expression of His love to us and of our gratitude to Him? Could the desecration and impiety be at all intensified if the elements were, according to the Romish view, the shrines and vehicles of the Saviour Himself? The participation of symbols which have a constituted meaning, understood alike by Christ and the communicant, in a spirit wholly alien from the truths and facts of which they are representative, is an acted insincerity and falsehood which nothing could aggravate. It does not require a spiritual mind to qualify a man to partake of the host. This, both according to the Romish and the Neo-Catholic view, is received alike by the devout and the undevout. Christ is there in an absolute and objective manner, and is manducated by sinner and by saint. But in the Supper, as set forth in the New Testament, there is no participation by the insincere communicant of aught but the bread and wine, for the spiritual conditions are lacking which alone can enable a soul to hold vital and fruitful fellowship with the Saviour. The depravation and impoverishment of the

Eucharist pre-eminently attach to those theories according to which a real reception may be wholly mechanical, neither demanding faith as a condition nor imparting it as a benefit.

It will be impossible to close the consideration of the nature of the Lord's Supper without glancing at some other accretions by which it has been disguised and perverted, and which have acquired in the estimation of some Churches a sanctity equal to that of the simple ritual as left by our Lord. They are, however, nothing more than ecclesiastical inventions, not only unsupported by apostolic practice, but at direct variance with it.

The Church of Rome, for example, in its catechism enjoins the practice of fasting, and alleges that it is not lawful to consecrate or partake of the Eucharist after food or drink, for this reason; because the "custom introduced wholesomely by the apostles, as ancient writers have recorded, was perpetually retained and preserved, that it should be taken only by persons fasting." This attempt to invoke apostolic example for the custom in question is but another of those audacious asseverations upon which the Church of Rome mainly rests. Of the introduction of this "wholesome" practice by the apostles, there is not the faintest trace, but, on the contrary, we have the historic certainty that when the Supper was first instituted it was after the Paschal meal; and as we must presume that our adorable Redeemer knew what was in harmony and what in dissonance with the sacredness of the Supper, we must regard the Romish observance as the meddlesome and unauthorised traditions of men. If fasting be an essential precondition of the right participation of the Eucharist, it must have been so at its inauguration, when, as we have seen, there was not a fast, but a feast.

The prominence which has been assigned to fasting in connection with the Eucharist, has undoubtedly arisen from the gross conceptions which have been formed of the doctrine of the real presence, and from the repugnance which has been felt at the amalgamation of the body of our Saviour with ordinary food. But it must again be maintained that such a conception would have no place in His mind who instituted the meal, and that too in immediate connection with the Paschal supper. He knew better than any of His disciples, and better than His Church in subsequent ages, what were the conditions upon which the efficacy of the sacrament depended; and in the light of His own practice, and therefore of His own authority, we set at naught the sacerdotal devices by which these are contravened. But if the devices in question are in the teeth of the original institution, they are equally opposed to the incontrovertible fact that in the Corinthian Church the Lord's Supper was preceded by the Agape, or feast of charity, in which, according to its original conception, the brethren sat down together at a social board, without distinction of rank or wealth. And though this preliminary feast and the Lord's Supper became at length the scene of flagrant disorders which the apostle severely reprehended, he does not employ what, according to the Church of Rome and her modern sympathisers, would have been the most decisive method of rebuke. He does not remind them that the Lord's Supper is to be partaken fasting, and He neither commands them to abandon the Agape nor to postpone it to the Eucharist. The importance which is attached to early morning communion arises in great measure from the same assumed necessity for taking the Mass with unbroken fast. But while I do not insist upon any inflexible rule as to the time of communion, and believe that that is left to the decision and convenience of each particular Church, I must insist on the fact that the original feast was not in the morning, but in the evening, and that if the highest precedent is to constitute a law, it must reverse the regulation of the Church of Rome.

In considering the various ecclesiastical customs which have been associated with the sacrament of the Lord's Supper, it is impossible to omit all reference to the posture of the communicants, and especially as the practice of Nonconformist Churches has in this respect been subjected to severe and unmerited censure. This practice has been charged with irreverence, and with evincing a serious misconception of the awful import of the Eucharist. But with what propriety or truth does such an allegation come from any persons who are not prepared to affirm the supremacy of tradition above the unquestionable authority of revelation itself? Repeating the principle which I have already advanced, that nothing can be essential to the sacrament which was not found to belong to it at its first appointment, and in the times of the apostles, it is indubitable that the position of our Saviour and His disciples was not that of kneeling, but of reclining. This was their position when the Saviour took bread and wine, and blessed, and gave to His disciples; and it was their position when they ate and drank the emblems of His love. Not only is no mention made of kneeling, but such an attitude is inconsistent with the whole narrative. Now, sitting in these days corresponds with reclining in the days of our Saviour. The former position is as reverent as the latter, and if the latter were consistent, as it must have been, with that devout and also grateful homage which was due to the Lord, who then inaugurated the commemorative meal, the former is equally consistent now. The charge of irreverence with which it has been branded mounts higher still, and implicates not only the apostles, but their Lord. Let not my purpose in these remarks be misunderstood. I am not accusing those Churches which have adopted the practice of kneeling with having thus corrupted the essential nature of the Lord's Supper. I am simply claiming that if in the details of the ordinance other Churches choose to swerve, for what they may deem sufficient reasons, from the forms which were incontrovertibly observed on the night when our Lord was betrayed, those Churches which respect these forms shall not incur the censure of profanation or irreverence. If any practice requires vindication, it is not that which conforms to a Divine precedent, but that which departs from it. Of other practices which obtain in some of the Churches of Christendom in connection with the Eucharist, such as the sign of the cross, prayers for the dead, and reservation of the host, I need not speak; for whatever *traditio apostolica* may be pleaded for them, it rests on no Scriptural authority, but is opposed alike to its letter and spirit.

The Lord's Supper is an ordinance designed for the Church, that is, for those who have received the Lord Jesus Christ as their Saviour, and who have consecrated themselves to Him. It is a feast of communion with Him, and with each other, because with Him. They partake of one body, and they are one body; they dwell in Him, and He in them, and they are members one of another. In the presence of the one Lord and the emblems of the one sacrifice, all distinctions melt away. There is neither barbarian, Scythian, bond nor free, rich nor poor, king nor subject, but Christ is *all* and in *all*. As there is one Lord, one faith, one baptism, so there is one loaf and one cup, before which all animosities and discords are to be healed and hushed, and one Divine peace fill all hearts. And this ordinance, thus speaking of the reconciliation of God with man by the death of Christ, is to be perpetuated in the Church through all ages until He come. To that glorious event the eyes and hearts of His disciples are yearning with passionate ardour as to the consummation of their highest hopes, when the sacrament that commemorates shall fade from view amid the glories of that heavenly banquet at which all the ransomed shall be gathered from all times and nations, and the Lord Himself in visible majesty shall feast them for evermore.

LECTURE VII.

THE PRIEST AND THE CONFESSIONAL.

LECTURE VII.

THE PRIEST AND THE CONFESSIONAL.

UPON no claim have the sacerdotalists insisted with greater emphasis and strenuousness than upon their possession of a distinct and exclusive commission to "retain and remit sins;" and there is no prerogative which has enabled them to wield a mightier, a more subtle, and a more disastrous and enslaving influence upon the nations of Europe. Associated with auricular confession, which has become, in fact, its necessary complement and correlative, it constitutes one of the seven sacraments of the Romish Church; "the second plank" (*secundam tabulam*), as it was figuratively designated by Jerome,[1] and it has been openly revived and defended by one of the writers of the "Tracts for the Day." "There is," he says, "none of the sacraments whose power and authority, as well as whose efficacy, is so strongly questioned, and in a great measure denied in our branch of the Church, as that of Absolution; yet there is not one of them that has its power and authority more strongly set forth, and more plainly stated in her offices. It is a matter well

[1] "Epist. ad Demetr."

worthy of note that when the divines of the sixteenth century rearranged the sacramental offices, they purposely left out the significant action of giving the paten and the chalice into the hands of the ordained priest, as symbolical of his receiving authority to offer the great sacrifice, together with the words conferring that authority, but they retained those which conferred the power of remitting and retaining sins. Whether the omission was wise and advisable, we are not now concerned to inquire; but we are concerned with the fact that there is nothing more clear in the whole office of ordination than that the power of absolution, the authority to forgive sins, is committed to every ordained priest. It is only by putting a manifestly non-natural sense on the words used, that they can mean anything else than that every ordained priest in his ordination receives power to forgive sins. And, indeed, a very little reflection will enable us to see that not only is this in the strictest accordance with the institution of Christ, as given us in the New Testament, but is absolutely necessary for the very purposes for which the Church was founded."[1]

The first tract in this remarkable series is occupied with the subject of priestly absolution, which it avowedly, and even ostentatiously, treats upon a scriptural basis; and as it seems to contain an argument which is designed to be exhaustive, I shall proceed to test the strength of its reasoning in the light of that revelation to which it so confidently appeals. Of the candour

[1] "Tracts for the Day," p. 152.

which distinguishes its citations and inferences, I shall say nothing at present, but leave the reader to form his own dispassionate judgment as the evidence unfolds itself in detail. The writer affirms that "under the law and the gospel the term 'confession' had a fixed technical signification, referring to what is commonly called 'auricular confession' (p. 10); and that auricular confession was ordered by God when He instituted the law, and it was practised by the chosen people to the time of Christ's coming" (p. 11).

This is the thesis, which has the advantage of being stated in bold and unambiguous language. It is always, however, unlucky to stumble at the threshold, and the first instance in proof is curiously wide of the mark, and cannot be made to reach it except by a process of straining which would do violence to the whole nature of evidence. "We read," he says, "in the law: 'The Lord spake unto Moses, saying, Speak unto the children of Israel, When a man or woman shall commit any sin that men commit, to do a trespass against the Lord, and that person be guilty; they shall confess their sin which they have done: and he shall recompense his trespass with the principal thereof, and add unto it the fifth part thereof.'[1] 'And if he do not utter it, then he shall bear his iniquity.'[2] The chapter continues with directions to the priest as to the kind of sacrifices, and amount of satisfaction for different sins. So also in Leviticus: 'It shall be, when he shall be guilty in one of these things, that he shall confess

[1] Num. v. 5-7.   [2] Lev. v. 1.

that he hath sinned in that thing: and he shall bring his trespass offering unto the Lord for his sin which he hath sinned'"[1] (p. 11).

Now the chapter from which the first testimony is adduced supplies even a superfluous refutation of the assumption that we have here the institution even in rudiment or shadow of auricular confession. The case in question is one which has manifest reference to property, and the trespass involves an overt violation of civil rights; and the confession is not stated to be to the priest any more than to the people, or to the man who has been the victim of the offence. "They shall confess their sin," is the simple statement of the sacred writer, and there is not a film of evidence that the confession was of a private and auricular character in the ears of a priest.

As to the circumstance which occupies the remaining portion of the fifth chapter of Numbers, namely, the conjugal infidelity of a wife, she is brought to the priest by her own husband, upon whom "the spirit of jealousy has come;" but she is not brought for the purpose of confession, but for the sake of undergoing the process of testing by a supernatural ordeal.

The next citation which the writer has given—"And if he do not utter it, then he shall bear his iniquity"—is another proof of the undiscriminating carelessness with which some of the modern defenders of sacerdotalism seize upon the most irrelevant evidence, and press it into service. It was needful but to give the citation

[1] Lev. v. 5, 6.

in full in order to supply the most convincing answer to the assumption which the essayist is seeking to maintain. "And if a soul sin, and hear the voice of swearing, and is a witness, whether he hath seen or known of it; if he do not utter it, then he shall bear his iniquity."[1]

Here we have neither priest nor auricular confession, but an open court with spectators, and we have a witness who possesses information, whether by actual observation or otherwise, that a certain sin has been committed by another, and who suppresses the evidence. The expression, "voice of swearing," קוֹל אָלָה, which is rendered by the Septuagint φωνὴν ὁρκισμοῦ, or voice of adjuration, does not relate to the obligation of informing against a common swearer, but to the case of a person who is adjured by the civil magistrate to answer upon oath, and who refuses to declare what he knows upon the subject. The essayist discovers in the word נָגַד, to declare, a "fixed technical signification," the existence of which is certainly not established by any evidence he has yet produced. He substitutes a priest for a magistrate or judge; secrecy for an open court; auricular confession for a formal deposition of testimony, which all could hear, and which was demanded in the interests of public justice; and it is by such unsifted precedents, alike in the teeth of etymology and inspired narrative, that he seeks to uphold modern sacerdotalism.

The writer fares no better in his allusion to the con-

[1] Lev. v. 1.

fession which David made to Nathan, when he said, "I have sinned against the Lord" (p. 11). Indeed, the whole paragraph in which he treats of this incident is characterised by its blunders, alike in facts and in the reasoning founded upon them.

"This confession," he says, "was therefore an authorised institution of the law; and it is of this which the Old Testament writers speak when they mention confession. Though made through the priest, it was made to God; and as God spake to the people through the prophet, so did He hear them through the priest. The Protestant seems to believe that when such an expression occurs in Scripture as 'I will acknowledge my sin unto thee, and mine unrighteousness have I not hid. I said I will confess my sins unto the Lord,' it proves that confession to a priest is not required by God, forgetting that David, who used those words, actually made that confession through Nathan, saying, 'I have sinned against the Lord;' and that when he adds in the psalm, 'And so thou forgavest the iniquity of my sin,' he received that absolution mediately through the prophet. 'The Lord also hath put away thy sin'" (p. 12).

Had the writer forgotten when he penned these words that the subject of his treatise was, "Priestly absolution, scriptural"? Now Nathan was not a priest, and never, so far as we can learn, exercised any specifically priestly function. He was a prophet, as the essayist himself acknowledges. But what had David to do with a prophet, instead of a priest, when he was making confession of sin? Has not the defender of auricular confession just announced the neat antithesis, that "as God spake to the people through the prophet, so did He hear them through the priest"? And in curious illustration—if contradiction can be called illustration—of this memorable discovery, he informs his readers that God heard David, not through the priest, but through the prophet. Nay, more, he deliberately reminds the Protestant of his error in supposing that confession to a priest is not required by God, by himself forgetting that David did not confess to a priest. Had he also forgotten that David did not go to Nathan, but that Nathan went to him, and charged him to his face with his double crime; and that the confession made by the king was such as any convicted and penitent man would make to another who had brought sharply home to him some deed of iniquity? With as much reason might auricular confession be grounded on the self-accusation of criminals to policemen, when conscience can bear its load of guilt no longer.

But perhaps the most extraordinary case which is adduced in favour of the scriptural authority of auricular confession is that of Achan, the man who had sorely troubled Israel. Let the reader bear in mind the modern apparatus of confession, as found in the Romish Church, and advocated by certain promoters of revived Catholicism in the Church of England—the seclusion of priest and penitent in close and whispering communication with each other—and then see what resemblance it bears to the confession of Achan, touching which the essayist says, "Nor did Joshua hesitate to exhort Achan—'My son, give, I pray thee, glory to the Lord God of Israel, and make confession unto him; and tell *me* now what thou hast done; hide it not from me.'"[1]

Here we have a public inquiry, solemnly, terribly judicial, in which all the tribes of Israel were profoundly interested. A presumptuous and daring trespass had been committed, which had been avenged by their disastrous defeat before Ai, and the nature of the trespass had been communicated by God Himself to Joshua, who by a process of inquisition, narrowing like a girdle of fire at every step of the scrutiny, at length encloses the culprit with a frightful and fatal precision. The eyes of the whole camp are turned to this method of detection. And when Achan is thus isolated, and pointed at as by the finger of God, Joshua acts as but the supreme judge, as he was the supreme leader of the people. He was not a priest, but a prophet and judge, and the confession which Achan made to him was not given under the seal of secrecy, never to be broken, but was made with the distinct understanding that it was to be published, and visited with the most open, summary, and condign punishment. It was an auricular confession practically made in the ears of a whole nation, and bears a strong resemblance to the confession made by a boy to his master in the presence of the assembled school, and which is afterwards followed by castigation or expulsion.

[1] Josh. vii. 19.

But extraordinary as this evidence for auricular confession may seem, worse remains behind. The essayist has discovered the time when this institution was revived. It was under Ezra, "who stood up, and said unto them, Ye have transgressed, and have taken strange wives, to increase the trespass of Israel. Now therefore make confession unto the Lord God of your fathers, and do his pleasure. Then all the congregation answered and said with a loud voice, As thou hast said, so must we do. But the people are many, and it is a time of much rain, and we are not able to stand without, neither is this a work of one day or two; so arrangements were made for the division of the people into sections, to go to separate parts of the city" (p. 12).

Now here we have to complain of a device which is the reverse of honourable, and which we regret to add is far from uncommon in the writings of sacerdotalists—we mean the abrupt termination of a quotation just at the point where it is followed by the completest refutation of the theory it was meant to sustain. If the writer had quoted the next verse, he would have enabled his readers to see something of the class of men who were to assist in inaugurating this process of reformation. "Let now our rulers of all the congregation stand, and let all them which have taken strange wives in our cities come at appointed times, and with them *the elders of every city, the judges thereof*, until the fierce wrath of our God for this matter be turned from us." The whole narrative, therefore, contains no express reference whatever to any auricular confession to a priest; and the examination, moreover, is one of the most legal, formal, and public character with respect to a sin which was, and must have been from its very nature, notorious and incapable of concealment. It presents to us the spectacle of a whole multitude, as far as possible, simultaneously and openly renouncing a practice into which they had fallen during their years of captivity; the priest having no more to do with this wholesale inquisition than "certain chief of the fathers, after the house of their fathers, and all of them by their names," who "were separated" for this work, and "sat down in the first day of the tenth month to examine the matter." Ezra the priest was one of the commission for inquiry and judicial separation, and nothing more; he and his co-assessors "making an end with all the men that had taken strange wives by the first day of the first month."[1]

The next witness he adduces is, if possible, more injurious to his cause than any of the previous ones, and is amenable to the same imputation of uncandid and incomplete quotation. It is taken from Nehemiah ix. 1–3, "Now in the twenty and fourth day of this month the children of Israel were assembled with fasting, and with sackclothes, and earth upon them. And the seed of Israel separated themselves from all strangers, and stood and confessed their sins, and the iniquities of their fathers. And they stood up in their place, and read the book of the law of the Lord their God one fourth part of the day; and another

[1] Ezra x. 16, 17.

fourth part they confessed, and worshipped the Lord their God."

The writer significantly omits the concluding phrase, "and worshipped the Lord their God," in order, we presume, considerately to provide more time for the "auricular confession," which he here assumes in the very teeth of the narrative, which clearly imports that the confession was corporate and public. He also fails to note that all Israel assembled that day, "the twenty-fourth day of this month," and that the confession, if auricular, took place within the fourth part of it, and even less, a marvel which would throw into the shade all the miracles both of the Old and New Testament. Nor is this all. The auricular confession of the sins of the fathers who were dead was all compressed into the same brief period. Think of a large modern city confessing auricularly all its sins and those of its fathers in the "fourth part" of one day! And yet, in this manner, with a haste and recklessness which cannot be too severely reprehended, does our author seek to extort from the Scriptures evidence which they refuse to yield; and then assuming that he has established his position, says, "Auricular confession being a recognised institution of the Jewish Church, to it would apply the words of Solomon, 'He that covereth his sins shall not prosper, but whoso confesseth and forsaketh them shall have mercy.'" Doubtless on this assumption many of the most general commands of the Old Testament to confess sin would be capable of a sacerdotal interpretation; but the samples of criticism just passed in review would avail to authorise any practice, however baseless, except in the estimation of reasonable men, who must see that such exegesis is calculated to bring the system which adopts it into contempt.

The writer then proceeds to announce another startling principle, viz., that under the Old Covenant "no provision was made for the forgiveness of sin;" and he further declares that in the sole case of David was absolution given. This astounding declaration is, of course, designed to exalt the function of the modern priesthood, with whom is lodged this gracious prerogative. Could the writer have forgotten that in the records of that Old Covenant it is written, "Blessed is the man whose transgression is forgiven, whose sin is covered;" and, "Thou wast a God that forgavest their iniquities, though thou tookest vengeance of their inventions;" and, "Let the wicked forsake his ways, and the unrighteous man his thoughts, and let him return unto the Lord, and he will have mercy upon him, and to our God, for he will abundantly pardon;" and, "Who is a God like unto thee, that pardoneth the iniquity, and passeth by the transgression of the remnant of his heritage"? Could he, in fact, have forgotten that when the Lord proclaimed His name to Moses at the giving of the Law, the Divine clemency was emphatically announced as one of the attributes of that name, and that too not as a clemency which was suspended and inoperative for long centuries, but as a clemency which was then and thenceforward in living energy? "The Lord, the Lord God, merciful and gracious, long-suffering, and abundant in goodness and truth, keeping mercy for thousands, *forgiving iniquity, transgression, and sin.*" The golden thread of Divine forgiveness, as a truth, a promise, and a fact realised through penitence and faith, and as a blessing for which the recipient offered devout and rapturous thanksgivings, runs through the old economy. If the writer who denies this had contented himself with declaring that the ground of that forgiveness was not yet fully disclosed, and was not laid until the Great Sacrifice for sin was made upon the cross, we should not have demurred to the representation; but nothing can justify the language by which he has sought to restrict an authoritative forgiveness to the New Dispensation.

The sore extremity to which some Romish theologians have been reduced, in their endeavours to sustain the practice of auricular confession, may be seen in the famous treatise of Cardinal Bellarmine, " De Pœnitentia," in which he proclaims the discovery that the sacraments of penance and auricular confession are "adumbrated" even in Paradise itself after the Fall, as well as in the history of Cain. "God," he says, "first exacted from Adam and Eve, and then from Cain, a confession of sin;" and this confession was "not only of the heart, but of the mouth; not only in the general, but in the particular."

But as if conscious that these cases render but a doubtful support to his thesis, and are manifestly more in harmony with Protestant than with Romish practice, he has to contrive some expedient which will supply the missing link. And his discovery is more subtle than ingenuous. He informs us without any authority that the "interrogation" of our first parents was made by an angel appearing in human form, as is obvious from the fact that he walked in paradise in the cool of the evening.[1] Now, not only does the narrative make no mention of the angel, but the designation is repeated again and again, "The Lord God." Accordingly his commentary, as is usual with him, does not so much expound the text as contradict it; and the reason he assigns for such an arbitrary and deceitful handling of the Divine Word, namely, that "he walked in paradise in the cool of the evening," not only involves an extraordinary oversight of the anthropomorphic language of the Old Testament, but, anthropomorphism apart, stumbles at a difficulty which no believer in the Incarnation of the Son of God ought ever to have felt. If the Cardinal had found *this* sublime fact "adumbrated" in the Mosaic narrative, he would have been nearer the truth than when, in order to construct the complete machinery of auricular confession, he has to repudiate the text, invent an angel, and to characterise as an adumbration of sacramental confession a conversation which took place, to all appearance, in the simultaneous hearing of both Adam and Eve; and in which, so far from there being any true, spontaneous, contrite confession, there was absolutely

[1] "De Pœnitentia," lib. iii. cap. 3.

nothing but evasive excuses and cowardly recriminations. The case of Cain is still more unfortunate for the Cardinal, inasmuch as instead of its being an exemplification of a confession "not only of the heart, but of the mouth" (*non solum cordis, sed etiam oris*), it was not a confession either of the one or of the other, but a sullen and defiant resentment of the Divine inquisition in words which disclose neither contrition nor attrition, but which were meant to disavow all knowledge of his brother's weal or woe. "Am I my brother's keeper?"

The theologian who could discover in these incidents "adumbrations" of sacramental confession, was a champion worthy of the Church he had to defend; a Church which has never been able, and since the decree of papal infallibility is less able now than ever, to dispense with the services of controversialists who respect neither modesty nor truth. In concluding this examination of Old Testament evidence I must give emphasis to the statement that in no single instance has the word "confession" such "a fixed technical signification" as will sustain any sacrament of penance.

I now proceed to the consideration of the evidence which is adduced from the New Testament. The writer whose statements have just been reviewed professes to see auricular confession in the conduct of the multitudes who came to the baptism of John and confessed their sins. Here again it is noteworthy that the confession was neither formal nor private, and therefore not "auricular;" but from the very necessity of the case, considering the vast numbers who submitted to the rite of baptism, must have been public. That Judas Iscariot should be cited as another exemplification of auricular confession, because he went to the priests and confessed his sin, and flung at their feet the price of blood, is but in keeping with that free handling of Scripture of which we have already seen such extraordinary specimens. His confession was in the presence of all the chief priests and elders; it was also the explosive and frantic utterance of burning remorse at a deed of which they were already aware, and in which they had been confederates. That an act so informal, so public, so tragical, to which Judas was driven by the furies of an outraged and avenging conscience, and which consisted of but one sentence of condensed and consuming agony—" I have sinned, in that I have betrayed innocent blood "—should be paraded as a case of " auricular confession," would have been deemed incredible had we not seen the extravagant distortions which the sacramentarian medium can impart to the simplest facts of Old Testament history. Such violent wresting of the record prepares us to find that Sapphira made auricular confession to Peter; and that the Ephesians who were converted under the preaching of Paul—and many of whom having used curious arts, " brought their books together, and burned them before all men"—made auricular confession to the apostle when they acknowledged and showed their deeds. We are not surprised that the same whimsical method of interpretation finds auricular confession in the injunction of St. James, " Confess your faults one to another," thus converting a broad Christian obligation into a shrivelled technical prescription. For this stupendous structure of auricular confession there is not one atom of evidence to be found within the pages of Scripture. There is not one instance of a layman closeted with a priest, and disclosing the sinful secrets of a lifetime, either spontaneously, or in response to the searching and prurient questions of a father-confessor. Such a practice was unknown to Judaism, and it is equally unknown to Christianity. And though we are not now concerned to extend the area of this discussion beyond the confines of the Scriptures, it is unquestionable that the practice of private confession, except in connection with public discipline, had no place even in the earlier periods of the post-apostolic Churches.

But it is alleged that, whatever defect of evidence there may be in Scripture as to the obligation of auricular confession, such confession is in fact indissolubly associated with the prerogative of absolution, with which it is affirmed our Saviour clothed His apostles and their successors. If, it is argued, confession is not commanded, it is at least involved in the official and ministerial remission of sins, which, in order to be valid, must rest on repentance, a repentance whose reality can be ascertained only through means of such a full and unreserved disclosure of sins as is denoted by auricular confession. The obligation of confession becomes thus an inference founded on certain assumptions of sacerdotal function and power, which themselves require to be established on an impregnable basis. Can such a basis be found, and can such a basis be found in the pages of the Divine Word?

This leads us to the second branch of inquiry, which will involve an examination of those passages of Scripture which are confidently pleaded as empowering sacerdotal absolution, and therefore by inference enforcing auricular confession.

When Peter made the wonderful confession, " Thou art the Christ, the Son of the living God;" Jesus answered and said, " Blessed art thou, Simon Bar-jona, for flesh and blood hath not revealed it unto thee, but my Father which is in heaven. And I say unto thee, Thou art Peter, and upon this rock will I build my church; and the gates of hell shall not prevail against it. And I will give unto thee the keys of the kingdom of heaven: and whatsoever thou shalt bind on earth shall be bound in heaven: and whatsoever thou shalt loose on earth shall be loosed in heaven."[1]

A passage strongly resembling this, and throwing light upon its meaning, occurs in the eighteenth chapter of Matthew. " Verily I say unto you, Whatsoever ye shall bind on earth shall be bound in heaven: and whatsoever ye shall loose on earth shall be loosed in heaven." The power which the first passage seems to restrict to Peter, is in the second extended to the other apostles. What is this power? To Gentile ears the phrases " binding " and " loosing " are peculiar. Were they

[1] Matt. xvi. 17-19.

equally so to Jewish ears, or had they acquired in their ordinary speech an idiomatic and unambiguous force which at once determines their meaning? To the Jews they were perfectly familiar, and the evidence which has been adduced by Rabbinical scholars, and especially by Lightfoot, proves that they are phrases which do not of necessity involve any allusion either to the "remission" or the "retention of sins."

"Binding and loosing," says Lightfoot, "in the language and style most familiarly known to the Jewish nation, did refer more properly to things than to persons, therefore he saith ὅ ἐὰν δήσῃς, and not ὅν; and in Matt. xviii. 18, ὅσα ἂν δήσητε, not ὅσους. The phrase to bind and loose, in their vulgar speech, meant to prohibit and to permit, or to teach what is prohibited or permitted—what lawful, what unlawful; as may appear by these instances, a few produced, whereas thousands might be alleged out of their writings.

"Our wise men say that in Judah they did work on the Passover eve till noon, but in Galilee not all; and as for the night, the school of Shammai bound it, that is, forbade to work on it. But the school of Hillel loosed it till sun-rising, or taught that it was lawful to work till sun-rise.

"They send not letters by the hand of a Gentile on the eve of the Sabbath, nor on the fifth day of the week. The school of Shammai bound it, but the school of Hillel loosed it.

"Women may not look in a looking-glass on the

Sabbath; but if it were fastened upon a wall, Rabbi loosed the looking into it, but the wise men bound it.

"R. Jochanan went from Tsipporis to Tiberias. He saith, 'Why brought ye to me this elder? for what I loose he bindeth, and what I bind he looseth.' The scribes have bound heaven, they have prohibited it. They have upon necessity loosed salutation on the Sabbath—that is, they have permitted it, or taught that it was lawful. Thousands of instances of this nature might be produced, by all of which it is clear that the Jews' use of the phrase was of their doctors' or learned men's teaching what was lawful and permitted, and what unlawful or prohibited.

"By this vulgar and only sense of this phrase in the nation, the meaning of Christ using it thus to His disciples is easily understood; viz., that He doth first instate them in a ministerial capacity to teach what bound and loose, what to be done, and what not—and this as ministers; and thus are ministers, necessarily, to the end of the world.

"But as they were apostles of that singular and unparalleled order as the like never were in the Church again, He gives them power to bind and loose in a degree above all ministers that were to follow; viz., that whereas some part of Moses' law was now to stand in practice, and some to be laid aside, some things under the law prohibited were now to be permitted, and some things then permitted to be now prohibited, He promiseth the apostles such assistance of His Spirit, and giveth them such power, that what they allowed in practice should stand, and what to fall should fall; what they bound on earth should be bound in heaven."[1]

The apostles were appointed to be legislators under the promised inspiration of Christ for His new spiritual kingdom. As a kingdom it must have laws, by which its order was to be secured and maintained, and the laws which with that infallible guidance they enacted were the binding and loosing on earth, which would be confirmed by a corresponding binding and loosing in heaven. Concerning doctrines, practices, and rules of discipline, they had authority within a certain definite range, the limits of which they would be prevented from transgressing by a spiritual illumination which would be vouchsafed to them by their ascended Lord; but of auricular confession and the forgiveness of sins, we find in the passage just considered not a word.[2]

The next passage upon which the Romanists and Ritualists build is our Lord's commission to His disciples, as recorded in John xx. 22, 23: "And when he had said this, he breathed on them, and saith unto them, Receive ye the Holy Ghost: whose soever sins ye remit, they are remitted unto them; and whose soever sins ye retain, they are retained."

This may be considered as the very citadel of the confessionalists, and candour constrains us to acknow-

---

[1] Lightfoot, vol. iii. pp. 99-101.

[2] Meyer says of the phrase (ἱέναι ἁμαρτιαν) that it is absolutely without authority—"gänzlich kein Sprachgebrauch."—"Commentary on Matthew," p. 324.

ledge that, viewing the words apart from other teaching of our Lord, and from the recorded practice of the apostles, they seem to convey the prerogative of absolution; nor can it, I think, be fairly contended as against this prerogative, that it is one which it is impossible for God to impart, either to the apostles or to any other class of men whom He may select as the official administrators of His kingdom. He who can endow the prophets with the power of prevision, and who can give to apostles spiritual insight which far transcends the range of their natural faculties, could invest them with the power of "searching the heart" and "trying the reins of the children of men," and of so infallibly discerning the precise spiritual condition of every man, as to enable them without hesitation or mistake to pronounce him absolved or unforgiven. Protestant writers wholly miss the question at issue when they suppose the priest to arrogate Divine powers, and to exercise them as if they were his own, and underived. He claims simply to stand as delegate of heaven, and as administrator of the grace of God. Now that such an order of spiritual officers is possible ought not, I think, to be denied by any man who believes in the power of God, any more than it can be denied that an ambassador may be invested with plenipotentiary powers to declare the fate or fortune of any subjects of a king. Having received from the monarch a clear statement of the principles by which his judgment and action are to be guided, and possessing, as he may, sufficient wisdom to discover the precise attitude of each subject to his sovereign, he can pronounce a favourable or unfavourable sentence, with the utmost assurance that it expresses the will, and will obtain the ratification, of the supreme power. No ambassador invested with such functions, and possessing such unfailing discernment, can be justly accused of arrogance or irreverence towards his royal master. He does not assume to be the fountain of authority, but its channel. He does not sway the king's decision, but officially declares and enforces it. I cannot, therefore, pretend to challenge the doctrine of auricular confession and priestly absolution on *a priori* grounds, as if it were impossible for God Himself to invest an order of men with such stupendous power. He who can communicate the gifts of tongues, and prophecy, and healing, and miracle, cannot consistently be regarded as incapable of deputing the ghostly function in question. And, further, I cannot imagine that on the supposition that such authority was confided to mortal men, it could have been conveyed in terms more precise or appropriate than those now under consideration. These concessions I make without reserve, as due in all candour to the confessionalists, whatever consequences they may be supposed to involve.

How far, however, this interpretation will stand the test of other lights, is another matter. The occasion on which our Lord spake the words, was on the evening of the day of His resurrection. The disciples were assembled together with closed doors, for fear of the Jews. Thomas was absent, and could not therefore, on that occasion, though an apostle, receive the breathing of his Divine Master, nor the commission which He imparted to the rest of the apostolate. Nor is there any subsequent mention of his receiving the same commission in the same form. He was not favoured with that gracious sufflation at the memorable interview at which his resolute unbelief in the Saviour's resurrection was so strikingly rebuked and vanquished.

Reserving for consideration in the sequel what was the precise nature and method of that remission and retention of sins which our Saviour here bestowed, let us look at the assumption that the apostles were at that time clothed with the prerogative which is claimed by the modern priesthood. Our Saviour then breathed on the apostles, ten of them, and on them alone; and simultaneously with that sacred symbolic act He endowed them with this special authority of forgiving and retaining sins. But of what avail is this concession (which, however, is made only provisionally) to those who in these times assume to themselves, without the same Divine sufflation, the same apostolic discrimination and judgment respecting the spiritual condition and destiny of men? There yawns an enormous chasm between the admission that apostles had this prerogative, and that the same prerogative is enjoyed by a modern priesthood, whatever may be its intellectual power or moral character; for it must be asserted again and again that neither ignorance nor depravity is supposed to disqualify a priest for the work of receiving confession and bestowing forgiveness. A Borgia and a Bourdaloue are on the same level as priestly confessors, the atrocities and nameless infamies of the former being no bar to his shriving souls for heaven, or sealing them for hell.

Now, whatever be the meaning of our Saviour's language when He breathed upon the disciples, it is not only significant, but absolutely fatal to all priestly pretensions, that these words were never again employed in the early Church; that there is no record of their use when Matthias succeeded Judas in the apostolate; that Paul himself, if ever he was ordained at all, was ordained not only without these words, but by a man who does not appear to have been either minister or deacon, but a certain disciple named Ananias, who imparted to him his sight and the gift of the Holy Ghost. Among all the qualifications specified in the New Testament as indispensable to the office of bishop or presbyter, that of receiving confession and pronouncing absolution has no place. The commission which our Lord gave to the apostles to preach the gospel was handed down to others, not silently, or by inference, but expressly, and in the most solemn terms; but of the command to forgive sins, or the permission to forgive sins, or the supposition that by them sins might be forgiven, we find not the faintest trace. If, therefore, it be conceded for the moment that the interpretation given of our Saviour's words by the Romanists and Ritualists is the true one, and that the apostles possessed the power of pronouncing with authority, and with an infallibly judicial decisiveness, the absolution and remission of sins, the great gulf which stretches between apostles and modern priests can be spanned only by an assumption more easily made than proved, that they inherit this tremendous prerogative in virtue of their lineal descent from the apostles.

But the question recurs with reference to the apostles themselves, Did they possess the power in question as a donation from Christ when He breathed upon them and said, "Receive ye the Holy Ghost"? And if they did then and there receive this marvellous gift, was it permanent, and so absolutely under the control of the apostles, that they could summon it into operation at will, or was it intermittent, and available only on some special occasions? The apostles had other gifts of a supernatural character, gifts of prophecy, tongues, and healing; but it is significant that Paul left Trophimus at Miletum sick, and that his beloved son in the faith, Timothy, whose life seemed so essential to the early work of planting and training the Churches, was not miraculously healed by the apostle, but was recommended to try the very ordinary dietetic regulation of "using a little wine for his stomach's sake, and for his often infirmities." The spirit of prevision seemed also to be as little under his control as the power of working miracles. Some things were within the reach of his prophetic ken, others were as certainly beyond it. If therefore the power of absolution were a miraculous endowment, this is no proof of its permanence even in the apostles themselves, unless evidence can be adduced to show that in this respect it was distinguished from other *charismata*. If however it were permanent, the apostles must have been able to forgive or retain the sins of any person with whom they might hold converse. But in this case, as we cannot imagine that they possessed the authority to acquit or condemn in an arbitrary manner, totally irrespective of the moral condition of the person before them, their scrutiny of the spirit must have been profound, searching, and unfailing. The souls of men must have "lain naked and opened to their eyes," as to the eyes of Him with whom they had to do. The very possibility of mistake in any individual case would fatally vitiate their claim to authoritative adjudgment in every case. Whether the supposed infallible scrutiny, which the confessionalist theory of apostolic prerogative necessarily involves, was accomplished by means of some supernatural illumination of the natural faculties, or by the impartation of some new one, is immaterial to the point before us. Had the apostles such power of penetrating the secrets of the soul, and had they such power not intermittently but continuously, not to meet some rare and exceptional emergency, but to qualify them for the ordinary duties of their apostolic commission? It is not denied that it might have been bestowed along with other miraculous powers, but the inspired records are not only silent as to such a gift, but are full of instances which discredit the assumption that such a gift was actually bestowed. Simon Magus was baptised along with other Samaritans professing sincere repentance and faith; but it was not until he offered to purchase the Holy Ghost with money that the apostles discovered him to be in the gall of bitterness and in the bonds of iniquity. Here, if anywhere, was an opportunity for the Apostle Peter to assert his sacerdotal power by enjoining upon this baptised neophyte the necessity of confession to him, accompanied by a course of penance. But the apostle imposed upon him no such obligation. He left him standing in the presence of God. He commanded him to repent, and to pray God if perhaps the thought of his heart might be forgiven him, thus significantly reminding him that his case was one wholly between himself and his Maker, and that his forgiveness must come, if at all, direct from heaven in answer to his own prayer. If it be urged in reply that here we have an instance, not of the apostle remitting sins, but retaining them, by his declaration that Simon had no part nor lot in the matter, and that his heart was not right in the sight of God, it is sufficient to answer that this was simply the asseveration of a fact which no inspiration was needed to discover in the case of a man who had with shocking profanity offered to buy the gift of the Spirit, and that in no sense can an apostle be said to "retain the sins" of another when he prescribes to him the only way in which they can be forgiven. The apostle does not undertake, in virtue of a sacerdotal power, to negotiate the reconciliation of the greedy and hypocritical magician with God, and Simon himself clearly reveals by his answer that he attributed no power to Peter which could render him service in his fearful extremity but that of prayer. "Pray ye the Lord for me, that none of these things which ye have spoken come upon me."

It has been supposed that in the history of Ananias and Sapphira we have an instance of apostolic power to read the heart. But even allowing that there was no other means of acquiring the knowledge that Ananias and Sapphira had agreed together to lie to the Holy Ghost, and that there was nothing self-convicting in the whole aspect and manner of Ananias, the utmost conclusion which the incident warrants is that there were rare occasions on which, for the purpose of impressing a solemn lesson on the infant Church, a special insight was granted to the apostles. But the occasions were manifestly infrequent even in their experience, and are nowhere promised to any others who may aspire to be their successors. When the Apostle Paul asks the question, "What man knoweth the things of man, save the spirit of man which is in him?" and when he says, "God which knoweth the hearts bare them witness, giving them the Holy Ghost, even as he did unto us;" in what more significant and conclusive manner could he disclaim such knowledge for himself? If he had been, as the sacerdotal theory must suppose, an official organ of the Divine Omniscience for the purpose of "remitting and retaining sins," this disavowal of the knowledge of the hearts of other men, and this ascription to God alone of the stupendous prerogative, would have been both incomprehensible and false ; and he might with as much truth and reverence have said, " I know the heart," as, " I preach Christ crucified," for he would have received for both, and for both equally, a Divine commission and qualification. To have concealed this supernatural endowment would have been an unpardonable dereliction. Its possession would have protected him from deception, and he was often deceived ; from treachery, and he was often betrayed. The history of the apostles and their letters combine to prove that whatever occasional assistance they might receive by which they could search the spirits of men, they were for the most part as dependent as others on the ordinary facts and processes by which men acquire the knowledge of each other's character. At times they might be endowed with supernatural insight, but they were generally left to the uncertainties of observation and inference.

That the apostles were not permanently possessed of the supernatural knowledge of the heart, we hold to have been incontrovertibly established; but even on the supposition that they were, there is an enormous disproportion between this foundation and the structure which Romanists and Ritualists have reared upon it. The foundation is that apostles were inspired to search the heart, and thus to acquire an infallible knowledge of its condition in the sight of God. The structure is that priests, whether the best or the worst, the purest or the most corrupt, the most enlightened or the most ignorant, but always fallible and never inspired, may judicially, and without any possibility of reversal in heaven, "remit or retain sins." We have apostles on one side, and men who are no apostles on the other; inspiration on one side, and no inspiration on the other; special prerogatives on one side, and no special prerogatives on the other; a knowledge of the heart preternaturally supplied on the one side, and no knowledge of the heart at all, except such as the professed penitent may choose to impart, on the other; an express authorization from the lips of Christ on the one side, and nothing but an assumed and indemonstrable commission on the other. And yet with all these differences, any one of which is fatal to modern sacerdotal pretensions, men are still found who can arrogate not only what, for the sake of argument, we have conceded to belong to apostles, but far more than any apostle ever dreamed of as appertaining to the ordinary duties of his office.

There is another passage which has been cited by a recent writer in support of the doctrine of priestly absolution, to which I should have made no reference but for the extraordinary manner in which it has been pressed into service. "In order," we are informed, "to show that God had given the power to men, in refutation of the Pharisees, who asked, 'Who can forgive sins but God only?' He worked the miracle of healing the paralytic, and to him he said, 'Man, thy sins are forgiven thee.' Then we are told that the multitudes glorified God, which had given such power unto men. In the case of the sinful woman, our blessed Lord pronounced a formal absolution—'He said unto her, Thy sins are forgiven.'"[1]

Could this writer be serious in the adduction of such a passage for such a purpose? A palsied man is brought to be healed, and the Saviour, instead of at once addressing Himself to the cure, exclaims, "Son, be of good cheer, thy sins be forgiven thee." These words sent a thrill through the crowd. Many countenances are seen pale with rage and horror; quick glances are exchanged from eye to eye, and there are whisperings, and murmurings, and hints of blasphemy. And the scribes, those eager and relentless enemies of Christ, ever listening for words which they could forge into accusations, found here, as they thought, enough to prove Him guilty of death, and angrily inquired, "Why does this man thus speak blasphemies: who can forgive sins but God only?"

Here a distinct question was raised. The Jews had had prophets before, and priests too, but never any who vaunted such a prerogative as this. Even Moses himself, whom God had raised up for the deliverance of His people, had affected no such tremendous claim. He had wrought miracles, divided the sea, turned the flinty rock into a fountain of waters, but he had never invaded the sacred rights of the Eternal, and presumed to determine the immortal destinies of man. On his face, with all the fervour of a heart that must break unless its prayer be heard, he had besought that God would forgive His rebellious people, but he had never

[1] "Tracts for the Day," p. 14.

pronounced with authority the words, " Thy sins be forgiven thee." And Aaron had stood between the living and the dead, and the plague was stayed ; and Elijah had closed and opened the windows of heaven ; but *sin* they had all left in the hands of Him with whom alone is the mercy that can forgive. There was not one truth which enthroned itself more firmly in the mind of a Jew, and the practical violation of which he was more disposed to resent and punish than this, that the high function of dispensing pardon was inalienably held in the hand of God. He shrank from the supposition that any one could share in the prerogative. So long as the priests and scribes were ignorant of the true nature of Christ, so long as they failed to behold enshrined within the veil of His humanity, true and essential Godhead, so long it was natural that their indignation should be enkindled against His assumption of powers which can reside only in the hands of the Supreme. They were right in maintaining that none can forgive sins but God only, and Christ meant to disclose on this occasion some rays of His Divinity.

This truth He first asserted, not by working miracles (for this would have established nothing beyond his being the executor of a Divine commission), but by forgiving sins. The claim was easy enough to make, for it had relation to an invisible effect. But who was there to verify the assumed prerogative by gazing into the Book of Remembrance and seeing whether the sins were indeed blotted out ? It has ever been an easier and safer thing to assume spiritual powers than material ones, because the latter are prone to suggest the necessity for demonstration, while the former appeal to faith or credulity. It is easier, for example, for a priest to limit or extend the duration of purgatorial fires than to cure the physical disorder of the votary for whom those fires are reserved; and the priesthoods of the world have, for the most part, been wise enough to place the sphere within which their thaumaturgic exploits are accomplished beyond the senses and the reason of man. But such was not the spiritual claim of the Son of man; or, at least, if the forgiveness was invisible, the demonstration was to be visible. And hence, while the bystanders were murmuring, the Saviour said, "That ye may know that the Son of man hath power on earth to forgive sins (then saith he to the sick of the palsy), Arise, take up thy bed, and go into thine own house. And he arose and departed into his house." The prerogative of forgiveness exercised by one in human form was a fact altogether new, and it required to be supported by miracle. The Saviour acknowledged the existence of such necessity by working the miracle, and from any modern pretender to absolving powers we require the same convincing authentication.

But we must enter the gravest protest against the manner in which the writer in question introduces this case of healing. He informs us that the miracle was wrought "in order to show that God had given the power (of forgiveness) to men, in refutation of the Pharisees, who asked, 'Who can forgive sins but God only'?" Could the words of our Lord have been more widely misconceived? He does not say that ye may know that "man has power on earth to forgive sins," but "the Son of man;" expressions which are not only not synonymous, but cannot be confounded without producing the most serious havoc in the interpretation of the language of the New Testament. Let the Catholic revivalist whose words are before us attempt the substitution of the word "man" for the "Son of man" in the Gospels, and see whether all that is predicated of the former can be equally predicated of the latter. Is it possible that he can have expended any care in tracing the expression, "Son of man," in its various connections, and have failed to discover with what extraordinary and even superhuman functions and glories it is associated? Of "the Son of man," but not of man, it is said that He hath "descended from heaven," and that He is "in heaven," even while on earth. "The Son of man," but not man, is "Lord even of the Sabbath." The Son of man, but not man, "shall come in his glory, and before him shall be gathered all nations, and he shall separate them one from another, as a shepherd divideth sheep from goats." "The Son of man," but not man, has "come to seek and to save that which was lost." "The Son of man," but not man, must be "lifted up, that whosoever believeth in him may not perish, but have everlasting life." "The Son of man," but not man, "came not to be ministered unto, but to minister, and to give his life a ransom for many." This is the Son of man that came, and that had power on earth to forgive sin, and it is not a little amazing that this writer should have virtually suppressed the Divine power and glory, which are so commonly and so conspicuously associated with the phrase, "Son of man," and without any warrant but the sore exigencies of an arbitrary theory, have confounded forgiveness of sin by "man" with forgiveness by the "Son of man."

It will not avail to adduce the statement that the "multitude marvelled and glorified God, which had given such power to men," for the multitude were no more aware of the real nature of Christ than were the apostles themselves, both then, and for a considerable period afterwards. The Divinity of the Saviour was disclosed by slow degrees, nor did He choose to unveil at once the mystery of His person, even though such concealment and reticence involved the disciples in temporary misapprehensions and errors. Moreover, there were subjective inaptitudes on the part of His hearers, which rendered the instantaneous revelation of His Divinity impossible. The undisciplined eye would have been blinded with the sudden and overpowering blaze. The multitude saw in Him a man, a wonderful man, but nothing more; and their astonishment was heightened when they beheld the prerogative of forgiveness which He claimed confirmed by the miracle of healing. It was not as man that He forgave, but as the Divine man, in whom dwelt the fulness of the Godhead bodily. In like manner, not as "man," but as "the Son of man," He sa to the sinful woman, "Thy sins are forgiven."

Now it is far from my purpose to allege that those who endeavour to found an argument for the practice of priestly absolution upon the passages just considered, see in the phrase, "Son of man," nothing more than a barren psilanthropy, but their reasoning is valid only on this supposition. If they hold, as they do, that "the Son of man" was "Emmanuel, God with us," and that it was in virtue of this, His unique and incommunicable nature, that He cancelled the transgressions of the paralytic and the fallen woman, it is an audacity which cannot be too gravely censured which prompts a merely human priest to usurp the same awful functions. He who forgave the paralytic, was "the Alpha and the Omega," "whose eyes are as flames of fire," "who searcheth the heart and trieth the reins" of the children of men; and who therefore saw, by an intuition direct and infallible, that the spiritual state of the palsied penitent was such as to justify the gracious absolution which he there and then received, alike without auricular confession, penance, and satisfaction. And sacerdotalism, unable to satisfy any one of these conditions, places on the same level of authority its forgiving prerogative and that of the Saviour, assuming all His power while possessing none of His qualifications.

The priestly claim in question, therefore, cannot establish itself on the example of Christ, nor, as we have seen, on any commission He gave to the apostles exclusively. Such commission, so far as the evidence supplied by the New Testament goes, was never exercised by the apostles in the form of private confession and judicial absolution, and we are compelled to ascertain the estimate which they formed of spiritual functions by the manner in which they discharged them. And what was that manner? It was twofold. It consisted in the proclamation of that gospel which announced the terms upon which forgiveness of sin was obtained, or forfeited; and it further consisted in the acts of discipline by which open and flagrant transgressors of Christian law were separated from the Church, or, on repentance, readmitted to its communion. The fulfilment of the commission in the former aspect was seen in every instance in which the terms of salvation were published, whether by apostle or private Christian; and the fulfilment of the commission in its latter aspect was seen in that memorable example of excommunication and readmission which is furnished by the Corinthian Church.

The expulsion of the incestuous person by the authority of Paul and the vote of the Church was a "retaining of his sin;" and the subsequent restoration of the offender, on the ground of his hearty repentance, was the "remitting of his sin." A grievous iniquity had been perpetrated, not only against God, but against the Church of God. The temple of the Holy Ghost had been polluted, and it became necessary for the members of the Corinthian brotherhood to mark their sense of abhorrence of a deed which, however consistent with heathenism, was an outrage on the fundamental ethics of the gospel. This they did, and what they bound on earth was bound in heaven, inasmuch as Paul was the inspired expounder of the will of Christ in regard of all such overt and fearful depravity. But the absolution which followed was so far from being sacerdotal, that there is no trace of any evidence that the penitent was ever confronted with any elder or bishop of the Corinthian Church (if any such officer at that time existed among them). And, moreover, the absolution was conferred by the whole Church. "To whom," says the apostle, "ye forgive anything, I forgive also in the sight ($\pi\rho\acute{o}\sigma\omega\pi\hat{\wp}$) of Christ;" the apostle thus according to the Church a power of absolution co-ordinate with his own. He was in fact the authorised expounder of the law of discipline, and the outraged community was charged with its administration. The examination of the evidence of the New Testament therefore yields the same result as that of the Old, and warrants us in affirming the conclusion, that in neither is there any trace of auricular confession to a priest, either as a practice or as an obligation. There is no mention of a priest as an official of the Christian Church, no mention therefore of confession to a priest, no mention of the intercession of a priest, no mention of absolution by a priest. The whole structure of the confessional is human, and that alone. It is one of the plants which the "heavenly Father hath not planted," and which will in due time "be rooted up."

It has been sufficient for my present argument to show that the practice of auricular confession is destitute of the authority of inspiration, and can never therefore become essential as a condition of salvation. It would be not less easy to show, if it came within the scope of my purpose, that this species of confession was equally unknown to the early Fathers. The confession technically called by them ἐξομολόγησις was quite another thing, and denoted either confession of sin to God, or public penance, and in the latter sense was restricted to those who had been guilty of notorious offences, on account of which they had been excluded from the communion of the Church, their confession being required as a condition of their restoration to ecclesiastical privileges.

"During the Decian persecution," says Riddle, "the number of penitents being very large, the bishop deemed it expedient to appoint certain presbyters to the special office of receiving their confessions, preparatory to public penance; it having been already recommended as a wholesome practice that persons suffering under any perplexities of mind or troubles of conscience should have recourse to some wise and skilful pastor for their guidance and satisfaction. The establishment of this office of penitentiary presbyters is related by Socrates,[1] from whom we learn also that it was never admitted by the Novatians; that it was abolished at Constantinople by Nectarius, the bishop, in the reign of Theodosius; and that this example was followed by almost all the bishops of the East, in whose Churches

---

[1] "Hist. Eccl." lib. v. cap. 19; and Sozomen, "Hist. Eccl." lib. viii. cap. 16.

the office accordingly discontinued; but that it continued in use in the Western Churches, and chiefly at Rome, to prepare men for the public penance of the Church. The appointment of these penitentiary priests may be regarded as having led the way to the institution of confessors, in the modern acceptation of the term. But these officers were by no means identical, and ought not to be confounded with each other. The office of penitentiary priests 'was not to receive private confessions in prejudice to the public discipline, much less to grant absolution upon bare confession before any penance was performed, which was a practice altogether unknown to the ancient Church; but it was to facilitate and promote the exercise of public discipline, by acquainting men what sins the laws of the Church require to be expiated by public penance, and how they were to behave themselves in the performance of it, and only to appoint private penance for such private crimes as were not proper to be brought on the public stage, either for fear of doing harm to the penitent himself, or giving scandal to the Church.'[1] The confession of sins was indeed private, but it was destined to be made public in order to the performance of penance. The private or auricular penance of later centuries is quite different from the confession made to those penitentiary presbyters. Confession was not made to them with a view of obtaining forgiveness from God, but in order to procure restoration to the former privileges of the offended Church. It was considered indeed useful and

[1] Bingham. "Antiq." book xvii. chap. 3, sec. 11.

necessary to seek for both kinds of forgiveness at the same time, but no Christian minister claims the power of pronouncing pardon in the name of God.'

"The regular establishment of the system of private confession and absolution is usually ascribed to Leo the Great, who represented not merely any particular penitentiary priests, but every priest, as possessing the power and authority to receive confession, to act as an intercessor with God on behalf of the penitent, and to declare forgiveness of sins in the name of God. But even the system introduced by this pontiff differed from that which has prevailed since the thirteenth century in the Roman Church, inasmuch as the confession of sins was left to every one's conscience, and penance was still regarded as an entirely voluntary act which no one could be compelled to perform; nor was the priest supposed to possess in himself any (delegated) power of forgiving sins. And subsequently to the age of Leo it was considered as a matter quite at the option of an offender either to confess his sins to a priest or to God alone."

¹ See Schroeck, "Kirchengeschichte," iv. 31, sec. 321.

LECTURE VIII.

THE PRIEST AND THE CONFESSIONAL (CONTINUED).

LECTURE VIII.

THE PRIEST AND THE CONFESSIONAL (CONTINUED).

HAVING in the previous lecture investigated at considerable length the nature of the evidence which Scripture supplies touching the sacerdotal doctrine of Confession and Absolution, I now proceed to examine it in that fuller ecclesiastical development which has been given to it by the Church of Rome, and which is being regarded with increasing favour by a certain influential section in the Church of England. Around the practice of confession has grown up a complex system of doctrine, some examination of which is indispensable to a right understanding of those priestly claims against which these lectures are directed; and I am sanguine enough to believe that this examination will serve to show, from evidence adduced from authorized Romish teachings, the precariousness of both the theory and practice of the sacrament in question.

It will be requisite for us to consider—

I. The subject-matter with which the priests profess to deal in confession.

II. To test the reality and validity of their decisions.

III. To glance at the moral tendencies and effects of the sacrament itself.

I.

The subject-matter with which the priest professes to deal in the sacrament of Penance consists of sins committed after baptism, but not necessarily of all such sins, for a distinction is made between sins that are venial (*venialia*) and sins that are mortal (*mortalia, lethalia*).[1] The confession of venial sins is left entirely at the option of the penitent. He may, for the sake of greater security, disclose them if he choose; but all his mortal sins he must confess, and this confession must not only be *general*, but *special*, involving a minute description of all the circumstances in which the sins were committed. The omission to reveal any one mortal sin, or any circumstance which serves to give it peculiar aggravation, will vitiate the act of confession, and invalidate the absolution which the priest pronounces, inasmuch as the absolution proceeds upon the supposition that there has been on the part of the penitent no conscious reservation. A mortal sin is defined as "that which of itself inflicts spiritual death on the soul, inasmuch as of itself it deprives the soul of sanctifying grace and charity, in which the spiritual life of the soul consists."[2]

This definition is designated the *a posteriori* definition, as it describes the sin in the light of its effects: *a priori*,

---

[1] This subject-matter is designated by the Romish theologians *materia remota*. [2] Dens' "Theologia," vol. i. no. 153.

it is defined as a sin grievously repugnant to the order of right reason and eternal law, and also a sin which turns away from its ultimate end or from God."[1] On the other hand, a venial sin is defined as "that which does not inflict spiritual death on the soul, or that which does not turn away from its ultimate end, or which is only slightly repugnant to the order of right reason."[2] The distinction is supposed to be still further elucidated by "differentiæ" like the following. "That man by mortal sin makes the ultimate end to rest interpretatively (interpretative) in the creature, not so, however, by venial sin; that by a mortal sin a man shows contempt (at least interpretatively) of God, but not by venial sin; that by this contempt a mortal sin acquires infinite wickedness which a venial sin has not; that mortal sin incurs the guilt of eternal punishment, while venial sin, of itself, incurs only the penalty of temporal punishment. And Thomas Aquinas adds, it is supposed, a valuable contribution to the *éclaircissement* of this point by the discovery that mortal sin is "against law" (*contra legem*), but venial sin is beside the law (*præter legem*). If the question be asked whether there is any *specific* difference between mortal and venial sins, the Church of Rome informs us that as to their formal objects they may not differ in species, inasmuch as the theft of one coin (which is a venial sin) and the theft of thirty (which is a mortal sin) are of the same species; but if these sins be considered in the light of their aversion from God, they are said to differ in their whole

[1] Dens' "Theologia," vol. i. no. 153.   [2] Ibid. No. 153.

kind (*toto genere*). Special rules have also been considerately furnished, by means of which these sins may still further be discriminated. But these are prefaced by a somewhat discouraging dictum of St. Augustine, who frankly confesses that "it is most difficult to find out what is mortal and what is venial, and most dangerous to define them; and that these are matters which are to be weighed not by human but by divine judgment."[1]

The theologians of Rome would have shown their wisdom if they had avoided the difficulty and the peril thus significantly indicated by the Bishop of Hippo, but they have ventured to formulate such rules as the following. That where Scripture attaches to any sin a grave appellation, such as "wickedness," "iniquity," "abomination;" or says it "deserves death," or is "hateful to God," or "excludes from the kingdom of heaven," or is marked by a "woe," it is mortal. If, however, it applies mild epithets, such as "mote," or "hay," or "stubble," then the sin is venial.[2] The allusion to "hay and stubble" is, by the way, an extraordinary instance of misinterpretation, inasmuch as the passage cited refers not to *sins*, but to men of unworthy character, whom the careless master-builder had put into the structure of the Church, or to doctrines repugnant to the Christian faith.

Another rule is supplied by tradition, which is to be ascertained by the decisions of councils and pontiffs,

---

[1] Dens' "Theologia." *De peccatis.* No. 156.
[2] Ibid. No. 156.

and from the writings of the holy Fathers. Here, however, the ground is felt to be treacherous, and we meet with the naïve acknowledgment that with respect to the holy Fathers and Doctors we must attend carefully (*caute attendendum*) to what was their mode of speaking, and what the "discipline of those times." The tradition is, in fact, not to be taken whole and entire. It must be sifted. For, as we are told, second marriages, which have only a certain unseemliness about them, were in the first ages of the Church sometimes called " crimes " and " beastly things " (*res bestiales*). In other words, the tradition concerning the distinction between " mortal and venial sins" is a variable quantity; and the tradition of the sixth century, though so much nearer the apostolic times, is set at nought by the tradition of the nineteenth, certain deadly sins having in the mean time crossed the ancient line of demarcation and become venial. Thus the Church of Rome, according to its convenience, repudiates the antiquity which it professes to revere. Another help in the task of discriminating "mortal" from "venial" sins is to be sought in the common and consenting opinion of bishops, superiors, and doctors or scholastics, though every reader of these worthies knows that a " common opinion " is a mere figure of speech. The fourth instrument of discovery is "natural reason," which considers the gravity of the object, its repugnance to the virtues, both the words and ends of the law, the penalties denounced against transgressors, and also the deliberateness of the act and the circumstances connected with it."[1]

If the mind of the layman is not sufficiently enlightened or obscured by these rules for distinguishing the mortal and the venial, more remains behind.[2] There is a process of addition in virtue of which venial sin may, *per accidens*, become a mortal sin by accumulation or coalescence. A thief, for example, may steal at

---

[1] Dens' "Theologia." No. 156.

[2] The following I translate from Bouvier's "Theological Institutes."

"Venial sins, *as* venial, cannot united make a mortal one; for since mortal and venial sins differ *essentially* from each other, venial sins, however multiplied, never constitute a mortal one. For example, a thousand lies, either in joke or official, are a thousand venial sins, and do not make one mortal sin. Nevertheless, very many observe that he who should be ready to commit all venial sins as they might turn up, and should propose to himself to avoid only mortal sins, even without formal contempt, does sin mortally, because such disposition of mind involves clearly the danger of sinning mortally.

"If the matters or effects of venial sins are able to coalesce into one, so that the object becomes grave in reference to the same precept, it becomes a mortal sin, not by the multiplication of venial acts, but because the *last* act has a grave object. For example, he who on the same Lord's Day often labours for a quarter of an hour, without sufficient cause, sins venially each time; but if at the last time he labours so long as to make a mortal sin, he sins mortally. On the other hand, however, he who works each Lord's Day a short time, or on each day in Lent takes a little before his meal, only sins venially, because the matters of this sort of transgression do not coalesce into one object against the same obligation. So he who steals articles of small moment from different persons, without the intention of enriching himself, sins only venially; but if he steals them from the same person, he will sin mortally, where, with due and sufficient union, he shall complete a grave matter, because then they constitute a grave object against the same obligation."
—Vol. v. pp. 44, 45.

different times small matters, and so long as he does not intend to reach a sum sufficiently large to be considered notable (*notabilis*), he is but a venial offender; but if he pilfers enough to bring his larceny up to such a point that he perceives, or might perceive, or ought to perceive, that it is "grave," then, though the prior acts are all venial, the last act by which the grave matter is completed is a mortal sin.[1] If, however, he designed from the beginning to effect a considerable embezzlement, then each act of the series is mortal, because each is tainted with the same guilty intention. But, touching the matter of coalescence, there is still another refinement which must be an unspeakable consolation to certain persons who have but confused notions as to the rights of property. For we are told that in order that separate and minute acts of theft may coalesce, it is necessary that they should be "morally continuous;" so that if the acts are separated from each other by an "ample time," they cannot constitute one whole sin.[2] But what is a "small matter," what a "grave one," what an "ample space of time"?

[1] Dens' "Theologia." No. 161.
[2] Bouvier says:—"Nevertheless authors agree that a greater quantity is required to constitute a mortal sin when minute thefts are perpetrated on different persons, or on the same person at great intervals, because the masters are less unwilling (!). *Billuart* thinks, with several other theologians, that as great an interval should be allowed between minute thefts, whether from the same or from different persons, as should keep them from being connected with each other; and then, however many they may be, they do not constitute a grave matter. Suppose if five asses [of coin] are stolen in one year, and five the next, and so on through many years, by the last theft the mortal sin is not committed on

There is a curious conflict of opinion among the Romish doctors touching all these points. Billuart and others contend that a grave matter is a *certain definite sum* absolutely considered, and, of course, the same in every case, irrespective of the condition of the person from whom the thing may be stolen. But this opinion is strongly contested by others, who maintain that theft should be graduated on a sliding scale, and should be viewed in the light of the circumstances of the loser. If, for example, a poor man be robbed of a franc, or even a half, the thief may commit a mortal sin. Several writers hold that it is a "grave" matter if it amount to what will suffice to maintain in food, raiment, and lodging, a man and his family for one day.

But Gury confesses this rule to be very obscure and confused,[1] and presents us with an edifying tariff, to which, however, he appends this significant caution, that though it applies to the chief parts of Europe, it will not suit every place. To rob a poor mendicant of half a franc is a mortal sin; to rob a digger of a

account of the defect of connection. It is presumed that the pilferer had no desire to enrich himself in this way, or to retain a notable sum thence arising. If several persons steal small sums at the same time from the same man, perceiving that a heavy loss will thence accrue, none of them sins mortally, unless they act by mutual agreement, because the heavy loss cannot be imputed to any of them in particular: it has befallen the master, by accident, so far as each thief is concerned."—Vol. v. pp. 475, 6.

It must be a delicious consolation to the master who has lost a "*grave*" sum to know that none of his servants are guilty of a "*grave*" sin. This must more than reconcile him to such ingenious robbery.

[1] "Comp. Theol. Moral." p. 257.

franc and a quarter, and an artificer of a franc and a half, is a mortal sin; to rob a man moderately rich of three francs or more, according as he lives more or less luxuriously, is a mortal sin; to rob magnates, or very rich persons, of six or eight francs, is a mortal sin; and it is a mortal sin to rob kings and millionaires of ten or twelve francs. It may occasion surprise that, inasmuch as the classification observed in this tariff clearly proceeds not on the basis of the condition of the thief, but on that of the circumstances of the defrauded party, the loss on the part of kings and millionaires of so small a sum should constitute a mortal sin. Gury, however, and his array of doctors are prepared with an answer. The scale is limited to that maximum point, for otherwise thieves might *enrich* themselves out of princes without committing a mortal sin, which would be inimical to the public good![1] In practice, however, we are informed, on the authority of Liguori, a grave matter of theft cannot be exactly determined; and, as the confessor is baffled, the decision must be left to the judgment of God.[2]

In this case the penitent must of course be left in uncertainty as to whether he is, or is not, the subject of a mortal sin. Liguori and others have held that thefts do not coalesce beyond the space of two months, although the matter stolen approaches by accumulation a serious sum. Other theologians, however, recognizing in sins a more desperately confluent proclivity, would insist upon the interval of one year; while

[1] Gury. "Casus Conscientiæ," p. 171.   [2] Ibid. p. 171.

some contend that the distance of a month, or even a shorter time, will prove a non-conductor, if the peculations be but very small. Gury, with judicial gravity, endeavours to strike the balance, and suggests that some of their casuists err on the side of rigour, and others on the side of indulgence. We are further graciously enlightened as to when minute thefts make up a grave matter. If they be committed at different times, *or* at the same time from different persons, the sum total becomes a grave matter when it exceeds by *one half the sum generally considered grave;* but if the minute thefts be perpetrated *both* at different times and on different persons, the larceny becomes "grave" only if it become *double* what is generally regarded as a grave theft.[1]

As to small thefts, or injuries perpetrated through a lifetime, it is generally held by the Romish casuists that unless there has been restitution, condonement, or almsgiving, in accordance with the intention of the persons defrauded and wronged, these petty sins coalesce into a mortal sin. But it is suggested, as if by way of consolation to the poor criminal, that as men are not accustomed to exact particular restitution of moderate purloinings, but to condone them, or, at least, to consent to their being given to the poor; and, moreover, as pious men often give alms to make satisfaction for their debts; small thefts, or injuries during a lifetime, need not constitute a mortal sin.[2]

---

[1] Gury. "Theologia Moralis," p. 238.
[2] Dens' "Theologia," vol. i. p. 371.

If a servant who did not intend by petty thefts to steal a grave matter, does, by misadventure, reach it, he is tenderly informed that it is quite enough if he restore only that small matter which finally completes the grave matter;[1] in other words, if, having stolen seven francs, he restore two or three, he escapes the mortal sin!

It is to be observed that much as the Church of Rome has written on sins, mortal and venial, it has never yet drawn up a complete and authoritative catalogue of these sins, so as to enable its votaries to determine the exact nature of their guilt. If it specify seven deadly sins, even these admit of so many modifications, due to a variety of circumstances, that they often become transformed into venial. And hence, what with the lack of exhaustive lists in which mortal and venial sins are respectively tabulated; and what with the transformations which turn venial sins into mortal, and mortal into venial; and what with the absence of all determinate definitions as to the precise weight of a light and of a grave matter, and of the length of an "ample distance" between separate acts of transgression; and what with the bewildering diversities of opinion which prevail among the Romish doctors; the whole question of mortal and venial sins is in the most chaotic condition. And seeing that the penitent is not required to confess venial sins, it is manifest that the discrimination of one class of sins from

---

[1] Gury. "Casus Conscientiæ," p. 172.

another must be largely left in his own hands. It is needless to add that, this being the case, the area of subjects upon which confession is made will vary according to knowledge, temperament, and tenderness of conscience; and that two penitents confessing the same day to the same priest, will, though guilty of the same sins, disclose a widely different series of offences. The impracticability of ascertaining in all cases what is a venial and what a mortal sin, is still further aggravated by the Romish doctrine of "probabilism," which is expounded by Father Gury in his "Compendium of Moral Theology."

According to this rule of judgment, if any person who is learned and upright holds any opinion which he knows he has diligently considered, and which he is prepared to defend on the strength of grave reasons, that opinion is to him probable.

Any one author of great excellence, even though he differ from the common opinion, provided he adduces a reason which others have not duly examined, makes his own opinion probable; and any man utterly ignorant, who hears another whom he accounts upright, and prudent, and learned, allege that any opinion is probable, may regard it as "probable."[1] And it is further maintained that if a penitent is bent on following an opinion contrary to that of the father-confessor, but still probable, the confessor is bound to give him absolution, even though the priest's opinion be the more probable.[2]

[1] "Compend. Theol. Moral." pp. 24, 25. [2] Ibid. p. 35.

These considerations will help to show the incertitude which envelops the whole teaching of the Church of Rome respecting the nature and distinction of sins; and it is not a little remarkable that councils and popes, who have pronounced unalterable decisions upon so many matters which the world deems of such infinitesimal importance, should to this day have abstained from a supreme and final judgment upon the questions at which we have just glanced, and which are still left unsolved by any final authority.

At present there are five different systems or principles of moral appraisement in vogue in the Church of Rome, designated by terms of most barbarous Latinity. There is the system of absolute safety (*Tutiorismus absolutus*); there is the system of mitigated safety (*Tutiorismus mitigatus*); there is the system of the greater probability (*Probabiliorismus*); there is the system of equal probability (*Æqui probabilismus*); and there is the system of probability (*Probabilismus*).[1]

The exposition of these develops a series of still further refinements, which it would be irksome to detail, but which reveal a microscopic casuistry which has contributed not a little to the debasement and corruption of the nations which have owned the domination of Rome. These gradations of probability through degrees and sub-degrees are to a large extent

---

[1] Gury. "Compend. Theol. Moral." p. 24. Gury mentions another school, denominated *Laxistæ*, which, however, has been condemned.

left to the adjudication of each priest, whose decision must inevitably be powerfully influenced by his moral character and his mental peculiarities; and hence arises the absolute impossibility of aught approaching to uniformity in the confessional rulings of the various priests throughout the world. The Fathers differ, the Doctors differ, the Priests differ—and these differences inevitably find their way into the sacrament of penance, and render it in great measure a Lesbian rule. So notoriously, indeed, is this the case, that where a choice is possible, priests are often selected by the penitents because of their special and accommodating qualities as father-confessors, a preference which would be equally without reason and justification if the confession, both as to what is elicited and what is adjudged, were the same, whoever the priest himself might be.

II.

We are now prepared to consider in the second place the assumed reality and validity of those decisions which are pronounced by the priests in the sacrament of penance. We say the "assumed" reality and validity, for it will become clearer as we advance that no ground can be more treacherous and deceitful than that upon which the penitent builds his faith that the absolution he receives either determines or expresses the final judgment of heaven. The sacrament now under consideration lacks, in truth, every element of certainty. In the priest himself there meet possibilities which may well destroy the confidence of the penitent in the efficacy of the absolving act. For while it is astounding to see what discreditable and revolting characteristics can consist with the validity of the sacerdotal order, it is scarcely less astounding to see how its acts can be practically nullified. It is not every priest in the Church of Rome who is a priest indeed; in other words, whose administration of the sacraments can convey with certainty the grace and the security which are alleged to be connected with them, for his orders may be affected by an incurable taint. No ordination is valid unless there be in the recipient of orders what is termed in the Church of Rome an habitual, or, at least, a virtual intention; and of the existence of such intention in the case of any priest whatsoever, no one knows but himself. A disastrous uncertainty therefore attaches to the claims of every priest in the Papal communion, and as the validity of the orders determines the validity of the sacraments, it is manifest that no penitent can be assured that the priest into whose ears he is pouring the secrets of his life has more authority to absolve or condemn than the first shoeblack or costermonger he encounters in the streets.

The uncertainty in question may not originate with the priest, but with the bishop who ordained him, or with the bishops from whom even he received his orders; and at whatever point in the chain the fatal element of defective intention crept in, it arrested thenceforward the flow of sacramental efficacy. To say that the penitent proceeds on the *assumption* that the father-confessor received an ordination which is untainted through the whole of its regressive line, is to say that he consents to believe that which not only he cannot prove, but the *proof* of which is absolutely necessary in order that to him the sacramental forgiveness may have any value. This flaw, possible in any case of ordination, must, if duly appreciated, destroy the confidence of every penitent in the absolute efficacy of the sacrament of penance. It is like a defect in the credentials of one who assumes to be an ambassador of an earthly monarch, the validity of whose actions and decisions depends upon the completeness of his authorisation. The defect may be subtle—indiscernible to the public eye—known only to himself and the king whose royal will he fraudulently presumes to represent; but none the less does it inspire both false hopes and false fears, and none the less will his decision be discredited when the monarch shall reckon with him. The man who wears the name of priest, but who had not due intention in the act of his ordination (a possibility which the Church of Rome distinctly allows), is not a priest, and he has neither consecrated the host, nor absolved a penitent, though he has been in the office of the priesthood for fifty years; and the faithful Catholic layman who has depended on his ministrations has returned home from Mass and confessional, saying, "Peace, peace, when there is no peace."

But the invalidity of sacerdotal orders is not the only element which renders the sacrament of penance a precarious thing. The ordination of the priest may be unexceptionable. It may, formally, empower him to discharge all priestly functions, and yet he may be so lacking in qualifications which no rite or ordination can confer, that it is at the layman's peril that he adopts him as his father-confessor. The teaching of the Church of Rome on this point is such as may well drive its votaries to despair.

They are, in the first place, informed that any parish priest is qualified, formally, or in virtue of orders, to be a confessor,[1] and then they are warned that all needful care must be taken in the choice of a confessor. But what is the liberty of choice possessed by hundreds of thousands who live in districts of the country but thinly populated, where priests are wide apart, where means of locomotion are but few and expensive, and where, therefore, by an insuperable necessity, the Catholic penitent must confess to his own priest or to none at all? Or why does the Church of Rome first pretend, by its collation of sacerdotal orders, to empower priests to receive confession, and then issue a monition that some of them had better not be trusted? It might well have been supposed that the qualifications of the priest and the obligations of the people were correlative, and that as all parish priests are authorized to receive confession, all their parishioners respectively would be safe in their hands. But we are informed by Dens that "the election of a confessor is a matter of the highest moment, on which the salvation of a penitent sometimes depends; and that for this reason St. Francis of Sales exhorts

[1] Dens. "De Confessione," p. 83.

the Catholic most earnestly to pray God that He would supply him with a man after His own heart." [1]

This affords but a cheerless prospect for those rustics who have but one priest at hand, and he possibly not "a man after God's own heart." We are further informed that where the confessor is at the same time to be the director of the spiritual life, then the difficulty of finding one who is equal to the two functions combined is one of the gravest character. "Avila says, Choose one out of a thousand; but I (Francis de Sales) say one of ten thousand, for fewer are found capable of this office." [2]

If this be so, that there is but one safe and efficient guide out of ten thousand Catholic priests, the laity must have but poor shepherding. But this is not all, for it appears from the acknowledgment of Dens that some confessors are "easy, silent, or lax," and that such are consulted by some of the faithful from an improper motive. But what becomes of the integrity and sufficiency of the priest's qualifications for the function of a father-confessor, if, in fact, he be not practically competent to discharge the duties of the confessional? "Easiness, silence, laxity," are not qualifications, but disqualifications; and to talk of "orders" without "fitness" in a spiritual kingdom is an insult both to God and man. No layman with an improper motive ought to be more able to meet with such a priest, than an ignorant and indolent scholar should be able to meet with an examiner who would weakly accommodate his

[1] Dens. "De Confessione," p. 133.   [2] Ibid. p. 133.

questions to his stupidity. Nor so much; for it appears from the testimony already cited that the salvation of the penitent may depend on the quality of the confessor. What is the value of orders which give to the laity, on whose behoof they are conferred, no security that their possessors can or will efficiently discharge the duties of their office? It is freely acknowledged by Catholic writers that a priest may be ignorant, and the question is asked whether the ignorance of the priest invalidates the absolution of the penitent? This question is answered in the negative. Here, again, it is a matter of wonder that orders can be divorced from qualifications.

But the precarious nature of confession and absolution does not end even here. For when the penitent has found a priest who will satisfy all the conditions desirable in such a functionary, goodness (*bonitas*), knowledge (*scientia*), and prudence (*prudentia*), another serious difficulty emerges. As the priest is not endowed with omniscience, nor even with such a modification of it as may give him direct access to the heart, he must depend on the penitent for his knowledge of what is within. And if the penitent be at all defective in the spontaneous disclosure of his life, inner and outer, then the priest may, and (if he do his duty) must probe him with questions until he has succeeded, as he thinks, in bringing to light all the hidden things of darkness. But he may be mistaken. Sins may yet remain unrevealed either through the failure of his skill for the nonce (*nemo mortalium omnibus horis sapit*), or through the forgetfulness of the penitent; and in either case there are some sins which are neither confessed nor forgiven, which might have been both confessed and (on the Romish theory) forgiven had the priest been more searching in his scrutiny. The conditions of salvation must, accordingly, vary enormously in different parishes with the laxity or severity of the priests, for not only will there be elicited a different catalogue of sins, but there will be imposed a different degree of penance or satisfaction.

And what must be the state of things when (no uncommon contingency) an ignorant penitent is shut up to an ignorant priest, and still more to one whose ignorance is combined with a demoralization of heart in which the light of conscience has become so dark, that the Lord said of it, "How great is that darkness!"

There have been times when such priests swarmed in the Romish Church. The pages of Catholic historians record their iniquities with an unsparing fidelity, and yet during those times such were the men who assumed to open and shut the kingdom of heaven. The sweeping maxim of Gury, which has also the authority of the blessed Liguori and others, that the confessor is in a state of damnation who without sufficient knowledge undertakes the duties of the confessional,[1] must work havoc among the priests of the middle ages, and among the people too, for what becomes of the judgments of such confessors? Does heaven stamp them with its seal? Does it accept and endorse their distinctions of mortal and venial sins?

[1] Gury. "Theologia Moralis," p. 564.

And are the faithful whom the priests in their ignorance, their laxity, or their drunkenness, have shriven, made sure of eternal life? The confessor, we are informed, ought sedulously to address himself to the study of "moral theology;" and Liguori insists that this study should never be intermitted, because out of so many different and disparate things which pertain to this science, many of them escape the memory, and require to be recalled by constant application.[1] But what was the study of moral theology pursued by the common priests of the dark ages, of whom many could neither read nor write? In the days of Charlemagne not one priest out of a thousand in Spain could address a common letter of salutation to one another. About the year 1000 scarcely a single person was found in Rome who knew the first elements of learning. In the days of Dunstan none of the clergy, it is said, knew how to write or translate a Latin letter.[2] And in the year 1551, in the diocese of Gloucester, out of three hundred and eleven of the clergy, consisting of dean, prebends, and other ministers, one hundred and sixty-eight could not repeat the commandments, thirty-one of them did not know in what part of Scripture they were found, forty-one knew not where the Lord's Prayer was written, and thirty-one were ignorant of who was its author![3] It is hard to conceive what knowledge the priests of these periods could possess of the science of

[1] Gury. "Theologia Moralis," p. 565.
[2] Hallam. "Middle Ages," vol. ii. p. 353.
[3] "Later Writings of Bishop Hooper," p. 151 (Parker Society).

moral theology, by which they were to be equipped for the tremendous duties of the confessional.

In this consideration of the elements which combine to render the absolution of the priest a precarious blessing, I have attached no importance to the nullifying circumstances which may pertain to the penitent so far as they are within his knowledge or will. For the Church of Rome is sufficiently explicit as to the fact that the conscious concealment of any known sin of a mortal kind renders the whole confession nugatory and the absolution void. For invincible ignorance she provides ample room, and for inadvertence too, but she demands that no consideration of shame, modesty, or fear, shall shelter a deadly sin. In other words, the absolution is valid only when the confession is complete. But the fact still remains that the sacrament of penance can afford no security to any penitent who duly considers the circumstances which can vitiate the orders of his priest, the confusion which still reigns as to the distinction between venial and mortal sin, and the difference which prevails between priest and priest even in adjoining parishes. Whether the judgment of the priest be supposed to rule and fix the judgment of God, or to be ruled and fixed by it and express it, the notion that a penitent obtains a trustworthy absolution is preposterous; for it is clear that a road or a river may, according to the divergent views of the priests on either side, modify the conditions upon which salvation is attainable, and a layman who is absolved on the right bank of a stream would be condemned on the left. Do both the priests in contiguous parishes equally represent the will of God when, from varying degrees of knowledge or ignorance, or from a different classification of sins *essentially the same*, they pronounce contrary decisions? It is impossible to characterise this with truth as a fancy picture, for the standard authorities of the Romish Church are replete with acknowledgments of the contentions that exist between various doctors as to whether a special form of sin shall be regarded as venial or mortal.

With these uncertainties, which by no means exhaust the list, uncertainties arising both from the side of the confessor and the penitent, I hesitate not to say that there is no proof, and from the nature of the case there can be none, that there has ever been a solitary instance of valid and irreversible priestly absolution in the Church of Rome from the beginning until now.

The claim of a minister of Christ to pronounce absolution must either be that of an authority to utter and decree the actual condition of the penitent in the sight of God, or it must be that of simple declaration that, on the supposition of certain spiritual qualifications being possessed, the penitent is absolved. In the former case, the confessor determines and fixes the state of the penitent, and might, had he so chosen, have determined and fixed that state in quite the contrary manner. In the latter case the confessor's declaration is only an uttered interpretation of what, so far as he can learn, is the moral and spiritual attitude of the penitent towards God. The former view of the function of the minister is, as we have seen, a monstrous invasion of the Divine prerogatives, from which prophets and apostles shrank with instinctive and sacred recoil; the latter view is harmless enough, for the absolution (if such it may be called) is but the announcement, on the authority of the Divine Word, that, given a certain attitude of soul towards God, there is a corresponding attitude of God towards the soul. Whatever exceeds the limits of this guarded declaration must proceed on the assumption, either that the priest knows more than he has obtained from the penitent in the confessional, or that apart from that knowledge he has a power vested in himself, and independent of the character of the penitent, to assign his destiny. This latter assumption is one which the Church of Rome has, so far as I know, never formally made, but it is unquestionable that popular sentiment in that Church invests the priests with the prerogative in question; and it is equally unquestionable that it is the formal doctrine of Rome, that be the piety of a layman what it may, the condition of his soul in the sight of God will not avail for his salvation unless, when opportunity serves, he receives priestly absolution on earth.[1]

---

[1] The following are the 6th, 7th, and 8th canons of the Council of Trent, respecting the indispensableness of sacramental confession.

"If any one shall deny that sacramental confession was either instituted by Divine command or is necessary to salvation; or shall say that the practice of secret confession to a priest alone, which the Catholic Church has always observed from the beginning, and does still observe, is alien from the institution and command of Christ, and is a human invention, let him be accursed.   ["If

III.

I have now to consider the moral tendencies and effects of the sacrament of penance.

In the treatment of this question it is not necessary to indulge in any unseemly impeachment of the motives by which the Romish authorities have been influenced in their enforcement of auricular confession. It is impossible to deny that this practice has been advocated by many upon the very highest grounds, nor can we reasonably dispute the testimony borne by hundreds of godly men in the Church of Rome, that they have found in confession spiritual help and consolation.

But we have not now to do with the occasional benefits which may accrue from any system to individual men. There is scarcely any practice which is so corrupt as not to produce some incidental good.

"If any one shall say that in the sacrament of penance for the remission of sins it is not necessary by Divine authority to confess all and each mortal sin of which, with due and diligent premeditation, the man is conscious, even the secret sins, and sins against the last two laws of the Decalogue, as well as the circumstances which alter the species of a sin, but that such confession is only useful for the instruction and consolation of the penitent, and was formerly observed simply as a canonical satisfaction imposed upon him; or shall affirm that those who labour to confess all their sins desire to leave nothing to be pardoned by the Divine mercy; or, finally, that it is not lawful to confess venial sins, let him be accursed.

"Whosoever shall affirm that the confession of every sin, according to the custom of the Church, is impossible, and merely a human tradition which the pious should reject; or that all Christians of both sexes are not bound to observe the same once a year, according to the constitution of the great Council of Lateran, and therefore that the faithful in Christ are to be persuaded not to confess in Lent, let him be accursed."

Where, however, systems have to be judged, not merely in the light of Divine commands, but in that of their actual working and influence, it is necessary to observe their operation over a large scale; and if their general results are evil, whatever plea might be urged for their being allowed to those who find them helpful, no defence can be made for their being rendered imperative on those who resent them, or who are injured by them. Few persons would deny that there is, at times, a great relief in unburdening to a friend the sins and sorrows of one's life. But the relief is not forgiveness. And few would deny that in times of difficulty and temptation the warnings and counsels of a friend may be of sovereign service, and thousands have known the value of having a director in the chief crises of their life. But for one priest who, taken at random, is qualified for this solemn function, there may be found a dozen laymen whose actual experience of life is far wider than that of the priest, and whose knowledge is all the more valuable that it is not derived from technical books on theology or casuistry. The confessional, however, has to be considered, not under some ideal aspect, but in the light of its actual form and history in the Church of Rome, and in the light of that strong gravitation towards evil from which it is so hard to restrain it. It is the enforced confession once a year, at least, on the part of every adult male and female, of all their mortal sins so far as remembered, to the priest, be his ignorance and moral character what they may—this it is for which not only no authority can be found in the Scriptures, nor in the earlier centuries of the post-apostolic Church, but which has been productive of the most disastrous results in those nations where it has had the most unrestricted sway. If the confessional be designed to instruct the conscience, to restrain the passions, to purify the life, and to develop a nobler manhood; if, as is alleged, its machinery is admirably adapted to promote these ends, it is, at least, extraordinary that no such favourable consequences result from its operation. For it is an indisputable fact that, looking at the moral life of those countries which have known least of the confessional, it contrasts triumphantly with that of those which have known the most of it, there being no sane man who would dream of inviting a comparison between England and Spain.

In considering the influence of the confessional, we must not attach too much value to the priests of exceptional excellence, in whose hands the sacrament of penance will be administered with gravity, prudence, firmness, and tenderness. For not only are such men exceptional, but the system of Romanism does not provide for their existence at all, at least as an indispensable necessity. They may not be found anywhere, and if there were not a single devout or godly priest in the world, the validity of the sacraments would not be impaired one jot or tittle. The moral character of the priest within certain limits is wholly an accident to the priesthood, and what these limits are may be surmised from the explicit statement that "neither faith, nor probity, nor a state of grace is required in a minister in order to the validity of sacraments."[1] The filthiness of the channel does not pollute the stream it conveys. This is the dogma of the Church of Rome, insisted on in every variety of language, and the character of tens of thousands of her priests has not left the dogma without abundant confirmation. If, therefore, no priest is bound to be moral, so all priests may be immoral, and it is notorious that many are so. And as is the priest, so will be the sacrament of penance as administered by him. He cannot drop his personal character when he enters the confessional box, and where he is a corrupt man it is hopeless to imagine that his corruption will not colour the nature of that catechetical scrutiny through means of which he probes the heart and life of the penitent. It boots nothing to say that instructions are given in works intended for the use of the priest that the questions he propounds are to be of a prudent character, and not to exceed what is necessary to elicit the sins of the penitent. For of what use are instructions of this nature when it is distinctly declared that prudence is not requisite to the validity of orders? and what is that limit at which the priest is to be presumed as having completed his knowledge of all the sins on which he has to adjudicate? The limit will vary with the confessor himself, for the Church of Rome has nowhere prescribed the full list of questions which he is to propound, and beyond which he is not

[1] Gury. "Theologia Moralis," p. 45.

to go. It is left to his own intelligence, of which he may have little; his own prudence, of which he may have less; his own modesty, of which he may have none. He, and not the penitent, is to determine the scope of the scrutiny, and if his queries are not answered he can refuse or reserve the absolution. With such powers in his hand the penitent is at his mercy.

And it is to us inconceivable that any person who duly ponders this consideration can fail to see that it would be a miracle if the confessional itself did not become, whether intentionally or inadvertently, an incitement to those very sins from which it pretends to restrain. The wise priest is supposed to respect the actual range of the penitent's sins, but he is also supposed to reach it. Now, there is not one man in a hundred endowed, either by nature or training, with such tact as to discover this faint boundary; and if the questions transcend it they cannot fail to become suggestions of the possibilities of evil to those who never dreamed of them before. Even though the priest be one of the holiest men such an examination becomes in itself an education in sin; a new series of transgressions is opened up to the mind of, perhaps, a susceptible youth, whose imagination is set on flame with this unexpected discovery, and he leaves the priest a worse man than he came.

I shall not defile these pages with any minute description of that loathsome and abominable process of investigation through which it is competent for any confessor to trail every penitent that kneels in the confessional. And it is impossible for me to find words which will adequately express the detestation which I have felt in examining the favourite casuists of Rome, whose pages are thickly bleared with filth and infamy. They shall lie masked in their congenial Latin. But my purpose in this lecture would be very imperfectly accomplished did I not, with as much of faithfulness as is consistent with delicacy, enable the reader to appreciate in some measure the power which the confessional possesses to disintegrate the conscience, and to debase the whole moral nature. Some faint idea has already been afforded in the first part of this lecture of the subtle casuistry which has grown up around the system of confession, the refinements upon refinements by which theologians seem to have vied with each other as to who possessed the keenest metaphysical blade. A glance has been given, and only a glance, into the philosophy of theft. We have seen the prescriptions which have been considerately drawn up for the purpose of keeping thievery within venial limits; and it will have been observed how the *essential* criminality of stealing is not only lost but practically denied in those graduated tariffs which make it *venial* to steal a penny and *mortal* to steal a pound. But a similar method of casuistry is applied to every sin that man can commit. A lie, for example, is heavy or slight according to the amount of loss which it occasions to one's neighbour;[1] so that if the falsehood contemplated

[1] Gury. "Theologia Moralis," p. 499.

the infliction of a heavy loss, but fails through circumstances beyond the control of the liar, the lie is insignificant. We are further informed that it is not a falsehood if we only declare that that is false which we believe to be true, but that it is a falsehood if we say that that is true which we believe to be false.[1]

A father confessor if interrogated by a tyrant whether Titius has confessed to the commission of a homicide, may and ought to answer, "I do not know," because the confessor does not know so as to reveal it. A wife who has been unfaithful to her husband, being interrogated by him, may answer in the first place that she has not broken the matrimonial tie; and when she has been absolved, if he ask her again, she may say, "I am innocent of such a crime." If the husband still persist in questioning her, she may say, "I have not committed it, so as to reveal it to you."

The woman is formally and elaborately defended in these answers by St. Liguori, Suarez, and others, and in the following manner as given by Gury in his "Casus Conscientiæ."[2] She may say in the first case of asking that she has not broken the matrimonial tie, since it still continues to exist. She may say in the second case that she is innocent of the crime, because, having made confession and received absolution, her conscience is no longer oppressed by it, since she has a moral certainty that it is forgiven—nay, further, she may even affirm on oath that she is innocent. In the

---

[1] Gury. "Theologia Moralis," p. 199.
[2] Gury. "Casus Conscientiæ," p. 129.

third place, she may deny with probability (*probabiliter*) that she has committed the crime imputed, understanding secretly with herself that "she has not so committed it as to reveal it to him."

This is the solemn deliverance of Liguori, a canonized saint of the Church of Rome, and of a host of others (*cum aliis bene multis*). Were it not that I write with the pages of Gury before me, such representations of the ethical teachings of that Church, or of any other Church, would have seemed to me absolutely incredible, and I can well believe that even now some might be disposed to regard them as Protestant calumnies. But *litera scripta manet*, and the incredulous reader will find the evidence at page 129 in the work of Gury on "Casus Conscientiæ," published in Ratisbon in the year 1865, and endorsed with the imprimatur of Montagnac and Reger.

From the cases just considered, it will be seen that two of the laws of the Decalogue are cheaply set at nought through the glosses of the priests whose influence is now predominant in the Church of Rome. The commandments which enjoin truth and connubial chastity and honour are practically abolished, and this too chiefly through the influence of sacramental confession and absolution; for it is the fact that the unfaithful wife has received absolution which is to justify her in the infamous falsehood of saying, "I am innocent of the crime." Thus it is that the sanctity of human language, the divinely appointed medium of communication between man and man, is trampled on, and its words deceptively employed in a double sense. Aided by this corrupt species of logic, there is not an adulteress in the world who cannot under priestly sanction, and even with a solemn oath, according to Liguori, protest her innocence, and carry on the double iniquity of unchastity and falsehood, the former finding its shield in the latter, and both in the immoral teaching of the priest.

Bouvier, the Bishop of Mans, in his " Philosophical Institutes" propounds the question whether it is lawful to take an oath of fidelity to a usurper, and accept an engagement under him? He justifies the oath, provided the man secretly resolves to be faithful, if the chance should happen, to the legitimate sovereign. And if at a subsequent period the legitimate prince should claim his services, he ought promptly to espouse his cause, and even assassinate the usurper to whom he had sworn obedience.[1]

The same prelate maintains that a man who, mounted on horseback or in a carriage, is not able otherwise to escape an enemy, may, if the path is narrow, trample under foot a lame man, a sleeping man, or a child that has been baptized, and still be excused from the crime of homicide.[2] The rights of the lame and the sleeping to life are not considered, nor does the learned casuist inform us how the frantic fugitive is to ascertain whether the child has been baptized, and how long he is to arrest his horse or chariot, to obtain such important information, when the pursuer is thundering at his heels. But indeed he need give

[1] Pp. 628, 630. [2] "Institutiones Theologicæ," vol. v. p. 452.

himself no trouble, for if he should happen to trample to death an unbaptized child or a drunkard, if he do it in good faith, this will excuse him (*bona fides excusabit*).

Sanchez declares that any one may swear that he has not done a certain thing, although he has done it, if he understands with himself that he did not do it on a certain day, or before he was born, or understanding some other similar circumstance, without the words having in them anything which makes the reserve known. "And this," he adds, "is very convenient in many conjunctions, and always just when it is necessary or useful for health, honour, or property."[1]

Gury informs us that if a thief, intending to steal cloth, enters a shop by night, and lights a candle, taking all care to avoid the danger of conflagration, but by some unexpected accident the candle falls into the straw, and the whole shop is burned, and the thief with difficulty just manages to escape, *he is liable for nothing*, because he did not in the least foresee the danger. Nay, further, he is not even accountable for the cloth which he was bent on pilfering, even though he had laid his hand upon it, because the loss of that too was involuntary. The seizing of the cloth was not the cause of the loss, nor was the carrying of the candle the immediate cause of the conflagration, because the burglar took sufficient care.[2]

It were easy, too easy, indeed, to fill scores of pages

---

[1] Sanchez. "Oper. Moral." part ii. lib. iii. chap. 6.
[2] "Theologia Moralis," p. 282.

with citations from Dens, Bouvier, Sanchez, Liguori, and Gury, in which there is the same shameless casuistry in the treatment of questions bearing upon almost every commandment in the Decalogue. Truly have they made void the law of God by their traditions. That which has been said of the Jesuits as an order, may be applied with scarcely any deduction to the whole of the Church of Rome; viz., that while recommendations may be found in their writings in favour of a strict observance of the moral code, "all these expressions of rigorous sentiment are reduced to mere figures of speech through the all-covering action of the principle of probabilism, which runs continuously through the whole volume of Jesuit doctrine, like a foot-note which thoroughly modifies the force of the text. . . . . Through the slides of a side proposition, artfully masked, the Jesuit doctors have provided a mechanism for converting at will the whole series of moral principles into a set of dissolving views."[1]

In short, the general principles which are enunciated in the writings to which we have referred, and in which we have left buried in deserved obscurity and ignominy the most revolting cases, are wholly evacuated of their worth when they come to be applied to the details. The virtue which is commanded in the rule vanishes as an obligation amid the endless exceptions which may be pleaded and defended, and which are not only so numerous, but so startling, that the wonder is what room is found for the rule at all. Theft, falsehood,

[1] "Quarterly Review." No. 275, p. 108.

adultery, and other sins are forbidden by these consummate sophists; but immediately that the prohibition is announced there follows a troop of dexterous evasions, by means of which any one must be a blundering transgressor who cannot manage to escape. " Sinning made easy and safe," might well be the title of the works to which we have referred; and while it is true that the various rulings of these authors have not received the *ex cathedrâ* authorization of the pope himself as dogmas *de moribus*, it is well known by him that such are the text-books from which his subordinates are being instructed for their sacerdotal work, and yet they are not condemned. So far as I can learn, they are in no index of prohibited books, nor have they incurred any of the anathemas which have been fulminated with such vengeance against far less questionable things in the famous Syllabus. The immoral teaching in his own Church which the pontiff does not censure he sanctions; and until the licentious and filthy casuistry, of which but a sample, and by no means the worst, has been given, is formally and authoritatively suppressed, and excluded from seminaries and colleges, the moral responsibility and odium must rest upon the pope himself.

No stronger proof of the demoralizing effects of the confessional need be sought than the edicts which have from time to time been issued by popes in condemnation of the iniquities for which the confessional afforded such facile occasion. What means the letter of Pope Paul IV., addressed on the 18th of January, 1556, to the Inquisition of Granada, in which he commanded that august body to prosecute the infamous clergy who had converted the sacrament of penance into an abominable orgie? Or what means the edict published in Seville in 1563, having the same object in view, which led to so many denunciations, that the police of the Inquisition was insufficient to receive them? One hundred and twenty days were required for the formal deposition and consideration of the charges, and the revelations which took place were so revolting, that the Fathers of the Holy Office in their alarm let many of the delinquents go free. Or what mean the Bulls of Gregory XV. and of Benedict XIV., which I shall not venture to translate, but which denounce the secret prostitution of the confessional to the most shameless vice? As the priests are but men, and according to the doctrine of the Romish Church need not be good men, they are liable to those infirmities and passions which no ordination can charm away; and it is no wonder that in the administration of a sacrament, which from its very nature engenders and foments temptations, they should be ensnared in sin. These two things, the confessional and sensual crime, have been historically associated from the beginning. If they are not respectively cause and effect, they are occasion and consequence. And what they have been they will continue to be as long as the sacrament of penance endures.

After this exposition of the doctrine and practice of the confessional in the Church of Rome, it is not without just alarm that we view the determination on the part of an energetic section of the Anglican clergy to revive it in the Church of England.[1] It is not necessary for us now to inquire at any length to what extent the practice is grounded on the teaching of the Prayer-Book. Dr. Pusey and his followers consider the service for the ordination of priests a mockery if it do not authorize the sacrament in question; and, further,

[1] "We have been concerned in this place," says the writer on sacramental confession in the first number of a series of "Studies in Modern Problems," "only with the teaching of the Church of England. That her teaching on absolution is too clear to be mistaken or explained away, and that her teaching is catholic and primitive, and therefore in accordance with holy Scripture, is our position. She sends her priests out with a real commission, and with real power to heal souls afflicted with the leprosy of sin, by applying to them in absolution the precious blood, which alone can cleanse the guilty soul. Even the power and efficacy of the atoning blood itself is limited by the dispositions of the soul to which it has to be applied, and the commission of the priest is strictly to *penitent* sinners. But wherever the true penitent is found, there too is ready the power to loose the bands of his sins. We say that this is the unmistakable teaching of the Church of England, and, if so, it must follow that those who exercise this ministry, so far from being unfaithful stewards, deserve to be upheld and encouraged by those in authority. . . . Their lordships [the bishops] are in a difficult position. If they adhere to the Prayer-Book they offend my Lord Shaftesbury and "The Times" newspaper. If they use the Prayer-Book with mental reserve, and in a non-natural sense, they injure the Church, the clergy, and their own souls; and in the long run they ensure for their successors disestablishment and disendowment. . . . We venture in this connection to recall certain words of the late Bishop Wilberforce in his first ordination service as Bishop of Oxford. After quoting the words, 'Receive ye the Holy Ghost. Whose sins ye remit, they are remitted,' he added, 'These same words are again to be spoken to-day as in His name, and as if He were present with us.' And all this is the most blasphemous frivolity if it is not the deepest truth. But truth it is."—P. 36.

that no words can more emphatically teach it than those which are found in the service for the "visitation of the sick." "By His authority committed to me, I absolve thee from all thy sins, in the name of the Father, and of the Son, and of the Holy Ghost." The inference in favour of priestly absolution seems to us inevitable, and the sacerdotalists have here an entrenchment from which they can never be dislodged. But the words in question do not cover the wider interpretation which would find in them periodical auricular confession, either as a rule or as a necessity. Nor is there, as we think, any office of the Church of England which empowers such an inference. The confession of the sick person is accompanied by two conditions, the first being his sense of some weighty matter by which his conscience is troubled, and the second his earnest desire to receive absolution. The confession is not therefore set forth as a universal and necessary obligation.

The same view is supported by the exhortation given by the minister to those who are about to partake of the Lord's Supper. "And because it is requisite that no man should come to the holy communion but with a full trust in God's mercy and with a quiet conscience, therefore if there be any of you who by this means cannot quiet his conscience herein, but requireth further comfort and counsel, let him come to me, or to some other learned minister of God's Word, and open his grief, that by the ministry of God's holy Word he may receive the benefit of absolution, together with ghostly counsel or advice, to the quieting of his conscience, and avoiding of all scruple and doubtfulness."[1]

Two positions, therefore, seem to us to be equally unwarranted by the teaching of the Prayer-Book. The first is that auricular confession is enjoined on all as a preparation for the sacrament of the Lord's Supper; and the second is that the priest does not possess an official and authoritative prerogative to absolve in the case of every person who may avail himself of the invitation to disclose any burden which may be resting on his conscience. The Ritualist errs as widely in the maintenance of the former view as the Evangelical in the maintenance of the latter. But the fact remains that touching both these points the Church of England is at present divided into two great hostile sections, who are carrying on an internecine war with an implacable bitterness which furnishes a strange commentary on that uniformity which the Prayer-Book was avowedly meant to secure. Meanwhile, whatever be the teaching of this book, the practice of auricular confession is spreading. With, or without authority, its network is being extended over the land for weal or for woe. In one year, we are informed, a single priest of the Church of England heard thirteen hundred confessions, and his case was not an exceptional one.[2] "Several well-known priests have been disabled by the strain which this work puts upon them;" and "not only an appreciable, but a large percentage of the communicants of

[1] See Appendix E.   [2] "Studies in Modern Problems," p. 1.

the Church of England, now confess their sins to a priest."[1]

Some abatement may fairly be made from the language of an ardent partisan like the author of the work just quoted, but of the steady advancement of the practice of confession there can be no reasonable doubt. And the details of the practice are elaborated in remarkable conformity with the rules laid down for the guidance of the confessor in the Church of Rome. The work published in 1869, and entitled "The Priest in Absolution: a Manual for such as are called into the Higher Ministries of the English Church," is little else than a condensation of the recognised textbooks in the Church of Rome. There is hardly one direction given to the Anglican priest which may not be found in spirit, if not in form, in Dens, or Gury, or Liguori.[2]

[1] "Studies in Modern Problems," p. 2.

[2] In "Hints to Penitents," a book written for members of the Church of England, and in the third section, I find the following among a "Hundred suggestions for a rule of life in Advent or Lent." "Take less, or no sugar, butter, sweets, or needless luxuries." "Do not smoke more than — daily." "Take more care of and wipe the dust off all sacred books and pictures, and emblems of the Lord's Passion." "Do some very decided act of humiliation or self-denial, such as kneeling and touching the ground with your forehead; lying on the floor with arms extended as on a cross; standing and smiting the heart; repeating the prayer of the publican; not defending yourself when unjustly found fault with; using cold instead of warm water sometimes; using a harder pillow; rising after having got into bed; kneeling and saying, 'Lord, I am not worthy to rest in peace.'" "Look less into shop-windows daily, much less on Fridays." "Resolve to keep silence one hour on Fridays." "Double your penances given in confession, if permitted." "Begin this Lent to practise some outward act of reverence, as, for instance, bowing to the altar, or at the Gloria."

And it is but a cold and barren consolation which the nation derives from the assurance of the Evangelical clergy, that this work and others like it, which now constitute an extensive literature, are private and unauthorised. For if the leaven of the confessional be evil, does there rest no responsibility on that Church, or on its superior officers, through whose help, connivance, supineness, or dread of disturbance or rupture, the mischief is allowed steadily to work? Have the prelates forgotten their solemn vow which they made at their consecration, "That they were ready, the Lord being their helper, with all faithful diligence to banish and drive away all erroneous and strange doctrine contrary to God's Word, and both privately and openly to call upon and encourage others to do the same"?

In his recent charge[1] the Bishop of London devoted a considerable space to the examination of the practice of auricular confession in the light of holy Scripture, and pronounced a strong judgment against it; but the priests in his diocese who both defend and administer it are left unmolested. Everywhere we see priestly defiance and prelatical terror, not one of the bishops, though administering a system based on law, daring to invoke the law against practices which he has the cheap courage only to denounce as Romish and corrupt. Remonstrances, warnings, entreaties in mild, hesitating, and equivocal encyclicals, exhaust, as yet, prelatical zeal for Protestant truth; while the refractory

[1] October, 1875.

priests smile at such indecision, and extend the work of perversion year by year.

What concern is it to these transgressors that the law is against them (if, indeed, it be against them), provided that the power to enforce obedience is held in hands that dare not employ it, lest a system cemented by compromise should be rent asunder? The common reverence for the idol of an establishment among parties separated far as the poles on great doctrinal questions, and inspired with the most implacable animosities against each other, may, for a season longer, prevent any of these antagonistic schools from forcing matters to an extremity. But what, meanwhile, is to become of the nation, if the Neo-Catholic body in the Church makes fresh encroachments with its Baptismal Regeneration, its Real Presence, its Prayers for the Dead, and its Confessional, crushing into smaller space and influence the Evangelical section, until, under the shelter of Protestant law, which no bishop has the courage to enforce, the people have become saturated with Romanism without having formally seceded to Rome?

Let not the people of this country solace themselves with the deceitful illusion that the confessional, as we have seen it to exist in the Church of Rome, can never re-establish itself in our own time and nation. This sense of security is one of our most imminent and formidable perils. The parable is repeating itself once more with an alarming precision and significance, that "while we sleep the enemy is sowing tares;" and they are tares which are remarkable for their astonishing quickness of growth, especially in that fertile and unpreoccupied soil of youth in which the seeds are being scattered broadcast with such a diligent hand. If the adult population are the despair of the priests, the children are their hope; and another generation will yield results that will startle those Protestants who have been disposed to regard the Catholic revival as nothing but a superficial and transient fashion, adopted by the more sentimental or imbecile sections of the English Church. No one expects that the nation will, in a night, make the transition from Protestantism to Romanism. Evils do not establish themselves thus abruptly, but the ratio of progress which has been made by the Catholic party within the last twenty years affords an alarming indication of what may be its relative strength when twenty years more have passed away. That it is growing, and growing rapidly, no one can doubt who has an eye to discern the signs of the times; and there is hardly one distinctive element in the Romish practice and discipline which it is not determined to acclimatize once more in these dominions. To allege with a serene complacency that the moral and intellectual climate of our time and nation is absolutely unpropitious for the development of such an exotic, is to exhibit a strange blindness to obtrusive facts, or a strange incapacity to appreciate their import; and it is to forget that already the charms of Romanism have fascinated some of the ripest and most cultured Englishmen whom this century has produced, and has obtained their most unquestioning and abject concession to its extremest claims, including the Immaculate Conception of the Virgin, and the Infallibility of the Sovereign Pontiff. Our vaunted "Anglo-Saxon common sense" and "shrewdness" may be deemed proof against the progressive prevalence of sacerdotalism, but these can be regarded as nothing better than flattering phrases in the light of passing events, and of the historic fact that for centuries these same wonderful qualities were prostrated before the very superstitions and usurpations which are now so cheaply and inconsiderately contemned. The numerous clergy, illustrious and obscure, who have seceded to Rome since the commencement of the Oxford Tract movement, are Anglo-Saxons; the thousands of laity who are following closely on their heels are Anglo-Saxons; and if it be supposed that little can be said for their "common sense" and "shrewdness," unhappily these are properties which are far from universal, and if they are to be the only antagonists of sacerdotalism, it has before it an unlimited scope.

The first duty of the Protestants of England is to awake to the fact that Romanism is, by its very instincts, aggressive, and that Ritualism is preparing its way before it, by familiarising the minds of the people both with its doctrines and its ceremonial. I say with its doctrines, for no mistake can be greater than that which would resolve the whole Ritualistic movement into a passion for scenic grandeur or musical display.

If it were nothing but a development of æstheticism it might be left to pursue its course, with its rich vestments, and floral wreaths, and banners, and decked altars, and processional and recessional hymns. But it is more than a development of æstheticism. This is not only not concealed, it is distinctly avowed by those who are the leaders of the movement. In his " Plea for Ritual," Mr. Skinner says: " Ritual and ceremonial are not only not defensible, they are intolerable, as mere ecclesiastical literature, or religious æstheticism, or the philosophy of worship, or any other formalism. They are not even to be endured as mere securities for decency and reverence. They are signs of realities or they are nothing. They are the expression of the mind of the Spirit or they are nothing. They are no mere accident to religion, they belong to the very substance of religion. They are not the mere adjuncts and decorations of religion, they are the natural and spontaneous exhibition of religion. The ancient vestments of the priest bespeak the dignity and holiness of his commission from God. The two lights before the sacrament bespeak the presence of Him who is God and Man, and the very Light of the world. The incense bespeaks the sweetness which that presence sheds on the one hand, and the sweetness of the odour of prayer and intercession on the other. The ceremonial of the Church is the provision by which she meets the craving of man's higher nature after the truly beautiful and the permanently satisfying. They are the helps by which she cheers and sustains her children in their patient waiting upon God all through the battle of life."[1]

And another leader of the same movement, writing in "Essays on the Church and the World," observes: "Ritual, like painting and architecture, is only the visible expression of divine truth. Without dogma, without an esoteric meaning, Ritual is an illusion and a delusion, a lay figure without life or spirit, a *vox et præterea nihil*. The experience of the last century shows that it is impossible to preserve the Catholic Faith excepting by Catholic Ritual; the experience of the present century equally makes manifest the fact that the revival of the Catholic Faith must be accompanied by the revival of Catholic Ritual; and still more, that the surest way to teach the Catholic Faith is by Catholic Ritual."

To treat the Neo-Catholicism of the Church of England henceforth as if it were nothing more serious than an æsthetic fashion, having for its object the creation of sensuous delights, is no longer possible except to those who are determined to be deceived. Ritualism is a thing of doctrine, and the doctrine is in all essential points the doctrine of Rome. With respect to the Eucharist this is emphatically avowed and vaunted by many Anglican writers, and notably by Mr. Cobb, whose work, the "Kiss of Peace," bears the following amplified title—"or, England and Rome at one on the Doctrine of the Holy Eucharist," and is thus significantly dedicated: "To John Henry

[1] "Plea for Ritual," pp. 24, 25.

Newman, D.D., of the Roman Communion, and Edward Bouverie Pusey, D.D., of the Anglican Communion, through whose instrumentality, more than that of any other living men, the Holy Ghost would seem at this day to be carrying on the work of Corporate Reunion, this humble effort to break down one of the barriers of separation between us is dedicated, in token of sincere admiration of their work, and of deep gratitude to God from whom all such works proceed." Nor is there one sacrament of the Church of Rome which is not deliberately vindicated and approved, and, so far as public sentiment or law will permit, quietly introduced into the pale of the Church of England. The single point of the Papal supremacy is now declared by many to be the only essential feature which separates the two communions; and it is difficult to say, after the rapid approximation which has been made on other matters of difference, how long even this will be allowed to stand in the way. By many who hold office in the Church which, in the ceremony of the Queen's coronation, is formally designated "the Protestant Reformed religion established by law," the very name of Protestant is insulted, vilified, and indignantly renounced, and the leaders of the Reformation pelted with epithets of infamy from which even Danton, Robespierre, and Marat are indulgently protected. This Romanising "net is" assuredly "spread in the sight" of the whole nation; whether "in vain" or not it remains for the people to determine, and that too with all possible promptitude and energy. That Romanism, whether full-blown or in the bud, shall be repressed by force of law, no one who respects the claims of conscience and the equitable rights of man will be prepared to advocate; but that it shall be illicitly fostered in a Church whose *raison d'être* is that it shall be a bulwark of Protestantism, is a proceeding against which we are compelled in the name of justice and religion to protest. But this protest will not suffice to cover the whole ground of obligation which rests upon us. The nation requires instruction, and it must be our aim, as God may help us, to diffuse, by all forms of teaching and influence, that knowledge of the "truth which is in Jesus," before which superstition and unbelief shall vanish as fabled spectres flee before the light of the rising sun. Amid all the conflicts of these times, so full of distraction and sadness, the one conviction which abides in us unshaken, is that, through all the tumult, the world is seeking and will surely find its way to rest in Christ, as the Prophet in whose words is eternal life; the Priest whose sufficient sacrifice has reconciled all things to God, whether they be things on earth or things in heaven; and the King before whose sceptre of right and mercy all nations shall render the homage of their obedience, and their reverent and adoring praise.

APPENDIX.

APPENDIX A.

Lecture I. Page 20.

"THE Parable of the Thieves teacheth us that Christ's coming hath disannulled all such priesthood as is called *sacerdotium*, but *presbyterium* remaineth. The Priests and Levites pass by, and leave the wounded man, which was robbed going from Hierusalem to Jericho, unholpen, unprovided for.

"Moreover, mark what I say unto thee. Read over all the New Testament, and thou shalt not find once this word. *sacerdos*—"priest," applied or spoken of any one sort of ministers (as the common sort do use it), but when it is referred to the Pharisees, and to such as do appertain without all doubt to the New Testament. It is referred always to all Christian people, which all be sacerdotes through Christ, and ministers have *no manner of sacrifice*, but common with the laity, both men and women; that is to say, the *sacrifice of thanksgiving*, and the quick and lively *oblation of their own bodies*. The New Testament requireth no other sacrifice."—*Roger Hutchinson*. "*Image of God*," pp. 49, 50.

"The word *priest*, by popish abuse, is commonly taken for a sacrificer, the same that *sacerdos* is in Latin. But the Holy Ghost never calleth the ministers of the Word and sacraments of the New Testament, ἱερεῖς, or sacerdotes. Wherefore the translators, to make a difference between the ministers of the Old Testament and them of the New, calleth the one, according to the usual acceptation, priests, and the other, according to the original derivation, elders. Which distinction, seeing the vulgar Latin text doth always rightly observe, it is in favour of your heretical, sacrificing priesthood, that you corruptly translate *sacerdos* and *presbyter* always, as though they were all one, a *priest*, as though the Holy Ghost had made that distinction in vain, or that there were no difference between the priesthood of the Old Testament and the New. The name of *priest*, according to the original derivation from *presbyter*, we do not refuse; but, according to the common acceptation for a sacrificer, we cannot take it when it is spoken of the New Testament."—*Fulke*. "*Defence of Translation*," p. 109.

"Wherefore, to pass by the name, let them use what dialect they will, whether we call it priesthood, a presbytership, or a ministry, it skilleth not; although, in truth, the word presbyter doth seem more fit, and, in propriety of speech, more agreeable than priest with the drift of the whole gospel of Jesus Christ. For what are they that embrace the gospel but sons of God? What are Churches but His families? .... The Holy Ghost, throughout the body of the New Testament, making so much mention of them (the presbyters), doth not anywhere call them priests. The prophet Isaiah, I grant doth, but in such sort as the ancient Fathers, by way of analogy."—*Hooker*. "*Eccl. Pol.*" vol. ii.

"It is a significant fact that in those languages which have only one word to express the two ideas, this word etymologically represents *presbyterus*, and not *sacerdos*: *e.g.*, the French *prêtre*, the German *priester*, and the English *priest*; thus showing that the sacerdotal idea was imported, and not original.

"In the Italian, where the two words *prete* and *sacerdote* exist side by side, there is no marked difference in usage, except that *prete* is the more common. If the latter brings out the sacerdotal idea more prominently, the former is also applied to Jewish and heathen priests, and therefore distinctly involves this idea. Wickliff's version of the New Testament naturally conforms to the Vulgate, in which it seems to be the rule to translate πρεσβύτεροι by 'presbyteri' (in Wickliff, 'preestes'), where it obviously denotes the second order in the ministry (*e.g.*, Acts xiv. 23; 1 Tim. v. 17, 19; Titus i. 5; James v. 14), and by 'seniores' (in Wickliff, 'elders,' or 'elder men') in other passages; but if so, this rule is not always successfully applied (*e.g.*, Acts xi. 30, xxi. 18; 1 Peter v. 1). A doubt about the meaning may explain the anomaly that the word is translated 'presbyteri,' 'preestes,' Acts xv. 2, and 'seniores,' 'elder men,' Acts xv. 4, 6, 22, xvi. 4, though the persons intended are the same. In Acts xx. 17 it is rendered in Wickliff's version 'the gretist men of birthe,' a misunderstanding of the Vulgate 'majores natu.' The English version of the reformers and the reformed Church, from Tyndale downwards, translate πρεσβύτεροι uniformly by 'elders.'"—*See Lightfoot. Philippians.*

"The name of the priest seemeth to be brought into the Church out of the synagogue, for otherwise ye shall not find in the New Testament the ministers of the Word of God and of Churches to be called *priests*, but after a sort that all Christians are called priests by the Apostle Peter. But it appeareth that the ministers of the New Testament, for a certain *likeness* which they have with the ministers of the Old Testament, of ecclesiastical writers are called priests, for as they did their service in the tabernacle, so these also, after their manner and their fashion, minister to the Church of God. For otherwise the Latin word is derived of holy things; a man, I say, dedicated and consecrated unto God to do holy things. And holy things are not only sacrifices, but what things soever come under the name of religion, from which we do not exclude the laws themselves, and holy doctrine."—*Bullinger's "Decades."* Vol. iv. Dec. 5, p. 108.

"That the English word priest is frequently employed for the rendering of two different words in Greek, viz., *hiereus* and *presbyteros* (from the latter of which our 'presbyter,' or 'priest' is derived), is a circumstance of which no scholar can be ignorant indeed, but which is not in general sufficiently attended to; for it is not the same thing to be merely *acquainted* with the ambiguity of a word, and to be practically aware of it, and watchful of the consequences connected with it. And it is, I conceive, of no small importance that this ambiguity should be carefully and frequently explained to those who are ignorant of the original language of the New Testament.

"Our own name for the ministers of our own religion we naturally apply to the *ministers* (in whatever sense) of any other religion; but the two words which have thus come to be translated 'priest' seem by no means to be used synonymously. The priests, both of the Jews and the Pagan nations, constantly bear, in the sacred writings, the title of *hiereus*, which title they never apply to any of the Christian ministers ordained by the apostles. These are called by the title of *episcopus* (literally, superintendent, whence our English word 'bishop'); *presbyteros*, literally, elder, and so rendered by our translators, probably to avoid the ambiguity just alluded to, though the very word 'presbyter' or 'priest' is but a corruption of that name; and *diaconos*, literally, 'minister,' from which our word deacon is but slightly altered.

"These titles, from their original vague and general signification, became gradually not only restricted in great measure to Christian ministers, but also more precisely distinguished from each other than at first they had been, so as to be appropriated respectively to the different orders of those ministers, instead of being applied indiscriminately. But no mention is made by the sacred writers of any such office being established by the apostles as that of 'priest' in the other sense, viz., *hiereus*; priest, in short, such as we find mentioned under that name in Scripture.

"Now this alone would surely be a strong presumption that they regarded the two offices as essentially distinct, for they must have been perfectly familiar with the *name*; and had they intended to institute the same office, or one very similar to it, we cannot but suppose they would have employed that name. The mere circumstance that the Christian religion is very *different* from all others would, of itself, have been no reason against this; for the difference is infinite between the divinely instituted religion of the Jews and the idolatrous superstitions of the heathen, and yet, from similarity of office, the word *hiereus* is applied by sacred writers to the ministers of both religions.

"The difference of names then is, in such a case as this, a matter of no trifling importance, but would, even of itself, lead us to infer a difference of *things*, and to conclude that the apostles regarded their religion as having no priest at all (in the sense of *hiereus*, in Latin, *sacerdos*) except Christ Jesus, of whom indeed all the Levitical priests were but types."—*Whately*. "*Bampton Lectures*," pp. 247-249.

APPENDIX B.

Lecture III. Page 88.

THE account given by Jerome of the identity of bishops and presbyters in the apostolic age, and of the subsequent exaltation of the bishops above their co-presbyters, is entitled to consideration; if for no other purpose, at least for the purpose of showing that even so late as the beginning of the fifth century the doctrine of the Divine right of episcopacy was by no means universally accepted.

"A presbyter is the same as a bishop. And until by the instigation of the devil there arose divisions in religion, and it was said among the people, 'I am of Paul, and I of Apollos, and I of Cephas,' Churches were governed by a common council of presbyters. But afterwards, when every one regarded those whom he baptized as belonging to himself rather than to Christ, it was everywhere decreed that one person, elected from the presbyters, should be placed over the others, to whom the care of the whole Church might belong, and thus the seeds of division might be taken away. Should any one suppose that this opinion—that a bishop and presbyter is the same, and that one is the denomination of age and the other of office—is not sanctioned by the Scriptures, but is only a private fancy of my own, let him read over again the apostle's words to the Philippians; 'Paul and Timotheus, the servants of Jesus Christ, to all the saints in Christ Jesus which are at Philippi, with the bishops and deacons : grace be unto you, and peace, from God the Father and from the Lord Jesus Christ, &c. Philippi is a single city of Macedonia, and certainly, of those who are now styled bishops, there could not have been several at one time in the same city. But because at that time they called the same persons bishops whom they styled also presbyters, therefore the apostle spoke indifferently of bishops as of presbyters.' The writer then refers to the fact that St. Paul, having sent for the *presbyters* (in the plural) *of the single city* of Ephesus only, afterwards called the same persons bishops (Acts xx.). To this fact he calls particular attention, and then observes that in the Epistle to the Hebrews also we find the care of the Church divided equally amongst many. 'Obey them that have the rule over you, and submit yourselves, for they watch for your souls, as they that must give account; that they may do it with joy, and not with grief, for that is [un]profitable to you.' 'And Peter,' continues Jerome, 'who received his name from the firmness of his faith, says, in his epistle, The presbyters who are among you, I exhort, who am also a presbyter, and a witness of the sufferings of Christ, and also a partaker of the glory that shall be revealed. Feed the flock of God which is among you, not by constraint, but willingly.' These things we have brought forward to show that, *with the ancients, presbyters were the same as bishops.* But in order that the roots of dissension might be plucked up, *a usage gradually took place that the whole care should devolve on one.* Therefore, as the presbyters know that *it is by the custom of the Church that they are subject to him who is placed over them,* so let the bishops know that *they are above presbyters rather by custom than by the truth of our Lord's appointment, and that they ought to rule the Church in common, herein imitating Moses," &c.* — Riddle's "*Christian Antiquities,*" pp. 236, 237.

Canon Lightfoot, in his excursus on the Christian ministry, says :—

"Nor was it only in the *language* of the later Church that this fact was preserved. Even in her *practice* indications might here and there be traced which pointed to a time when the bishop was still only the chief member of the presbytery. The case of the Alexandrian Church, which has already been mentioned casually, deserves special notice. St. Jerome, after denouncing the audacity of certain persons who 'would give to deacons the precedence over presbyters, that is, over bishops,' and alleging scriptural proofs of the identity of the two, gives the following fact in illustration. At Alexandria, from Mark the Evangelist down to the time of the bishops Heraclas (A.D. 233-249) and Dionysius (A.D. 249-265), the presbyters always nominated as bishop one chosen out of their own body and placed in a higher grade ; just as if an army were to appoint a general, or deacons were to choose from their own body one whom they know to be diligent, and call him archdeacon. Though the direct statement of this Father refers only to the *appointment* of the bishop, still it may be inferred that the function of the presbyters extended also to the *consecration*. And this inference is borne out by other evidence. 'In Egypt,' writes an older contemporary of St. Jerome, the commentator Hilary, 'the presbyters seal (*i.e.*, ordain or consecrate) if the bishop be not present.' This, however, might refer only to the ordination of presbyters, and not to the consecration of a bishop. But even the latter is supported by direct evidence, which though comparatively late deserves consideration, inasmuch as it comes from one who was himself a patriarch of Alexandria. Eutychius, who held the patriarchal see from A.D. 933 to A.D. 980, writes as follows :—' The Evangelist Mark appointed along with the patriarch Hananias twelve presbyters, who should remain with the patriarch, to the end that, when the patriarchate was vacant, they might choose one of the twelve presbyters, on whose head the remaining eleven laying their hands should create him patriarch.' The vacant place in the presbytery was then to be filled up, that the number twelve might be constant. 'This custom,' adds this writer, 'did not cease till the time of Alexander (A.D. 313-326), patriarch of Alexandria. He however forbade that henceforth the presbyters should create the patriarch, and decreed that on the death of the patriarch the bishops should meet to ordain the (new) patriarch,' &c. It is clear from this passage that Eutychius considered the functions of nomination and ordination to rest with the same persons.

"If this view, however, be correct, the practice of the Alexandrian Church was exceptional, for at this time the formal act of the bishop was considered generally necessary to give validity to ordination. Nor is the exception difficult to account for. At the close of the second century, when every considerable Church in Europe had its bishop, the only representative of the episcopal order in Egypt was the Bishop of Alexandria. It was Demetrius first (A.D. 193-233), as Eutychius informs us, who appointed three other bishops, to which number his successor Heraclas (A.D. 233-249) added twenty more. This extension of episcopacy paved the way for a change in the mode of appointing and ordaining the patriarchs of Alexandria. But before this time it was a matter of convenience and almost of necessity that the Alexandrian presbyters should themselves ordain their chief. Nor is it only in Alexandria that we meet with this peculiarity. Where the same urgent reason existed, the same exceptional practice seems to have been tolerated. A decree of the Council of Ancyra (A.D. 314) ordains that 'it is not to be allowed to country bishops (χωριπισκόποις) to ordain presbyters or deacons, nor even to city presbyters, except permission be given in each parish by the bishop in writing.' Thus, while restraining the existing license, the framers of the decree still allow very considerable latitude. And it is especially important to observe that they lay more stress on episcopal sanction than on episcopal ordination: provided that the former is secured, they are content to dispense with the latter."—"*Philippians*," pp. 229-231.

The following remarks of Ritschl are worthy of observation, in further exposition of his views touching the identity of bishop and presbyter, and their plurality in the early Churches.

"Den Grund der Einrichtung dieses kollegialischen Vorstandes braucht man nur in der Rücksicht auf die Autonomie der Gemeinde und in dem Vorbilde der Synagogenverfassung zu suchen. Denn die Hypothese hat sich nicht bewährt dass die Mehrheit der Vorsteher ursprünglich der in grösseren Städten bestehenden Mehrheit der Hausgemeinden entspreche, dass das Amt der Vorsteher demnach ursprünglich monarchischen Charakter getragen habe, und das derselbe dem kollegialischen Charakter erst gewichen sei, als die Stadtgemeinden aus den Hausgemeinden zusammenwuchsen.

"Diese ursprüngliche Verfassung der Gemeinde unter einer mehrzahl von Episkopen oder Presbytern hat sowohl innerhalb der Apostolischen Zeit Bestand behalten, als auch noch längere danach fortgedauert. Für die Zeit der Wirksamkeit des Apostels Johannes in Kleinasien bezeugt es Clemens von Alexandria, indem er angiebt, der Apostel habe die Umgegend von Ephesus besucht, ' um hier Episkopen einzusetzen, dort ganze Gemeinden einzurichten, dort dem Klerus je einen der vom Geiste Bezeichneten hinzuzufügen.' In dem verhältniss dieser verschiedenen Geschäfte zu einander liegt die Gewähr, dass in dem ersten Gliede nur die Anstellung einer Mehrheit von Episkopen in Einer Gemeinde ausgesagt ist. Und in der an jene notiz angeknüpften Geschichte von dem Jüngling, den Johannes einem Gemeindevorsteher besonders empfohlen hatte, der aber Räuber geworden war, und den der Apostel persönlich wiedergewann, wechseln die beide Amtstitel so, dass der, den Johannes als ἐπίσκοπος anredet, von dem Erzähler als πρισβύτερος eingeführt wird."—Pp. 399, 400.

Whitaker, doctor in divinity, and the King's Professor and Public Reader of Divinity in the University of Cambridge, in his answer to Campian the Jesuit, says : "It is strange that you deny that which Jerome directly affirmeth in the beginning of the same epistle, namely, 'That the apostle doth plainly teach that a bishop and a priest are all one,' and this he proveth by many testimonies of the Scripture. And upon the first chapter to Titus he affirmeth plainly that a bishop is above a priest by custom, not by God's ordinance."—P. 163.

Again he says : "I confess that there was originally no difference between a presbyter and a bishop. Luther and the other heroes of the Reformation were presbyters even according to the ordination of the Romish Church, and therefore they were *jure divino* bishops. Consequently, whatever belongs to bishops, belongs *jure divino* to themselves. As for bishops being afterwards placed over presbyters, that was a human arrangement for the removal of schisms, as the historians of the times testify."

And again he says : "If Aerius was a heretic in this point, he had Jerome to be his neighbour in that heresy: and not only him, but other fathers both Greek and Latin, as is confessed by Medina. Aerius thought that a presbyter did not differ from a bishop by any Divine law and authority, and the same thing was contended for by Jerome, and he defended it by those very scriptural testimonies which Aerius did."—*Works*, vol. i. pp. 509, 510.

Field, in his book of the Church, says : "It is most evident that that wherein a bishop excelleth a presbyter is not a distinct power of order, but an eminence and dignity only, specially yielded to one above all the rest of the same rank for order sake, and to preserve the unity and peace of the Church. Thence it followeth that many things which in some cases presbyters may lawfully do are peculiarly reserved unto bishops, as Hierome noteth, 'Potius ad honorem sacerdotii quam ad legis necessitatem' (Rather for the honour of their ministry than the necessity of any law). And therefore we read that presbyters, in some places and at some time, did impose hands and confirm such as were baptized, which when Gregory, Bishop of Rome, would have forbidden, there was so great exception taken to him that he left it free again. And who knoweth not that all presbyters, in cases of necessity, may absolve and reconcile penitents, a thing in ordinary course appropriated unto bishops? And why not, by the same reason, ordain presbyters and deacons in cases of like necessity.'"—Vol. i. p. 322. London, 1853.

APPENDIX C.

Lecture IV. Page 169.

"BUT then, that he (Bellarmine) may not seem to give up the cause of his Church and desert it as wholly desperate, he pretends that the change that was made by the Council of Constance, and confirmed by the Council of Trent, was against no Divine law ; for communion in both kinds was neither instituted by God, nor did the ancient Fathers ever teach it to be necessary to salvation. One would wonder to see discerning men so infatuated. What words can be able to express a Divine institution if those of our Saviour are not, 'Drink ye all of this'? or how should the Fathers believe communion in both kinds not to be necessary, who thought it necessary for children, and actually communicated them in both kinds whenever they were capable of receiving it. . . . .

"But he was sensible some of their popes have called it a grand sacrilege to divide the mystery. *Gelasius* complains that some received the bread but abstained from the cup, whom he condemns as guilty of superstition, and orders that they should either receive in both kinds, or else be excluded from both, because one and the same mystery cannot be divided without grand sacrilege. *Leo the Great* declaims against them after the same manner. 'They receive the body of Christ with an unworthy mouth, but refuse to drink the blood of redemption. Such men's sacrilegious dissimulation being discovered, let them be marked, and, by the authority of the priesthood, cast out of the society of the faithful. It is in vain to say here, as *Bona* does, that these decrees were only made against the Manichees, who believed wine to be the gall of the prince of darkness and the creature of the devil, and therefore refused to drink it. For their reasons are general against all superstition whatsoever, and in their opinion the sacrament may not be divided without grand sacrilege and thwarting the rule of the first institution, which Bona might also have learned from another decree related in their canon law under the name of Pope Julius, who says: 'The giving of the bread and the cup, each distinctly by themselves, is a Divine order and apostolical institution, and that it is as much against the law of Christ to give them jointly, by dipping the one into the other, as it is to offer milk instead of wine, or the juice of the grape immediately pressed out of the cluster; all of which are equally contrary to the evangelical and apostolical doctrine as well as the custom of the Church, as may be proved from the fountain of truth by whom the mysteries of the sacrament were ordained.' Does not this plainly imply that communicating in both kinds distinctly was according to the laws of Christ and agreeable to His rule and doctrine, as well as His example? With what face, then, could Bona say that communion in both kinds was neither instituted by God, nor did the ancient Fathers judge it necessary, when even some of their ancient popes have told us so plainly that communion distinctly administered in both kinds is a Divine order, and that it is a grand sacrilege to divide them? And the ancients always administered in both kinds upon this principle, because it was the law of Christ, whatever Bona or his partisans can say to the contrary."—*Bingham's "Antiquities,"* vol. i. pp. 787, 788.

APPENDIX D.

Lecture V. Page 191.

I HAVE purposely abstained in the body of the preceding lectures from any discussion of the testimony of the Fathers touching the nature of the change which is alleged to ensue upon the consecration of the elements in the Eucharist. For upon such a question their authority can carry no such weight as will entitle it to absolute deference, even on the supposition that it was marked by perfect consentaneousness, which it is not, or even by uniform consistency in the utterances of each individual Father, a circumstance which no patristic scholar whose judgment is of the slightest value will venture to avow. It does not require more than a few years' acquaintance with the literature of those doctors of the Church to see that for purposes of controversy they are comparatively valueless, because capable of being suborned indifferently as witnesses for the impeachment or the defence of some dogmas which are contested even down to the present day. Nor can the fact of this equivocal testimony be a matter of wonder to any one who remembers that these dogmas had not been hardened into formulas at the time when the Fathers wrote, and therefore were not treated by them as questions requiring strict statement or logical inference. The Fathers accordingly wrote in ignorance of the mischievous process of congelation which would hereafter be applied to their fervid and impassioned utterances, turning their loving rapture into stern and inflexible propositions, by which they would have been revolted. Their very ecstasies have been converted into syllogisms, their aspirations into weapons of war. And by no modern writer has this unfair treatment of patristic language been more extensively sanctioned than by Dr. Pusey, in his work on the "Real Presence." If the citations contained in that work were sifted and classified, and none of them were allowed to stand as materials of evidence but such as could be proved to have been uttered or penned by the Fathers in deliberate and argumentative vindication of some definite dogma, his imposing array of authorities would shrivel into the smallest dimensions. Of what use is it, either for Romanist or Ritualist, to cite the inflamed and exaggerated rhetoric of Chrysostom, or Basil, or Cyril of Alexandria, in favour either of Transubstantiation or Consubstantiation, or of any objective change whatever in the sacramental elements of the Lord's Supper? On three conditions only can such impressment of witnesses be justified with the view of establishing any doctrine. The first is that they shall be accordant. The second is that similar extravagance of language employed by them in connection with any other rite shall be interpreted in the same literal manner. And the third is that their works shall not contain any statements uttered in a calm and didactic fashion by which their more rhetorical and impassioned utterances are expounded and defined.

The limits of this note will not admit of my considering how far the Fathers conform to the first condition, nor is it necessary. The remaining tests are amply sufficient to show that the hyperbolical language of the Fathers has not been impartially pressed into service for the support of elemental transmutation equally in baptism and in the Lord's Supper, and that their writings do contain expressions which serve to reveal their real opinions undisguised by that tumid declamation in which they were so prone to indulge.

Bingham has collected a small sample, out of an ample field rich in similar productions of rhetoric, which neither Rome, Constantinople, nor Canterbury has ever adduced in proof of a substantial change in the matter of baptism. The whole passage is worth citing :—

"I observe concerning the effects of this consecration, that the very same change was supposed to be wrought by it in the waters of baptism as by the consecration of bread and wine in the Eucharist. For they supposed not only the presence of the Spirit, but also the mystical presence of Christ's blood to be here after consecration. Julius Firmicius, speaking of baptism, bids men here seek for the pure waters, the undefiled fountain where the blood of Christ, after many spots and defilements, would whiten them by the Holy Ghost. Gregory Nazianzen and Basil say, upon this account, 'that a greater than the temple, a greater than Solomon, a greater than Jonah is here;' meaning Christ, by His mystical presence and the power of His blood. St. Austin says, 'Baptism or the baptismal water is red, when once it is consecrated by the blood of Christ, and this was prefigured by the waters of the Red Sea.' Prosper is bold to say 'that in baptism we are dipped in blood, and therefore martyrs are twice dipped in blood; first in the blood of Christ at baptism, and then in their own blood at martyrdom.' St. Jerome used the same bold metaphor, explaining those words of Isaiah, ' Wash you, make you clean'—'Be ye baptised in my blood, by the laver of regeneration.' And again, speaking of the Ethiopian eunuch, he says, 'He was baptised in the blood of Christ, about whom he was reading.'

"After the same manner Cæsarius says: 'The soul goes into the living waters, consecrated and made red by the blood of Christ.' And Isidore says: 'What is the Red Sea, but baptism consecrated in the blood of Christ?' Others tell us that we are hereby made partakers of the body and blood of Christ, and eat His flesh, according to what is said in St. John's Gospel: 'Except ye eat the flesh of the Son of man, and drink his blood, ye have no life in you.' Upon which words Fulgentius founds the necessity of baptism: 'Forasmuch as it may be perceived by any considering man that the flesh of Christ is eaten and His blood drank in the laver of regeneration.' Hence Cyril of Alexandria says: 'We are partakers of the Spiritual Lamb in baptism.' And Chrysostom: 'That we thereby put on Christ, not only His divinity, nor only His humanity, that is, His flesh—but both together. And Nazianzen: 'That in baptism we are anointed and protected by the precious blood of Christ, as Israel was by the blood upon the doorposts in the night. St. Chrysostom says again: 'That they are baptised, put on a royal garment—a purple, dipped in the blood of the Lord.' Philo-Carpathius says: 'The spouse of Christ, His Church, receives in baptism the seal of Christ, being washed in the baptism of His most holy blood.' Optatus, as we have heard before, says, 'Christ comes down by the invocation, and joins Himself to the waters of baptism.' Nay, Chrysostom, in one of his bold rhetorical flights, scruples not to tell a man that is baptised that he immediately embraces his Lord in his arms, and that he is united to His body—nay, compounded or consubstantiated with that body which sits above, whither the devil has no access.' Some tell us, as Isidore, 'that the water of baptism is the water which flowed out of Christ's side at His Passion;' and others, as Laurentius Novariensis, 'that it is water mixed with the sacred blood of the Son of God.' Others tell us 'that the water is transmuted or changed in its nature by the Holy Ghost to a sort of Divine and ineffable power.' So Cyril of Alexandria, who frequently uses the word μετastοιχείωσις (transelementation), both when he speaks of the water in baptism and the bread and wine in the Eucharist, or of any other changes that are wrought in the mysteries of the Christian religion. Cyril of Jerusalem and Gregory Nyssen have the same observations upon the change that is wrought in the oil after consecration, which they make to be the same with that of the bread and wine in the Eucharist. 'Beware,' says Cyril, 'that you take not this ointment to be bare ointment, for as the bread in the Eucharist, after the invocation of the Holy Spirit, is not mere bread, but the body of Christ, so this holy ointment, after invocation, is not bare or common ointment, but it is a gift of God that makes Christ and the Holy Spirit to be present in the action.' In like manner, Gregory Nyssen makes the same change to be made in the mystical oil and in the altar itself, and in the ministers by ordination, and in the waters of baptism, as in the bread and wine of the Eucharist, after consecration. 'Do not contemn,' says he, 'the Divine laver, nor despise it as a common thing, because of the use of water. For great and wonderful things are wrought by it. This altar before which we stand is but common stone in its own nature, differing nothing from other stones wherewith our walls are built; but after it is consecrated to the service of God, and has received a benediction, it is a holy table, an immaculate, not to be touched by any but the priests, and that with the greatest reverence. The bread is also at first but common bread, but when once it is sanctified by the holy mystery, it is made and called the body of Christ. So the mystical oil, and so the wine, though they be things of little value before the benediction, yet, after their sanctification by the Spirit, they both of them work wonders. The same power of the Word makes a priest become honourable and venerable when he is separated from the community of the vulgar by a new benediction. For he who before was only one of the common people, is now immediately made a ruler and a president, a teacher of piety and a minister of the secret mysteries.

And all these things he does without any change in his body or shape, for to all outward appearance he is the same that he was, but the change is in his invisible soul, by an invisible power and grace.' Pope Leo goes one step further, and tells us 'that baptism makes a change not only in the water, but in the man who receives it, for thereby Christ receives him, and he receives Christ, and he is not the same after baptism that he was before, but the body of him that is regenerated is made the flesh of Him that was crucified.'"

These are patristic testimonies on the wonderful effects produced by consecration on the waters of baptism, and Dr. Pusey may safely be challenged to produce any language from the same Fathers which affirms a more Real Presence in the Eucharist than is here affirmed in the so-called sacrament of regeneration. If such language exists, let it be cited. Until it is forthcoming I shall persist in declaring that the Fathers believed in no transformation in the elements of the Lord's Supper which was not effected by consecration in the waters of baptism, and that they assigned no greater efficacy to the former than to the latter. If Dr. Pusey plead the tropical language of the Fathers in extenuating explanation of the extravagance which marks the passages just adduced, the plea is admissible only on the ground that it be consistently applied to their corresponding rhetoric when treating on the Eucharist. On no fair principles of interpretation can any sacramentarian, whether Romish or Anglican, deduce Transubstantiation, Consubstantiation, or Real Presence, from the ancient doctors of the Church when expatiating on the wonders of the Mass, and resolve into mere figure statements of similar import touching the ordinance of baptism. There is figure in both or in neither. If in both, what becomes of the stupendous claims which have been made on behalf of the Eucharist; if in neither, why has not the Church of Rome, and why have not Dr. Pusey and his followers, vindicated for baptism in its elements and efficacy all that is so boldly assigned to it in the Fathers? It will be observed that I am not here justifying the extravagant and hyperbolical language in which these ancient writers were accustomed to speak either of the one sacrament or the other. It is incapable of justification, and has been the fruitful source of errors and conflicts in the Church down to the present day. I am insisting only on a consistent and impartial method of interpretation, and am affirming that this method has been systematically violated by those who have accepted the language of the Fathers concerning the Eucharist in its literal signification, and have resolved their language on baptism into figure.

But it may be asked, Were the fathers always on the soaring wing of rhetoric when they treated on the Eucharist, or were there seasons when they indulged themselves in calm, didactic exposition? The latter is the case, and it is in such exposition that we must seek for the key to their audacious metaphors.

What, for example, can be more explicit than the following language of Clement of Alexandria?

"How think ye that the Lord drank, when for us He became a man? As shamelessly as we? Was it not with decorum and propriety? Was it not deliberately? For know well He *partook of wine*, for He was man. And He blessed the wine, saying, 'Take ye, drink, this is my blood,' blood of the vine. He *allegorically* speaks of the Word who was shed for many, for the remission of sins, the holy fount of joy. . . . But that what was blessed was wine, He showed again, saying to the disciples, 'I will not drink of the fruit of this vine.' But what was drunk by the Lord was wine, He Himself says of Himself, upbraiding the Jews with hardness of heart."—"*Pedag.*" lib. ii. cap. 2. Colon. 1688.

Tertullian says: "Having declared 'with desire have I desired to eat this passover' as His own (for it were unworthy of God to desire anything not His own), He made the bread which He took and distributed to His disciples His own body, by saying, 'This is my body,' that is, the *figure of my body*. But it would not have been a figure unless His was a real body" (*veritatis corpus*).—"*Adv. Marc.*" p. 248. Lipsiæ. 1841.

Augustine abounds in language of calm exposition. He says: "We often so speak as to say, when Passion-tide, PASCHA, the Passover, draws near, that to-morrow or the day after is the Lord's Passion, although He suffered so many years ago, and THAT Passion hath not actually taken place more than once. Again, on the Lord's day, we say to-day hath Christ risen, whereas so many years have passed by since He rose. Why is it that no man is so foolish as to charge us with falsehood in thus speaking, save that we name the days from their correspondence (*resemblance, similitudinem*) with those on which the events took place; and so that is called the actual day which is not the actual day, but answers to it in the revolution of time, and that is said to be done on that day because of the celebration of the sacrament which is not done on that day, but was done long ago?

"Was not Christ sacrificed once in His own person, and yet in the sacrament is sacrificed for the people or by the people (*populis*), not only through all the festivals of Easter (*Paschæ solemnitates*, solemnities of the Passover), but every day? And it is clear that he sacrificed. For if sacraments had not a certain resemblance (*similitudinem*) to those things of which they are the sacraments, they would not be sacraments at all. But from this resemblance they receive, for the most part, the names even of the things themselves. As therefore after a certain manner (*quendam modum*) the sacrament of the body of Christ is the body of Christ, the sacrament of the blood of Christ is the blood of Christ, so the sacrament of faith is faith."—"*Epist.* xxiii. *ad Bonifacium.*"

"If a form of speech is preceptive, forbidding either a disgraceful thing or a crime, or commanding what is useful and beneficent, it is not figurative. But if it seems to command a disgraceful thing or a crime, or to forbid what is useful or beneficent, it is figurative. 'Except ye eat the flesh and drink the blood of the Son of man, ye have no life in you.' He seems to command a disgraceful thing or a crime, therefore it is figurative, commanding us to communicate in the Passion of our Lord, and sweetly and profitably to treasure up in our memory that His flesh was crucified and wounded for us."—"*De Doct. Christ.*" lib. iii. c. 16.

"This which ye see on the altar of God, ye saw last night also; but what it was, what it meant, of how great a thing it contained the sacrament, ye have not yet heard. What ye see, then, is bread and a cup, what your eyes also report to you; but what your faith requires to be taught, the bread is the body of Christ, the cup the blood of Christ. This, indeed, is but briefly stated, and it may suffice for faith, yet faith requireth instruction. For the prophet saith, 'If ye will not believe, ye shall not understand' (Isa. vii. 9). You may, therefore, say to me, Thou hast bidden us to believe:

explain, that we may understand. But some such thoughts as this may raise in the mind of some one. 'Our Lord Jesus Christ, we know whence He took flesh, of the Virgin Mary. He was nursed as an infant,' &c. (going briefly through His life, death, and resurrection). He ascended into heaven; thither He lifted aloft His body; thence He is to come to judge the quick and the dead; there He is now sitting at the right hand of the Father. How is the bread His body? And the cup, or what the cup contains, how is it His blood? These things, brethren, are therefore called sacraments, because in them one thing is seen, another understood. What is seen hath a bodily form (*speciem*), what is understood hath a spiritual fruit."—"*Sermon of Augustine, as explained and applied by Fulgentius*," pp. 185, 186.

"In the history of the New Testament, so great and marvellous was the patience of the Lord, that He endured him as if he had been a good man, though He knew his schemes, and admitted him to the banquet in which He commended and delivered to His disciples the figure (*figuram*) of His flesh and blood."—"*Enarra. in Psalm* iii."

"Christ instructed His disciples and said unto them, 'It is the spirit that quickeneth, the flesh profiteth nothing. The words which I speak unto you are spirit and life. Understand what I have spoken to you spiritually. You are not going to eat this body which you see, you are not going to drink that blood which my crucifiers will pour forth. I have commended a certain sacrament to you, and, spiritually understood, it will vivify you. Though it must of necessity be celebrated visibly, it must be understood invisibly.'"—"*Enarra. in Psalm* xcviii."

Lecture V. Page 235.

For the substantial identity of the Romish and Neo-Catholic doctrines of the Eucharist, we may cite the charge of the Bishop of Durham, October, 1870.

"The doctrine of the Church of Rome, as laid down by the Council of Trent, is that 'the substance of the bread and wine is changed into the substance of the body and blood of Christ, not naturally, but truly, really, and sacramentally; so that while the accidents remain in appearance, the elements are substantially the body and blood of Christ.' The doctrine of the new school of theology in our Church is that the elements are changed by consecration, and become after a spiritual manner the body and blood of Christ; so that Christ is not only present in the ordinance subjectively in the hearts of the faithful, but objectively also in the natural substances of the bread and wine, which become in some ineffable way, through the consecration of the priest, 'not mere channels through which Christ is conveyed to those who properly receive Him, but there and then Christ Himself, whether received or not.' Now there is, of course, a verbal difference in these statements, but they are one and the same in their essence and in their results. The whole doctrine which can be logically derived from the one, can be as logically derived from the other. Each confers on the consecrator the power of changing the elements into the body and blood of Christ. It may be said that the sacrament of the Lord's Supper is a rite so solemn and devotional that it should never be the subject of controversy, and that it is a matter of no great moment what may be the views of a Church or of individuals as to the nature of Christ's presence in His Supper. This was not the judgment of those brave and well-instructed reformers who, three hundred years ago, earnestly contended for the faith. It was on account of their abhorrence of the doctrine now commonly termed the objective presence, or, in other words, the actual presence of Christ in the elements, whether by transubstantiation or consubstantiation or impanation, that they resolutely laid down their lives. And why this, but because they clearly discerned in the history of the past that this doctrine was the key-stone of the whole fabric of Papal error. And now that three centuries have passed away, notwithstanding all the scriptural knowledge vouchsafed to us during that period, it would seem as though that fundamental error respecting the nature of our Lord's presence, which had been so boldly resisted and amply refuted by the reformers, and which has been well described as 'the central power which binds the Roman system together, and regulates every motion, and acts upon every particle, and invests the priesthood with more than human character,' is again being openly taught in all its essential corruption by the school of Ultra-Ritualists; and the battle won of old must again be fought, if our Church is to preserve its scriptural light and liberty, and not fall back again into the darkness and slavery of mediæval sacerdotalism."

APPENDIX E.

Lecture VIII. Page 386.

The following declaration, signed by Dr. Pusey and many others of the clergy of the Church of England, including some of her ripest scholars and ablest preachers, is worthy of note.

"We, the undersigned priests of the Church of England, considering that serious misapprehensions as to the teaching of the Church of England on the subject of confession and absolution are widely prevalent, and that these misapprehensions lead to serious evils, hereby declare, for the truth's sake and in the fear of God, what we hold and teach on the subject, with special reference to the points which have been brought under discussion.

"I. We believe and profess that Almighty God has promised forgiveness of sin, through the precious blood of Jesus Christ, to all who turn to Him with true sorrow for sin, out of unfeigned and sincere love to Him, with lively faith in Jesus Christ, and with full purpose of amendment of life.

"II. We also believe and profess that our Lord Jesus Christ has instituted in His Church a special means for the remission of sin after baptism, and for the relief of consciences, which special means the Church of England retains and administers as part of her Catholic heritage.

"III. We affirm that—to use the language of the Homily—'absolution hath the promise of forgiveness of sin; although the Homily adds, 'By the express word of the New Testament it hath not this promise annexed and tied to the visible sign,' which is imposition of hands, and therefore it says, 'Absolution is no such sacrament as baptism and the communion are.' We hold it to be clearly impossible that the Church of England in Art. xxv. can have meant to disparage the ministry of absolution, any more than she can have meant to disparage the rites of confirmation and ordination which she solemnly administers. We believe that God, through absolution, confers an inward spiritual grace, and the authoritative assurance of His forgiveness, on those who receive it with faith and repentance, as in confirmation and ordination He confers grace on those who rightly receive the same.

"IV. In our ordination as priests of the Church of England, the words of our Lord to His apostles—'Receive ye the Holy Ghost; whose soever sins ye remit, they are remitted unto them, and whose soever sins ye retain, they are retained,'—were applied to us individually. Thus it appears that the Church of England considers this commission to be not a temporary endowment of the apostles, but a gift lasting to the end of time. It was said to each of us, 'Receive the Holy Ghost for the office and work of a priest of the Church of God, now committed unto thee by the imposition of our hands;' and then followed the words, 'Whose sins thou dost forgive, they are forgiven, and whose sins thou dost retain, they are retained.'

"V. We are not here concerned with the two forms of absolution which the priest is directed to pronounce after the general confession of sins in the morning and evening prayer and in the Communion Service. The only form of words provided for us in the Book of Common Prayer for applying the absolving power to individual souls runs thus:—'Our Lord Jesus Christ, who hath left power to His Church to absolve all sinners who truly repent and believe in Him, of His great mercy forgive thee thine offences; and by His authority committed to me I absolve thee from all thy sins, in the name of the Father, the Son, and the Holy Ghost. Amen.' Upon this we remark, first, that in these words forgiveness of sins is ascribed to our Lord Jesus Christ, yet that the priest, acting by a delegated authority, and as an instrument, does through these words convey the absolving grace; and, secondly, that the absolution from sins cannot be understood to be the removal of any censures of the Church, because (*a*) the sins from which the penitent is absolved are presupposed to be sins previously known to himself and God only; (*b*) the words of the Latin form relating to those censures are omitted in our English form; and (*c*) the release from excommunication is in Art. xxxiii. reserved to 'a judge that hath authority thereunto.'

"VI. This provision, moreover, shows that the Church of England, when speaking of 'the benefit of absolution,' and empowering her priests to absolve, means them to use a definite form of absolution, and does not merely contemplate a general reference to the promises of the gospel.

"VII. In the service for 'The Visitation of the Sick,' the Church of England orders that the sick man shall ever ' be moved to make a special confession of his sins, if he feel his conscience troubled with any weighty matter.' When the Church requires that the sick man should, in such case, be moved to make a special confession of his sins, we cannot suppose her thereby to rule that her members are bound to defer to a deathbed (which they may never see) what they know to be good for their souls. We observe that the words 'be moved to' were added in 1661, and that, therefore, at the last revision of the Book of Common Prayer, the Church of England affirmed the duty of exhorting to confession in certain cases more strongly than at the date of the Reformation, probably because the practice had fallen into abeyance during the Great Rebellion.

"VIII. The Church of England also, holding it 'requisite that no man should come to the Holy Communion but with a full trust in God's mercy, and with a quiet conscience,' commands the minister to bid 'any' one who 'cannot quiet his own conscience herein' to come to him, or to some other discreet and learned minister of God's Word, and open his grief, that by the ministry of God's holy Word he may receive the benefit of absolution, together with, and therefore as distinct from, 'ghostly counsel and advice;' and since she directs that this invitation should be repeated in giving warning of Holy Communion, and Holy Communion is constantly offered to all, it follows that the use of confession may be, at least in some cases, not of unfrequent occurrence.

"IX. We believe that the Church left it to the consciences of individuals, according to their sense of their needs, to decide whether they would confess or not, as expressed in that charitable exhortation of the first English Prayer-Book, requiring such as shall be satisfied with a general confession not to be offended with them that do use, to their further satisfying, the auricular and secret confession to the priest; nor those also which think needful or convenient, for the quietness of their own consciences, particularly to open their sins to the priest, not to be offended with them that are satisfied with their humble confession to God and the general confession to the Church, but in all things to follow and keep the rule of charity, and every man to be satisfied with his own conscience, not judging other men's minds or consciences, whereas he hath no warrant of God's Word to the same.' And although this passage was omitted in the second Prayer-Book, yet that its principle was not repudiated may be gathered from the 'Act for the Uniformity of Service' (1551), which, while authorizing the second Prayer-Book, asserts the former book to be agreeable to the Word of God and the primitive Church.'

"X. We would further observe that the Church of England has nowhere limited the occasions upon which her priests should exercise the office which she commits to them at their ordination; and that to command her priests in two of her offices to hear confessions, if made, cannot be construed negatively into a command not to receive confessions on any other occasions. But in fact (see above, Nos. VII., VIII.) the two occasions specified do practically comprise the whole of the adult life. A succession of divines of great repute in the Church of England, from the very time when the English Prayer-Book was framed, speak highly of confession, without limiting the occasions upon which, or the frequency with which, it should be used; and the 113th Canon, framed in the Convocation of 1603, recognized confession as a then existing practice, in that it decreed, under the severest penalties, that 'if any man confess his secret and hidden sins to the minister for the unburdening of his conscience, and to receive spiritual consolation and ease of mind from him, . . . the said minister . . . do not at any time reveal and make known to any person whatsoever any crime or offence so committed to his trust and secrecy (except they be such crimes as by the laws of this realm his own life may be called into question for concealing the same).

"XI. While then we hold that the formularies of the Church of England do not authorize any priest to teach that private confession is a condition indispensable to the forgiveness of sin after baptism, and that the Church of England does not justify any parish priest in requiring private confession as a condition of receiving Holy Communion, we also hold that all who, under the circumstances above stated, claim the privilege of private confession, are entitled to it, and that the clergy are directed, under certain circumstances, to 'move' persons to such confession. In insisting on this as the plain meaning of the authorised language of the Church of England, we believe ourselves to be discharging our duty as her faithful ministers.'

UNWIN BROTHERS,
PRINTERS BY WATER POWER.

www.ingramcontent.com/pod-product-compliance
Lightning Source LLC
Chambersburg PA
CBHW020538300426
44111CB00008B/719